Weekend MBA For Dummies®

The Right Way to Delegate Tasks

Delegation is essential for tasks to be completed effectively. Here are steps for doing it the right way:

1. **Communicate the task.** Describe exactly what you want done, when you want it done, and the end results you expect. Be clear and invite your employees to ask lots of questions until you're convinced that they understand what you want done.

2. **Furnish context for the task.** Most people want to know the reasons why they need to do something. Explain to your employees why the task needs to be done, its importance in the overall scheme of things, and any possible complications that may arise during its performance. Again, invite questions, and don't get defensive if your employees push you for answers.

3. **Determine standards.** We all need to know when we cross the finish line. Agree on the standards that you use to measure the success of a task's completion. These standards need to be realistic and attainable, and avoid changing them after performance has begun.

4. **Give authority.** Give employees the authority necessary to complete the task without constant blockages or disputes with other employees.

5. **Provide support.** Determine the resources necessary for your employees to complete the task and then provide them. Successfully completing a task may require money, training, advice, and other resources.

6. **Get commitment.** Make sure that your employees have accepted the assignment. Confirm your expectations and your employees' understanding of the commitment to completing the task.

Customer Care

Whatever line of business you're in, customers are always at the centre. Make sure that you look after them as well as possible, and remember the following points:

- Gaining a new customer costs far more than retaining an existing one.
- Dissatisfied customers always shout more loudly than satisfied customers.
- Never forget that the customer has a choice.
- Listen to the customers to find out what they want.
- If you don't look after your customers, someone else will.

For Dummies: Bestselling Book Series for Beginners

Weekend MBA For Dummies®

Cheat Sheet

The Basics of Managing Risk

Risk management is the process of understanding and anticipating risks and then taking steps to minimise their impact on a business and the people within it. Here are the five steps for managing risk:

1. **Identify potential risks.**

   The possibilities for loss are almost endless. What risks is your business exposed to?

2. **Assess and prioritise potential risks.**

   Make sure that you include everything that could conceivably go wrong, and make sure that people are trained and briefed in risk management. *Always* pay attention to any risks inherent in technology failure.

3. **Select the right risk management tools to deal with each potential risk.**

   Develop a risk management process and plan with specific strategies for dealing with risk in your business. In some cases, prevention is the right course of action. In other cases, employee training may do the trick. Always make sure that you're fully and comprehensively insured.

4. **Evaluate the results of your risk management strategies and revise or renew them as appropriate.**

   Write down your risk management strategies and processes, and keep them under constant review. Especially when things go wrong, evaluate the ways in which risk management strategies are operated, and tighten them up if necessary.

5. **Put someone in charge.**

   Make sure that someone is in charge of risk management at your organisation, and make sure that they have sufficient authority to ensure that all strategies are implemented and delivered effectively.

Creating a Marketing Plan

A good one-paragraph marketing plan has the following seven components:

1. **Purpose:** What is the marketing plan supposed to accomplish?
2. **Benefits:** How do your products and services satisfy the needs of the customer?
3. **Customer:** Who is your primary customer and what is your strategy for building long-term relationships with that customer?
4. **Company:** How does the customer see your company? Remember that customers are some of the many people who contribute to positioning your company in the marketplace.
5. **Niche:** What is the niche in the market that your company has defined and serves?
6. **Tactics:** What specific marketing tools are you going to use to reach the customers?
7. **Budget:** How much of your budget are you going to allocate to this effort?

For Dummies: Bestselling Book Series for Beginners

Weekend MBA

FOR

DUMMIES®

Weekend MBA
FOR
DUMMIES®

by Richard Pettinger, Dr Kathleen Allen, and
Peter Economy

BICENTENNIAL
1807
WILEY
2007
BICENTENNIAL

John Wiley & Sons, Ltd

Weekend MBA For Dummies®

Published by
John Wiley & Sons, Ltd
The Atrium
Southern Gate
Chichester
West Sussex
PO19 8SQ
England
E-mail (for orders and customer service enquires): cs-books@wiley.co.uk
Visit our Home Page on www.wileyeurope.com

Wiley also publishes its books in a variety of electronic formats. Some content that appears in print may not be available in electronic books.

British Library Cataloguing in Publication Data: A catalogue record for this book is available from the British Library.

ISBN: 978-0-470-06097-1

Printed and bound in Great Britain by Bell and Bain Ltd, Glasgow.

10 9 8 7 6 5 4 3 2 1

WILEY

About the Authors

Richard Pettinger (BA, MBA, DipMktg) has taught at University College London since 1989, where he is senior lecturer in management. He teaches on the foundation courses, organisational change, and construction marketing courses. He has also taught strategic and operations management; the management of change; human resource management; and leadership to a wide range of undergraduate, postgraduate, professional, and international students. Richard is also enhancing and developing Management Studies Centre activities and courses, including the directorship of the new Information Management for Business course.

Since 2005, Richard has been a visiting professor at the Jagiellonian Business School, Krakow, teaching strategic management and developing a common UCL/Jagiellonian syllabus in strategic management and organisational change.

Richard is the author of over thirty business and management books and textbooks, including *Managing For Dummies*, and also writes journal, conference, and study papers.

Kathleen Allen is Professor of Entrepreneurship at the Greif Entrepreneurship Center of the Marshall School of Business at the University of Southern California, and has helped hundreds of entrepreneurs start their ventures. As an entrepreneur herself, Allen was involved in commercial real estate development for 10 years. She is the cofounder and CFO of Gentech Corporation.

Peter Economy is associate editor of *Leader to Leader*, the award-winning magazine of the Peter F. Drucker Foundation for Nonprofit Leadership, and author of numerous books. Peter combines his writing expertise with more than 15 years of management experience to provide his readers with solid, hands-on information and advice. He received his bachelor's degree (with majors in economics and human biology) from Stanford University and his MBA at the Edinburgh Business School.

Authors' Acknowledgements

From Richard: I acknowledge three managers who have had great influence on the ways in which things have turned out: John Taylor, who set very high standards all round, and who remains a close colleague and friend; Jack Cadogan at the Manpower Services Commission, who let me do things my way; and Graham Winch, who started me off at UCL. I have had wonderful support and enthusiasm all the way through from Ram Ahronov, Peter Antonioni, Roger Cartwright, Kelvin Cheatle, Frances Kelly, Paul Griseri, Jacek Klich, Robert Pringle and Andrew Scott – great colleagues all. Thanks for the great work of Rachael Chilvers and everyone at Wiley in making this project into something that we can all be proud of. Finally, I would like to dedicate this book to my wife Rebecca, without whom nothing is possible.

From Kathleen: Thanks to my MBA students at the Marshall School, University of Southern California, for their constant inspiration, and my husband and children who have put up with having an author in the house with great humour and patience. I could not accomplish everything I do without you.

From Peter: Thanks to my family for their ongoing support and Pannikin Coffee and Tea for many double espresso mochas.

Publisher's Acknowledgements

We're proud of this book; please send us your comments through our Dummies online registration form located at www.dummies.com/register/.

Some of the people who helped bring this book to market include the following:

Acquisitions, Editorial, and Media Development

Executive Editor: Jason Dunne

Executive Project Editor: Martin Tribe

Project Editor: Rachael Chilvers

Content Editor: Steve Edwards

Copy Editor: Kate O'Leary

Technical Reviewer: Graham Beaver, Professor of Strategic Management, Brighton Business School

Proofreader: Martin Key

Special Help: Jennifer Bingham

Cover Photo: © GIPhotoStock/ Alamy

Cartoons: Ed McLachlan

Production

Project Coordinator: Jennifer Theriot

Layout and Graphics: Claudia Bell, Carl Byers, Brooke Graczyk, Denny Hager, Joyce Haughey, Stephanie D. Jumper, Alicia B. South

Proofreader: Jessica Kramer

Indexer: Aptara

Publishing and Editorial for Consumer Dummies

Diane Graves Steele, Vice President and Publisher, Consumer Dummies

Joyce Pepple, Acquisitions Director, Consumer Dummies

Kristin A. Cocks, Product Development Director, Consumer Dummies

Michael Spring, Vice President and Publisher, Travel

Kelly Regan, Editorial Director, Travel

Publishing for Technology Dummies

Andy Cummings, Vice President and Publisher, Dummies Technology/General User

Composition Services

Gerry Fahey, Vice President of Production Services

Debbie Stailey, Director of Composition Services

Contents at a Glance

Table of Contents

Introduction

*W*hether you work in industry and commerce, or in public services, or in the not-for-profit sector, a good chance exists that you either already have a Masters in Business Administration (MBA), or are considering getting one. If you want to progress and develop your career, or do a better job at work, or get an excellent and comprehensive business and management education, then gaining an MBA is a great choice. Together with diplomas and other qualifications from professional and management bodies, the MBA forms the foundation of professional management expertise.

But is it the degree itself that's important, or is what you actually learn during your studies more relevant? Of course the qualification means a lot. The MBA is a mark of excellence and high achievement, especially if it's from a top business school.

However, what you gain along the way is also of immense value; and *Weekend MBA For Dummies* introduces, presents, and explains all of the topics that you encounter on a full MBA programme at any top quality business school. We cover strategy, leadership, accounting and finance, human resource management, marketing, and economics – exactly as you find at business school.

Your present level of leadership or management experience doesn't matter. Without having to enrol – and pay for – a top MBA programme, all of the course material is here. Having read this book, you can decide for yourself whether or not you need or want to go on and do the real qualification at business school. And if you already have an MBA, *Weekend MBA For Dummies* is a useful refresher and reference point that you can pick up at any time you choose. If you're on any programme of study, whether the MBA itself or any other management course – certificate, diploma, specialist foundation programme, or professional education scheme – you can read this book alongside your studies to help you.

Why Weekend *MBA For Dummies*? Well, you have to put some of your own time and effort into developing yourself, and that means a bit of studying and reading at weekends. We hope that this book is attractive and readable enough for you to *want* to pick it up at weekends. You can easily read it from cover to cover in a single weekend, thereby picking up and digesting a lot of knowledge and understanding very quickly. And if you're coming to business and management as a field of study for the first time, by the end of a good read during a single weekend, you'll have a very realistic idea of what you're letting yourself in for.

About This Book

This book provides the basis for acquiring and developing the substantial body of knowledge, skills, and understanding that's required of any manager, leader, pioneer, or entrepreneur; and this knowledge forms the basis on which you can build practical excellence and expertise.

Weekend MBA For Dummies is full of examples, tips, checklists, and other vital and useful information. Everything that we include in the book is tried and tested. Of course we introduce organisation and management theories – but only because they work in practice. We concentrate on what is *useful* and *valuable*: The aspects that will make you a better leader or manager.

However you approach the book and your own professional development, always note the examples, applications, and illustrations. Be inspired by the success stories, and understand the expertise and principles on which they were based so you can take steps to become a better leader, director, or manager. Becoming a better leader, director, entrepreneur, or manager is in itself intrinsically rewarding and fulfilling in whatever sector you happen to work. The best directors and managers in the world have reached their positions because of their own personal and professional commitment, as well as their ability to deliver their expertise.

How This Book Is Organised

Weekend MBA For Dummies is organised into six parts. The chapters in each part cover specific topic areas in detail, making finding the topic you want simple and straightforward.

Part 1: The New World of Business and Management

Business and management are going through times of great and rapid change and uncertainty. In this part, we consider what business is today – and what it is not. We take a close look at the power of technology and how to use it to your advantage. We consider also the global business environment and the hows and whys of strategic planning.

Part II: Leading and Managing in the New World

A working knowledge of the nuts and bolts of how to manage an organisation and the people within it is a very important part of business success. In this part, we consider the difference between managing and leading an organisation, and the latest trends in leadership. We look at how to best motivate and reward employees, and we show you how to recruit and retain the best employees, and organise them into effective teams and groups. And we consider the complex question of business and management ethics.

Part III: Money: What You Don't Know Will Hurt You

Understanding where a business's money comes from – and where it goes to – is a vital skill for all entrepreneurs, pioneers, and managers. In this part, we present the basics of accounting, as well as look at the most important and widely used financial statements – the balance sheet and profit and loss statement. We decipher the mysteries of financial analysis and evaluating annual reports. And we look at raising finance and why people might invest in you and your organisation.

Part IV: Marketing in the New World

In this part we help you to understand your customers' needs, and we show you how to provide top class and excellent customer service. We discuss the best approaches to developing a marketing plan, and we take an in-depth look at advertising and promotion. Finally, we look at the most effective and successful sales methods and techniques.

Part V: The Last Pieces of the Jigsaw

In this part, we take a look at manufacturing, distribution, and service, and how technology has had a major impact on each; and we explore the most important concepts of risk management. Finally, we reveal the secrets of successful negotiation.

Part VI: The Part of Tens

Every *For Dummies* book ends with a Part of Tens, a quick and fun read full of concise and snappy information. Here, we present tips that can help you to quickly become an effective participant in *any* organisation. We show you how to avoid the most common mistakes that managers make, the best ways to market your products and services, and how to improve your cash flow. And as if this book isn't enough, we suggest ten inspiring books to read.

Icons Used in This Book

We use icons next to blocks of text to draw your attention to particular nuggets of information throughout the book:

The bull's-eye highlights a good idea or shortcut that can save you time or trouble.

This icon draws your attention to a piece of information about business and management that you shouldn't forget.

Information that can help you avoid disasters.

The world of business is full of inspirational stories of business successes and failures, and this icon highlights them.

Sometimes a bit of advice stands out from the rest – a pearl of wisdom. Scattered throughout this book you find such pearls prefaced by this icon.

Where to Go from Here

For Dummies books are easy to access. We break up the subject matter into easily identifiable and manageable chunks. The book is structured so that whatever you want to look up, you can find it easily. *For Dummies* books are designed so that you can start anywhere you like. If you're new to business – perhaps a new employee, supervisor, or manager – then you may want to start at the beginning and work your way through to the end. A wealth of information and practical advice is awaiting you. Simply turn the page and begin!

If you already have plenty of experience, then you may want to turn straight to a particular topic or question, such as understanding accounts or motivating employees. You can simply go straight to that section by using the table of contents or index. And if you have any questions at all, then we'd love to hear from you. Please write to us at: Kathleen: kallen@marshall.usc.edu, Peter: bizzwriter@stanfordalumni.org, or Richard: r.pettinger@ucl.ac.uk.

Part I
The New World of Business and Management

'OK – Here's the business plan. Nigel takes charge of marketing, Tristram sales, Keith accounts and Psycho makes sure clients pay on time.'

In this part . . .

We consider what business is today – and what it *isn't*. We take a very close look at the power of technology and how to use it to your advantage. Finally, we consider the global business environment and discuss the hows and whys of strategic planning.

Chapter 1

Embracing Change

· ·

In This Chapter

▶ Looking at the new world of business

▶ Planning for change

▶ Walking confidently into the future

· ·

*T*oday, business owners and managers face a perplexing array of management practices and a variety of off-the-wall theories on how businesses should be run. In the past ten years alone, over 1,900 books have been published on the subject of change in organisations! Most of the authors purport to have seen the light, and to have found at last the latest and greatest management tools. The reality is that most of those 'innovative', 'state of the art' tools are merely elaborate makeovers of fundamental management theory. *A rose by any other name is still a rose.* How many different ways can we talk about total quality management or empowered work teams? It's no wonder that many managers resort to tried and tested ways of doing things. People find comfort in the familiar. The proponents of these new theories and practices echo a shared truth: The world has changed, but the way managers run businesses has not always kept pace.

As a whole, the business world has recognised the need to change – or to be left behind. Business schools and management studies centres have long preached this truth, and it's practised by the best and most forward-looking organisations. Every good MBA programme and many undergraduate business studies courses have modules and course units on change and uncertainty, and the need to be able to survive in a turbulent and uncertain world.

The best and most forward-looking and dynamic organisations lead by example. Pioneering owner-managers such as Richard Branson at the Virgin group of companies show that bucking trends in such diverse sectors as bridal wear, publishing, and financial services, as well as the airline and music ventures for which the company is best known, is possible. Entrepreneurial and visionary people such as Michael O'Leary at Ryanair show that it's possible to transform not just a company, but the whole sector in which it operates, if you have the expertise, are prepared to work hard – and to learn.

Yet many companies and organisations still fail to note all these developments in the business world, or else try to carry on in the old ways. Without any exception, these are companies and organisations that will fail unless they change. In relation to the competition and to the forward-looking firms, these companies deliver their products and services less quickly, more expensively, and to fewer customers and clients. They carry higher overheads and *on-costs* (that is, everything that they have to pay for as a direct consequence of being in their line of business and structured the way that they are); and in many cases are driven by demands that they follow their own procedures rather than serve customers.

In this chapter we delve deeper into the process of change, the make-up of successful companies, and how to plan to move your company into embracing change for the better.

Welcome to the New World

So what are the main things that are going on in the business world right now? Well, here's a list:

- ✔ Successful entrepreneurs are making vast fortunes with start-up companies whose share values have shot through the roof.

- ✔ Internet companies such as Amazon, Google, and eBay have higher capital values than banks, supermarket chains, and department stores.

- ✔ New business models, new communications technologies, and new distribution methods allow people to get their products and services from wherever they choose – and whenever they choose.

- ✔ Outsourcing and subcontracting have led to opportunities for specialists to provide high quality and expert services to companies that previously had to run these things themselves. For example, many companies that used to engage their own security and cleaning staff now outsource these activities to specialist firms.

- ✔ Flexible working, together with access to technology, means that people can work at any time, doing the hours that suit them, subject only to meeting deadlines and output targets.

Of course, none of these developments are completely new. Industrial revolutions occurred throughout the history of civilisation; and although technology is advancing faster than ever, past generations were very used to economic and social changes.

So revolutionary changes, or *paradigm shifts*, aren't today's exclusive property. They've occurred many times over the centuries and will continue to do so. Without these revolutionary changes societies would stagnate and flounder in their own safe and traditional ways of doing things. Change is a good thing! And change is certain to happen, so embrace it gladly and willingly.

What's so great about change?

Have you ever ridden a monster rollercoaster or done a bungee jump? These activities are exhilarating, terrifying, and glorious all at the same time. What makes doing them so great is that you don't know exactly what's coming next, but you do know that something's going to happen. So you try to prepare. You hang on tight, and you may close your eyes because you're feeling pretty vulnerable. Or you may throw your arms up, toss your head back, and scream as loudly as you can. What a rush! And what another rush when you've actually done it! Welcome to the real world.

The world is all about change and uncertainty – expected and unexpected – and change is as unavoidable as death and taxes. You can't put your business into a vacuum and escape the changes (although, like death and taxes, you may try to avoid them for as long as you can). Instead of seeking in vain to avoid change, welcome it, savour it, and use it to your advantage, because change is a fact of life.

Things are only going to get more chaotic and less certain in the future, as technology moves at the speed of light to provide businesses with quantities of information, contacts, and opportunities that no one thought possible even a few years ago. The best business schools and management studies centres know and fully understand the speed of change; and MBA programmes and other courses of study make sure that they cover entrepreneurial management, pioneering, and new product and service development because their customers demand it. Writing twenty years ago, management guru Tom Peters predicted the dynamic uncertainty in which we live today in his prophetic book *Thriving on Chaos.* He said, 'excellent firms of tomorrow will cherish impermanence – and thrive on chaos.' The reason is that out of impermanence and chaos come the opportunities that keep businesses revitalised and growing.

Dealing with this new global and technological – and volatile – environment requires a forward-thinking vision and mindset. No longer is it enough to be able to operate procedures, clear an in-tray, or simply produce stated product and service volumes. Today, you have to design, produce, and deliver the best possible products and services; and it all has to be done at speed, to high quality, value, and reliability standards – otherwise you lose out to those who offer more. Outmoded, expensive, and cumbersome organisational structures and hierarchies invariably don't allow organisations the option of responding quickly and effectively. So companies and their managers have to be prepared to change their whole approach, not only to the ways in which business is conducted, but also to the ways in which it operates. Companies of all sizes have to be prepared to be much more flexible, dynamic, and responsive, and most important of all, they need to include the customers' needs, wants, and demands every step of the way.

Size doesn't matter

The best companies have discovered that size doesn't matter when competing in a global economy. Don't forget that all the best companies started out as tiny garage-based businesses, market stalls, and single outlets. The most famous companies in the world and some truly innovative products and services have come from these beginnings. Remember these tiny companies?

- ✔ Virgin
- ✔ Dreamworks
- ✔ Sony

Richard Branson started the Virgin empire selling second-hand records and producing a student newspaper. Steven Spielberg started his film production companies, Amblin and Dreamworks, with a telephone and borrowed desk in a remote corner of the Universal Studios property empire. Akio Morita founded what is now the Sony Corporation in his father's garage and for over ten years this remained the company headquarters until the first product – magnetic recording tape – was of a fully commercial standard. If you're looking longingly at this kind of success, realise this: You need to really know what you're doing; you need to take the opportunities when they come along – and you need to work very, very hard!

Checking out the characteristics of successful companies

We don't have a crystal ball that allows us to predict what successful companies will look like over the coming years. Nevertheless, you can be pretty certain that they'll have some (if not all) of the following characteristics that enhance their chances of competing effectively in a dynamic and global market. Here's what successful businesses and their owners will do:

✔ **Spot fundamental changes in the world and create opportunities from them before these changes take hold in the general business population.** These entrepreneurial companies will also create strategies to exploit these opportunities, and develop new forms of business practice and organisational structures to implement their strategies.

✔ **Look and act flexibly and dynamically to respond quickly to change.** Even huge conglomerates such as the Nationwide Building Society and Legal and General are looking for opportunities and ways to re-invent themselves as conglomerates of smaller businesses to encourage innovation and creativity in their employees.

✔ **Create niches in markets that they can dominate.** Why go head to head with large, established companies in your market unless you have a death wish? Instead, the best entrepreneurs create niches of customers who have needs that aren't being met by their larger competitors.

✔ **Put the customer at the centre of everything that they do.** Without customers, you have no business. So why don't more companies involve customers in their businesses? Businesses that involve their customers in product and service design and development, quality issues, distribution – in fact in every area of the business – are among the most successful companies in their industries. Exemplary companies include:

- Sandals, the exclusive holiday company

- Body Shop, the cosmetics company (which also involved suppliers when owned by the Roddicks)

- IBM, in its corporate communications and systems divisions

✔ **Use teams to innovate and develop products quickly.** People from all the functional areas of business (production, marketing, finance, and engineering) comprise these teams so that businesses can develop products and services more quickly and effectively. For example, a design engineer won't create something that manufacturing can't produce.

An aircraft company once built a hangar to house the production of a new plane that the engineers had designed. Unfortunately, when the hangar was completed, the engineers learned too late that it wouldn't encompass the wingspan of the plane! This will never happen in the new business world.

✔ **Plan for total quality in every area of the business.** Quality isn't something you inspect for at the end of a process. Quality is something you build into every area of the business, into every process, and into every product. Customers today expect quality, no matter how much or how little they pay for something. Successful companies in the future will have to go above and beyond that expected standard of quality in every aspect of their businesses.

✔ **Implement flatter and more team-based structures.** Hierarchies are out; teams are in. Decision-making that has to fight its way through dozens of layers of hierarchy slows things down, and creates inertia. Companies that can't or won't respond quickly are in a dangerous position. It's time for bureaucrats to join a team!

✔ **Form strategic partnerships with other companies in their industry.** Companies are forming teams with other companies, including competitors! Adversarial business relations have no place in a market that's too complex for any one business to handle alone. Successful companies join forces with others that have what they need. For many years before they merged, Compaq and Digital collaborated on an extensive range of hardware and software projects – and this included jointly managing the sales and distribution sides.

✔ **Create real value.** Businesses create value when they provide products or services that the customers perceive as valuable, and when the company builds worth beyond what its founders contributed. We use the word *real* because the jury is still out on whether the Internet companies that have such high values at present are creating value that's sustainable, or merely part of a huge stock market boom. Time will answer that question.

Making predictions: What you can count on in the future

We don't want to give the impression that the world of business is in total chaos. You can count on a few sure-fire developments over the coming years. The following trends will affect your business and your job, so note them well:

✔ **A continuing decline in the birth rate in the developed world, and a change in age distribution.** This means that finding highly-skilled workers will become harder. Moreover, the aging population will impact on pension schemes, health care provision, retirement ages, and the ability of individuals to support themselves through their later years.

   • Other challenges related to the aging population will become apparent, and will be met by companies and organisations prepared and willing to move fast and first.

   • Working life will become longer. Already the Government is considering proposals to push the retirement age up to 68, and to allow people to work on beyond the age of 65 with no restrictions or caveats.

✔ **Changes in how disposable income is spent in the four primary sectors: government, health, education, and leisure.** These changes will produce opportunities in a variety of areas:

- *Social responsibility*, or giving something back to the community.

- Fitness and health (as the baby boomer generation ages).

- Sheltered and assisted housing.

- Collective and individual social service and living support.

- Retail and leisure (from the consumer power of those over 50 years of age).

- Managing finances and booking travel arrangements and other entertainment and leisure online will develop further.

✔ **A shift in power and ownership of business and property to pension funds and institutional investors.** This will have direct effects on business strategy, property development, usage, and management.

✔ **Review and evaluation of employment responsibilities, especially in terms of long-term commitments to those on standard contracts of employment.** The onus of responsibility is increasingly being shifted to companies wherever possible or feasible.

- The trend to work from home, on the hoof, or wherever work is actually required will continue; as will the need to work non-standard hours.

- Organisations will have to manage career flexibility. Individuals are going to have to be prepared to change careers, and re-train where necessary at different stages of their working life.

✔ **More global competition.** Many businesses began manufacturing and out-sourcing in other countries because labour was cheap and plentiful. And many businesses are finding that doing so didn't deliver the advantages that they sought. If productivity and quality are the watchwords, then more *skilled* staff are needed, and so you have to be absolutely clear that *skilled* staff are available if you do decide to move elsewhere. You need to look very carefully at all opportunities available in the global marketplace to make sure that they are indeed opportunities and not illusions!

Coping with Change

All the changes happening in the business world may appear overwhelming and even threatening, especially if you're a manager in a large company and wondering how these changes may affect your career and your future. Or as a business owner, you may be concerned about how long you can keep your business moving ahead in the new marketplace.

Undoubtedly, enormous, pervasive, and radical changes are taking place in the business marketplace and society. Accept that fact and begin to prepare yourself and your business for the changes to come. As soon as you get into the mindset of change, you'll feel comfortable with it and actually relish the thought that you don't know for sure what will happen tomorrow. Well, perhaps you can't relish that prospect just yet, but it certainly won't be as frightening. Surprises can be fun!

Planning for change

The idea of planning for change may seem oxymoronic – the two concepts just don't go together. How do you plan for something you don't know is going to happen? Well, you start by preparing your organisation and the people in it to respond quickly to change when it happens, and you develop ways to scan the economic, business, and market environment so that you become better at predicting what may come along. Here's a seven-step plan to help you and your company take advantage of change.

Step one: Out with the old, in with the new

Face it: We all get set in our ways, especially if they seem to be working, and we benefit from them. Everyone maintains a false sense of confidence about the ways in which they do things, and businesses are no different. After a system is put in place, it seems to get set in stone. We see this situation every day in the businesses we work with.

No matter how well something works, it can always be improved. An easy way to find out if you need to change something you're doing is to ask yourself: 'If I had to do this again, would I do it this way?' If the answer is no, then don't waste time working out what's wrong. Find a new way to do it. Do this for every area of your business and you'll make a really positive difference. You have to start somewhere. 'A journey of a thousand miles always starts with a single step.' So do *something* – and use it as a starting point – and don't go back.

Admit it – do you still have some of your childhood toys? Businesses often cling on to old products, services, and ways of working that you may feel attached to, but are now totally obsolete. These products and services have reached the very end of their life-cycles but continue to drain the limited resources of the business – time, money, and effort – to keep them going, to squeeze the last drop of revenue from them, and to avoid the uncomfortable question of how and when to kill them off. This practice is called throwing good money after bad. Instead, put your time, effort, and resources into finding new products and services to offer that are at the beginning of their life-cycles.

You need to take a critical look at your business and decide what is working and what is not. You may be spending too much time taking care of old products, services, systems, and processes. Concentrate your efforts on looking for new ways of doing things, and new products and services that will help you to be more competitive in the fast-paced global market. Get rid of the stuff that's not working – now!

Step two: Make a plan to improve

Continuous improvement, the constant re-evaluation of every aspect of your business to find ways to make it better, needs to become a part of the culture of your business. To accomplish this situation, create a plan that includes some goals, things that you want to improve, deadlines, and ways to measure the level of improvement you achieve.

Studies have found that people who write down their goals are much more likely to achieve them than people who don't put them in writing. That idea makes sense if you think about it. Writing goals down symbolises a commitment on your part to make them happen. But how will you know when you've achieved your goal? You also need to establish some measures of achievement, some specific ways to determine and demonstrate that you've reached the goal. For example, if one of your business goals is to improve the productivity of your employees, you have to define specifically which activities need to be improved, and how you can measure improvement in those activities.

Suppose you notice that productivity among the people who package your products has been slipping and they're not packaging as many products per hour as they have in the past. Here are some steps you can take:

✔ Come up with a realistic expectation for the number of products that can be packaged per hour. This figure is usually based on what's been done in the past when you've been meeting the goals set. It may also be a benchmark figure based on your best packagers.

✔ Check the productivity of all your packagers over a period of, say, a week, and compare the results against your benchmark. That way you will know quickly when productivity has increased.

✔ Talk to your employees to get input on how their production processes can be improved. Productivity may have declined for reasons that are unrelated to the packaging task itself. For example, the air temperature in the packaging area may be too warm due to lack of ventilation, making the employees lethargic.

Define your plan in terms of: 'Change from what, to what, when, where, how, and why'. Publish your plan in these terms, and make sure that all your employees know it and what you expect of them. And get their input – they know what the opportunities are, and also what the problems are.

The bottom line is, if you don't know where you're going, how will you know when you've arrived? Make a plan.

Step three: Celebrate wins over problems

Have you ever noticed that finding fault is much easier than recognising something good? At board meetings or in reports, companies often focus on what's wrong with the company and not what's right. They detail the problem areas and give little attention to the company's successes.

Celebrate everything that your company does right. Make sure that everyone knows when a good job has been done. Dave Sullivan, owner and CEO of Sullivan Development Services, a human resources (HR) development consultancy, always ordered food and drinks for everyone at the end of days in which successes (however small) were achieved. Doing so kept everyone together and made sure that everyone knew what had been achieved.

If you do have to find fault, then use it as a lever for putting things right. Celebrate when the problem is resolved. And never ever wallow in the mire of problems and faults.

Step four: Set aside money for change

Edwin Land, founder of the Polaroid Corporation, once said that you need to be the one to make your products obsolete. In other words, don't wait until others come along with a replacement product or service.

Of course, developing something new and implementing change costs money. So you need to budget for these developments and make sure that the resources are available. Of course, if you control the purse strings yourself, you'll know what's available as well as what's required. Otherwise, you need the support of your top management and backers, so make sure that they know what's required, the outcome – and how much the change is going to cost them! You need to get resources devoted to change and development, and that allocation of resources makes everyone more committed to actually finding ways to change.

Step five: Build a strong, consistent culture

In these turbulent times, companies need something they can count on for a sense of continuity, and employees find their stability and comfort in the culture of the company. *Culture* is simply the personality and norms of the company – how the company works and comes together.

Make sure that the company culture is strong, positive, and cohesive, especially in times of great change, and that everyone has confidence and knows where they stand, whatever's going on in the world around them. The last thing you want when you're trying to implement change for the good of all, is resistance based on the fact that people are frightened of the future. Get them used to change, and build a company in which everybody welcomes and embraces the excitement of it.

Scanning the environment

Environment scanning means understanding trends and developments in your industry, locality, and in the world around you, and is critical to your company's success and its ability to respond quickly to the innumerable changes it faces.

Make sure you read your local press, trade journals, and magazines, and the national daily press especially *The Times*, *The Telegraph*, and *Financial Times*. Make sure you have regular access to specialist journals such as *The Economist* and *Management Today*. You'll start to become better informed immediately; and you then soon get into the habit of questioning the received wisdom or general perception of your company and industrial sector. You also get into the habit of making sure that you know what you're talking about in meetings!

Reading widely in this way means that you find information about economic, political, and legal changes that might affect your business. You get advance notice of likely and possible booms and recessions. You find out what others are doing – in your sector and elsewhere – and you gain good ideas that you can try out for yourself.

Use the Internet as an environment scanning source. Make yourself familiar with sites specific to your industry and locality. Take a regular look at least some of the following Web sites:

✔ www.FT.com: The Web site of the *Financial Times* has excellent information on all companies, organisations, and sectors. The site provides a subscription service for more specialist information.

✔ www.cmi.org.uk: The Web site of the Chartered Management Institute (CMI) provides economic, business, and political information; and carries company profiles and success (and failure!) stories from all sectors.

✔ www.businesslink.gov.uk: This site lists local Business Links in all areas, a Government initiative that provides resources and support for company and organisation initiatives, as well as detailing local information and contacts.

✔ www.bbc.co.uk: The BBC's Web site carries a large and detailed range of current and historic information on companies and organisations, and also economic and (especially) political initiatives and proposals. Click on the Business and Money link on the homepage.

If you're incredibly busy (who isn't!) and don't have time to do this – then make time. Get out into the field, get out among customers, and get out into the community. Make yourself familiar with everything that's going on; find out what's important to people, what the burning issues really are – and soak it all up! You'll be amazed at what you find out when you make environment scanning a habit. You'll soon become an expert in gathering, analysing, and evaluating the information that you need.

Step six: Become an environment scanner

Information is the key to success, but the company with the most information doesn't necessarily win in the end. Instead, the company that wins knows how to use the information it collects to develop a competitive edge, improve the company, find new customers, find ways to keep old customers, and stay on top of change.

Having the ability to scan the environment for information about current trends is part of the equation, and a big part of your commitment (see the sidebar 'Scanning the Environment'). You then need the ability to analyse the information to see how it can help your business.

Step seven: Celebrate failure; reward change

Why on earth would a company want to celebrate failure? The answer is: *You can't achieve great success without learning from failures along the way.* As Napoleon said: 'Anyone who never made a mistake, never made anything.' Sony still celebrates the invention of the Betamax video system, even though it was swamped by the universally available VHS system. You may try to insulate your company from mistakes and errors, but in doing so you're certain to stifle progress and initiative. You can only fail if you try – and you can only win if you try. (Does that sound like a catch-22?)

Finally: Don't look back!

The challenge for businesses today is to stop wasting time on the past because it's no longer relevant, unless you enjoy the nostalgia of the good old days. And if you look really hard at 'the good old days' you normally find that they had their problems too. Who among us now wants to give up our mobile phones, laptop computers, or Internet access? The good old days are here and now. Over a hundred years ago, Oliver Wendell Holmes stated: 'I see it all perfectly; there are two possible situations – one can either do this or that. My honest opinion and friendly advice is this – *do it, or do not do it – you will regret both.*' So we say – do it. Start right now to accept and use change to your advantage.

Chapter 2

Information Technology and Competitive Advantage

. . . .

. . . .

*I*f you ask anyone in business or management whether they're technology aware and literate, they'll always answer 'yes' – whether they are or not. However, most technology is under-used and under-exploited overwhelmingly because it is chosen, designed, installed, and implemented by the wrong people, for the wrong reasons, in the wrong place, at the wrong time.

Misusing or under-using your Information Technology (IT) systems is extremely expensive. Doing so is also ultimately very damaging – in some cases, fatal – to the long-term future of the business.

You have to know what you want to do with your business in a business sense before you can begin to think about what kind of technology you may need. Chapter 4 helps you understand the strategic planning process better and gives you suggestions for how to go about it.

This chapter covers the four basic steps for preparing your business to maximise the opportunities afforded by technology:

✔ Know your business.

✔ Create a technology-competitive advantage.

✔ Develop a plan.

✔ Get some help.

Technology and You

The seeds of destruction are sown by anyone in any executive capacity who tries to bluff their way through the technology minefield rather than admit that they don't know enough about it and hand the job – or at least the groundwork – over to someone who does. We've all met people in business and management who say: 'Yes, but I simply don't have the time to sit down for long enough to know and understand the technology and what it can do.'

Our response is the same to everyone: 'Can you afford to fall behind your competitors? Can you afford to have something installed, the capacity of which you don't know or understand? Can you afford technology that nobody can use to its full potential?'

The number one reason for business failure is poor management. And creating a technology strategy is most certainly a management issue.

Technology has changed our fundamental perceptions about how business can, and should, be conducted. Customers now expect immediate transactions. Everyone expects immediacy of access to information, and if they can't get it from you, they'll get it elsewhere. Indeed, people expect everything faster today, and they expect instant responses, satisfaction, and questions answered, wherever in the world the particular contact person or manager happens to be. Technology has made everyone capable of conducting business or work from anywhere in the world. No wonder you see so many people with mobile phones and laptop computers at airports and railway stations; many workers reckon to stay in touch with their organisation and work even when on holiday.

If you're not using technology to its fullest extent today, you won't be in business five years from now. Not only that, you may well be overtaken by an entrepreneurial business that's using technology to its fullest advantage. And if you carry out work supplying to large or dominant customers, they may insist that you use technology their way or even to their design. *Supply side management* (which means doing your best to assure the volume and quality of everything that is supplied to you) has become an area in which many organisations have successfully cut costs and improved quality at the same time – overwhelmingly through the use of standardised technology – and they refuse to do business with anyone who does not install this technology or make it work effectively.

So you have no choice in the matter – sorry! You can't sit around deciding if and when you're going to invest the time and money to make technology work effectively for you – you must do it and you must do it now.

Knowing What You Need from Technology

To decide what you need from technology, you have to know and understand every aspect of your business and its environment. You need to know who your customers are and what they expect from you in terms of quantity, quality, and reliability. You need to know what your competitors are providing that you aren't, and what you're providing that your competitors aren't. You need to look at the supply side in full detail. You then have to look at each and every aspect of the business and see where investment in technology and the expertise needed to maximise its potential will make a difference.

In the detail, this process will vary among organisations. However, each of the following areas always needs a full evaluation in relation to IT:

- ✔ Communications among staff, departments, divisions, and functions
- ✔ Customer, supplier, and distribution management
- ✔ Manufacturing if you're in production; service delivery management if you're in services
- ✔ Information management
- ✔ Advertising and marketing
- ✔ Service delivery and support, and customer and client liaison
- ✔ Project work and project management

Think carefully about where you can improve or tighten your operations and activities, and what contribution technology is to make in support and pursuit of this.

Become your competitors' customer

Dealing with your competitors as a customer means that you can find out a lot about how they do business and how they treat their customers. Today, the chances of your having a product or service that no one else has are little or none. The best chance of differentiating yourself from your competitors lies in how you do business and how your company looks. Getting inside the operations of a competitor's company is difficult unless you're a customer. As a customer, you find out how your competitor treats customers, how their billing works, what they do when customers have a problem, and so forth. In short, you gain a much more informed view of your competitor rather than some meaningless statistics that someone else gathered. And when you've done it, record the information, and make sure that it's used to best advantage at all times within your organisation.

Look for ways to improve your competitors' operations

Looking at your competitors' operations gives you a chance to find holes. And when you find holes in *their* operations, that means finding opportunities for *your* business. Suppose you discover that your competitors have no means of getting input easily from customers. This detail provides an opportunity for you to consider ways to give customers access to your company, perhaps with a free-phone number or a Web site. So make sure that you see the possibilities in your own situation, and use them to your best advantage.

Discover how your business interconnects

Every business has many processes that go on inside it and you have to understand how they all interconnect before you can pinpoint how technology can improve them. One way to identify all the various activities and processes that take place is to put yourself into the shoes of the customer and walk through the front door. What's the first thing you see? Depending on the business, it may be a reception desk. Now ask yourself three questions:

- ✔ What work is taking place here?
- ✔ Who is doing the work?
- ✔ What do they need to do the work?

Now think about the work that starts at the reception desk and moves to some other point in the office. Maybe an order comes in, and it needs to go to the person in charge of recording orders and then to the warehouse to prepare for shipping. A copy may also need to go to accounting if the order creates an account. Each one of these activities is a process that probably has a technological procedure attached to it. As you walk through your business, you'll probably find that it's more complex than you realised, with many interacting and interlocking tasks. Understanding how your business works is the first step in looking for ways to make it better with the help of technology.

We're great believers in making your customer part of your team, so be sure to get their input on all the aspects of your company that they touch, from billing to manufacturing to shipping and customer service. The perspective and needs of your customers can form the basis for new opportunities to improve your business and make it more competitive. They may also give you ideas on how to grow your business. Technology can enhance all these activities.

Know the technology experts

You can invest in new technology, but you also need people on board who are willing to learn and able to use it. Making technology part of your company culture isn't as easy as saying, 'This is what we're going to do'. You encounter a lot of resistance from some people who don't want to give up their old, comfortable ways. You also encounter resistance from people whose careers have been built by following the old ways – and so you have to give incentives if you want them to change.

To get support from your employees, consider these suggestions:

- ✔ Ask your employees what tools they need to do their jobs better.

- ✔ Have them create a wish list of these tools.

- ✔ Show them how technology can make their lives easier and more productive and rewarding by ensuring that they are properly trained and briefed in its usage, and by making clear that this is the new way of working.

- ✔ Provide incentives for using the new technology, and ensure that people are rewarded for progress and advancement in technological proficiency and effective output.

- ✔ Make the process as enjoyable and rewarding as you can.

Creating a Competitive Advantage with Technology

When we've asked business owners what their competitive advantage is, they usually respond with at least one of the following points:

- ✔ Niche market
- ✔ Customer relationships
- ✔ Unique product

What we don't often hear is how these business owners are using technology as a competitive advantage to propel them ahead of their competitors. Why is that? With everything in the media today about technology, why are these business owners so unaware? Most business owners still see computer technology as an efficiency tool rather than an investment in the future success of their businesses, and doing so is a critical mistake. You can't afford to think like a traditional business owner any longer. Continuous advancements in computer technology have opened up new customer and geographical markets for many small businesses. But in creating a more accessible and integrated global economy, technology has also exposed a business's current customer base to competitors located thousands of miles away.

What technology can do for you

As a competitive advantage in any business, technology can be used to:

- Compete with other companies by marketing on a nearly level playing field – the Internet.
- Build and develop loyal relationships with customers.
- Link with strategic partners to speed up processes such as product development and manufacturing.
- Link everyone in the company with everyone else, as well as with necessary sources of information within and outside the company.
- Provide immediate information on pricing, products, and services to suppliers and customers.
- Provide speedy responses to customer and supplier complaints, and product and service problems.

Familiarity and effectiveness

Make yourself as familiar and knowledgeable as you can with the technology. That way, you'll know and understand what everyone is talking about, and you'll become more comfortable with the technology itself. Doing so is important because whatever line of work you're in, you're going to have to know, understand, and use technology.

- Use experts when you have to. Don't be afraid of not knowing something or not being able to do something – and when experts do come in to advise you, make sure that they show you what they're doing so that you understand it.

- Don't worry about asking even the simplest of questions, and asking what particular technological terms mean.

- If you need to know how to use something or do something, get someone to show you. If necessary, get them to write out a series of instructions for you to follow so that you can build up good and effective habits.

- Make sure your administrative, support, and back office staff are also up to speed. Back office and administrative staff are essential for the effective running of your organisation and your business, so make sure that they work as effectively and efficiently as possible.

Honda UK: Using technology to make better cars

When Honda UK set up its car production plant at Swindon, technology was used wherever possible to ensure quality and volume of production, effective information systems, and the best possible supply side management. Everything was fully integrated and supported by an extensive and continuing training programme in which all staff were required to participate. Everyone understood every aspect of the business and their position in it, and everything that had to be done to ensure that the cars carried on rolling off the production lines as fast as possible, and without faults.

An electronic re-order system was (and still is) used to monitor stocks of components; and as soon as a certain level of each is reached, a fresh order is automatically transmitted to the suppliers. The order includes component volumes, delivery schedules, and deadlines.

This full integration of technology, supported by the extensive staff training, reinforces the fact that technology is an investment on which returns are demanded; and it also makes sure that the cost base is managed as efficiently and effectively as possible. This in turn helps to ensure that Honda remains one of the top quality brands in the UK car industry.

When you have the capability to link everyone in your business to a central source of information and then let your customers and suppliers tap into certain areas of that information centre you gain enormous power. Information is power. The company who has the most information wins is, however, no longer true. Now the company who can *manage* the most information wins. You manage information with technology.

Killing the technology myths

As more advanced technology became available to businesses, the large corporations first had the capital to invest in and take advantage of all the benefits technology had to offer. But now businesses of all sizes see the value of investing in technology. However, both business people and managers get bogged down in things that they don't know or don't understand, and this gives rise to some myths and legends that we can lay to rest.

Networks and Web sites are for big organisations

This myth has largely disappeared – many individuals now have their own Web sites and *blogs* (personal, departmental, and company newsletters and opinion boards), as do businesses of all sizes. Any company that needs to reach its customers, whether those customers are local or on the other side of the world, can benefit from a Web site.

The three key benefits of using your Web site and the networks created to best advantage are:

- ✔ You can share information with other company computers, even if they're in remote locations.
- ✔ You can share resources and expertise.
- ✔ You can share programmes, and ensure that all your staff are trained to use them so that you're instantly flexible and responsive when required.

Networks and Web sites are cheap

A good Web site isn't cheap, but you can put together a pretty cheap network by just using a spare PC as your *server* (information storage centre) if it has enough disk space. However, you need to purchase and install the server software, *network cards* (to link the computers together digitally), hubs, and cables. If you want to go further with this topic, take a look at *Networking For Dummies*, 7th edition by Doug Lowe (Wiley).

At present, everyone expects you to have a Web site. Your commitment therefore is to ensure that your Web site is visually good, easy to use, and bang up-to-date. If you don't commit to this ideal, and your site looks sloppy and unkempt, customers and clients will assume that the rest of your business is sloppy also. If people have to wait longer than a few seconds for the pop-ups to appear, they will forget you and go to someone else. So invest in the quality and usability of your networks and Web sites, as well as their technological merit.

Make sure that your own staff know and understand how to use the Web site and network. It's bad business – and very expensive – to have staff spending unproductive time trying to navigate their way through a Web site that's difficult to use or, worse still, giving bad directions to customers, suppliers, and other interested parties.

Build a Web site and people will visit it

Some people are under the mistaken assumption that if they design and build a stellar Web site, potential customers will swarm to it like bees to clover. Don't be seduced by this myth. Remember, millions of Web sites compete on the Internet, and unless you find creative ways to let people know that yours is there, you may remain in exile for a long time. For instance, Boo.com, the online footwear retailer, failed to market itself effectively except on the Internet; and so few people bought their shoes.

Here are just three of the many ways you can attract people to your site:

✔ Register with search engine companies such as Yahoo!, Google, and MSN. You need to contact these and similar companies from a business point of view, and reach agreements with them ensuring that they put your company's name on the first page or two of any search. And be sure to use keywords that bring up your company's site near the top of any search list. (*Keywords* are typical words people think of when looking for your product or service.)

✔ Partner with compatible Web sites and create links so that someone who goes to your partner's site can easily find your site as well. For example, a travel agency can link with a resort site.

✔ Put your Web site address on your business cards, stationery, and all promotional material or advertising that you do offline, including the *Yellow Pages*.

Networks require an Internet connection

Actually, you don't need a connection to the outside world to run a network within your business. In fact, the newest operating systems look and feel like Internet Web sites, so you can have browsers, chat rooms, news, and mail servers that serve only your employees. These *intranets* are very valuable for keeping employees connected.

Networks aren't secure

If you don't allow people to dial in to your network server, then you have little to worry about in terms of someone from the outside gaining access. However, most businesses provide some sort of dial-in access so that employees can work from home or get information when they're away from the office. If you do allow access, then you can protect the security of your network with passwords and other types of security devices. Networks *can* be secure.

Thinking Ahead: Having a Plan

As with everything, the implementation of new technology requires planning. Remember, technology is an investment on which you are seeking returns, and so start planning from this point of view.

Don't upgrade or replace technology simply because doing so is fashionable, or because 'everyone else in the industry is doing it'. Take a step back, reflect, and decide what contribution you require from the technology.

Technology is no longer an operating expense for businesses. It has become a strategic investment that helps owners run their businesses more efficiently and effectively. Technology is an asset, just like equipment and employees. Nevertheless, your technology investment must support your business goals. Technology has value only when it is connected to a defined objective.

Before investing in technology, you need a plan. Start by evaluating your current information system.

How good is your information system?

Here's an easy quiz to test the status of your current information system:

1. Are you using electronic formats as well as paper forms and memos?
2. Can you remember where all your information is stored, and retrieve it easily?
3. Do all managers have the same information?
4. Can you easily find all your information on a particular customer?
5. Are your partners (suppliers and so on) part of your information system?
6. Can everyone come together to respond to a crisis quickly?
7. Can everyone easily access the technology if they need to?
8. Is the technology fully integrated (and this includes video-conferencing and tele-conferencing facilities where appropriate)?

If you can answer 'yes' to all these questions, then leave your system well alone. But many businesses can't do all these things at present. Remember, the problem isn't getting information but managing the information so that you can do something with it – and that's where technology can help you.

Refining your technology plan

The goal of a technology plan is to identify the areas of the business that can be improved and the specific technology – hardware and/or software – that can do the job. The plan usually covers a period of time into the future and adds the technology in stages so that the company isn't burdened with buying it and retraining employees all at once. Many businesses purchase computers and software without looking to the future and often without considering what they already have. Then when they reach the point where they're trying to link everything together, nothing is compatible, and they end up spending much more time and money than they would have if they'd planned carefully.

Here are some points to remember:

- ✔ Don't buy technology just because it's the latest and greatest thing. It has to make sense for your business and the kinds of activities and processes you have.

- ✔ Plan for the right period of time. Some business environments are pretty stable and predictable, so it makes sense to plan for three to five years into the future. In more volatile business environments, such as high-tech businesses, that planning timeframe may be reduced to as little as six months.

- ✔ Make the planning process a team effort. Get the input of all the people who will use the new technology to do their jobs. And don't forget to include feedback from your customers. Try asking, 'What can we do to make dealing with us easier and more pleasant?'

- ✔ Balance the costs of upgrading your old system versus going to a new system. In particular, make sure that you know and understand fully the length of a system's useful life before it requires upgrading and replacement.

- ✔ Train everyone. This technology is part of your investment. And remember that the technology won't work itself – you need capable and qualified staff to do that.

- ✔ Always see technology as an investment on which you have projected and demanded returns.

When you develop a technology plan for your business, think of technology as your competitive advantage and use it to accomplish the following:

- ✔ Speed up product development.

- ✔ Speed up processes.

- ✔ Access and manage information.

- ✔ Access and manage relationships.

- ✔ Build a network of strategic partners.

- ✔ Most importantly, survive!

Calling in an Expert: Getting Help

One of the best-kept secrets of management is that you don't have to do it all yourself – you can always summon help if, and when, you need it. So make your mind up that, whenever you need help on the technology front, you'll ask for it. The main source of help and advice comes from specialist consultants and information technology and services organisations. The best of these are always expensive; however, when needs must, you have to be prepared to pay for this (it becomes much easier to pay if you envisage the matter as an investment with eventual returns).

This section shares other sources of help available, many of them inexpensive, and in many cases, bringing the additional benefit of organisation development.

Students

Today's university and college students were weaned on computers. Technology is second nature to them, and they're a great source of technical help for you. For example, most business schools, engineering schools, and computer science departments are populated with highly-skilled college students who are often looking for part-time jobs to help pay their expenses and beef up their CVs. You can usually hire these students for very reasonable rates. Contact your local college or university about the best way to reach students looking for such work. Most colleges also have internship programmes where students are placed in a company to work part-time and are given college credit for it. Working with a student under that arrangement often means you don't have to pay for their input.

Don't forget sixth-formers. Even big high-tech companies hire them during summer holidays, and they report huge successes with these young employees.

Teachers, professors, and academics

If what you need to accomplish requires the maturity and experience of an older person, consider taking on those with expertise in IT and its applications, especially school teachers, lecturers, professors, and other academics. As well as being generally available in the summer, schools, colleges, and universities now experience pressure to build links with industry and commerce.

Send employees on training courses

You may have someone working for you who's eager to gain some new skills and become the resident techie for the company. Every community has places, including further and higher education colleges, private and commercial providers, and evening classes, where employees can begin to improve specific technology skills. Reward your employee's motivation by sending him or her on the relevant courses, and then make sure that they're able to practise and share their new skills and knowledge while working back at the company.

Chapter 3

Going Global

- -

In This Chapter

▶ Making the decision to go global

▶ Deciding whether your business has what it takes

▶ Choosing and getting to know compatible countries

▶ Finding a good intermediary

▶ Getting the money and resources to start exporting

- -

*W*hether you're a small retailer in a shopping centre in Maidstone or a large plastics manufacturer in Leeds, the global marketplace affects you. In countries from Kenya to South Korea, people around the world may want your products and services. In years past, going global meant a huge outlay of capital to fund facilities and hire people, but today, going global can be as easy as getting on the Internet.

Heading Overseas

Everyone's talking about international this and global that. Now that people have the capability to reach another country with the click of a mouse, the world seems quite a bit smaller and more accessible. You can go around the world virtually without leaving the comfort of your chair. Granted, that method's not the most exciting way to access the world, but it's a start.

Increasing competition in domestic markets and saturated markets in some industries are prompting business owners to examine the international marketplace where demand is great for domestic products and services and where, in some parts of the world, money is not an issue. In the international marketplace, businesses have found new markets for their products, partners for their businesses, and complementary products that help increase their sales in their local markets.

The global market is attractive to businesses at the moment for several reasons:

- ✔ With relatively low interest rates, businesses have had an easier time financing their overseas opportunities.
- ✔ Exporting to Europe has become easier due to the continued enlargement of the European Union.
- ✔ The opening up of new markets in China, India, and southeast Asia has attracted many UK businesses.
- ✔ Initiatives are continually going on in many parts of the world, driven especially by mega project activity, such as the development of Dubai.

Of course, reasons closer to home also exist for considering the global market:

- ✔ It allows you to build a broader customer base, which can minimise the impact of economic problems at home.
- ✔ You may be able to reduce the effects of seasonal market swings, because countries south of the equator are in opposite seasons to those north of the equator.
- ✔ If you have excess capacity in your manufacturing facility, you may be able to use it by finding more products to produce for global markets.
- ✔ You may find new life for a product that's losing ground in the domestic market, although doing so is not as easy today as it used to be. The Internet has made countries around the world aware of the latest products on the market in the developed world.

As in any marketplace, you must offer high quality products and services at competitive prices. Nobody will welcome you with open arms unless you have products and services that are of benefit to them, and you deliver positive benefits to the communities and locations into which you are going to try and work. Beyond those necessities, researchers have found that most successful global businesses have some common characteristics:

- ✔ **A strong global vision.** In other words, their plans consider the influence, effects, and opportunities found in the international market.
- ✔ **Management with some international experience.** Gaining an understanding of other countries and how they do business is easier than ever.
- ✔ **Strong international networks of people and businesses that can help them.** One of the cardinal rules of going global is to find partners in the country in which you want to do business. These partners know how things really work and can save you a lot of time and effort, not to mention money.

Whatever product or service you plan to offer, it must be something that you can modify to meet the needs of the customers in whatever country you're considering doing business with. If you're introducing a new product that has never been on the market before, you probably want to start domestically first to establish yourself. That way, your systems and controls can be in place and you have fewer problems when you expand to another country.

Making the World Your Oyster

With all the countries in the world, how do you know which are best for your products and services? You need to do your homework. Do your market and environment research thoroughly, and find out who else is operating in the particular locality. And after you've established that there's a market for your products and services, you need to know and understand any barriers that may exist in terms of:

- Product and service specifications, especially local restraints on things such as emissions.
- Cultural barriers, making sure that you've understood that no social or religious reasons prevent people from using your products or services.
- Employment practices, including minimum and maximum hours regulations, and any constraints on wage levels.
- The banking and finance systems, and especially the rules that may prevail upon overseas organisations trading in particular locations.
- Technology barriers and the ability to access information systems and networks.

Never be afraid to ask for help. You can find specialist consultancies dealing with most products and services in most countries of the world; and you may also find that the retail and clearing banks and other finance houses, trade federations, and even the UK Department of Trade and Industry can answer your questions.

Why go global?

The first thing you need to establish is the reason for going overseas – and easy short answers such as 'increasing sales', 'developing markets', or 'exploiting opportunities' won't do! You need to go into full detail on each of these reasons.

✔ **Increasing sales:**

- By how much, and by when?

- Why will the overseas markets and customers buy from us?

- What is their attitude to foreign organisations (especially Western organisations)?

- What can go wrong?

- Are others interested in the market, and if so, what are the potential consequences for us?

- How much will we need in order to establish a presence?

- How much will we need to invest in order to generate the sales volumes we seek?

✔ **Developing markets:**

- Are the markets really capable of being developed?

- How long will it take?

- What investment in marketing will it take?

- What other factors do we need to take into account?

- How will we manage the supply and distribution sides and networks?

- What are the preferred modes of transport in the country?

- In what order of priority do the products and services we have to offer really figure in the proposed markets and locations?

✔ **Exploiting opportunities:** You need to precisely define the opportunities. Part of this definition must involve calculating:

- A return on investment.

- The best, medium, and worst outcomes.

- What can possibly go wrong, and what contingencies are in place to provide the necessary help.

You may think that all of this analysis looks easy and obvious. In theory, all managers answer the questions carefully. In practice, however, as anyone who's ever participated in a failed overseas venture can tell you, the truth is very different. Top and senior managers of large organisations get the excitement of the chase and evaluate only the opportunities and prospects of success, and seldom the pitfalls. Many of these ventures then degenerate into exciting, glamorous, messy, dangerous – and expensive – adventures in locations about which they know and understand very little, and often care even less.

Simply assuming that because you're a large and effective domestic player you will become a successful international organisation is no basis for going overseas. Just because you have the production services and financial capacity to serve overseas markets, doesn't mean that they'll want to be served by you.

For smaller businesses, the status and kudos of having overseas customers and contracts must not detract from the core domestic market, unless the overseas market generates enough revenue to give it a life of its own.

Talk to other global businesses in your chosen location – they'll normally be only too ready and willing to share their experiences with you, to tell their war stories, and to point out to you the pitfalls, as well as the opportunities, in that location.

After you've evaluated all these considerations in full detail and you're satisfied that everything stacks up, you can then establish your own focal points on which you can base your overseas expansion.

Focal points for going global

Globalisation in a business sense is the process whereby organisations seek to establish a presence in the majority of countries, markets, and communities of the world. The following sections cover the things you need to be able to move into any new market; and they apply whether or not you do indeed intend ultimately to go global.

Global physical presence

Only three companies – ABB (the engineering company Asea Brown Boveri Ltd), Coca-Cola, and Microsoft – have carried out commercial activities in all the countries of the world. Transport, travel, and logistics firms have the capability of a truly global physical presence in terms of their ability to make deliveries and accept orders. Many banking and finance companies are able to access all parts of the world through partnerships, networks, and relationships. Oil and energy companies also supply to all countries of the world through networks and local providers. So the chances of having a genuinely global presence are clearly limited by the nature of the industry in which you happen to be operating; and to gain a physical presence across the whole world takes enormous amounts of finance and other resources.

Global reputation

Global reputation comes in many forms – not all of them good! On the positive side, companies such as The Body Shop enjoy a high global reputation for humane and fair business and employment practices. On the other hand, many European, North American, and Japanese companies are widely perceived to move into developing markets purely to exploit them – and then get out. If this has been the experience in the area in which you intend to try and work, then you'll have to convince the communities that you're different. The most successful global companies spent years investing in their global position and gaining returns on this, rather than seeking short-term entry into markets in the hope of making a quick profit.

 In order to understand the sheer range of activities necessary to gain a physical global or international presence, have a look at the Web sites of companies such as Sony, Nissan, Toshiba, Dell Computers, and Microsoft, and follow the links to 'About Us', 'Investor Relations', and 'Product Performance'. These links explain the nature of products and services demanded in different parts of the world, and the differences in specifications necessary to ensure that these products and services remain effective wherever they are delivered.

Global influence

Global influence, setting the standards for one or more specific area of activity or performance, arises from one or more of the following issues:

- Your technological standards, meaning your ability to command technology and make it easy for people to use your company in preference to others.

- Your product and service quality and standards, which are high enough to transcend any local considerations in different parts of the world.

- Your product and service volumes and accessibility, based on your ability to flood or dominate markets and charge prices that are acceptable to particular localities.

- Your manufacturing and service delivery standards, based on your capability to establish particular facilities, such as warehouses and depots, in different parts of the world.

- Your ability to get hold of finance, information, and other key resources in desired locations.

- Your command of rare or desirable raw materials (for example, oil in Norway, Canada, and the Middle East, or diamonds in southern Africa).

Your global influence may also extend to the supply and manufacture of key components for specific industries or the delivery of globally desired quality of products and services (for example, Microsoft software; Coca-Cola soft drinks). Global influence may also be commanded by your capability to establish one or more of the following:

- ✔ **Global icon status**, such as that achieved by Walt Disney in the film and entertainment industries.

- ✔ **Standards of consumer goods manufacturing, quality, and durability**, as established by Japanese manufacturing companies.

- ✔ **Industry norms and customs**, for example, the fashion industry, which is dominated by exhibitions and trade fairs in London, Paris, Milan, and New York. Other industries dominated and driven by such norms include aerospace, defence, and finance.

- ✔ **High industry standards**, such as the hotel standard established by Hilton, and subsequently developed and adopted by hoteliers who want a sustainable competitive position and commercial advantage in this sector.

Global access, reach and coverage are claimed by the major telecommunications, transport, and delivery companies of the world through their networks of suppliers, local distributors, and subcontractors. Some Internet companies also have a genuinely global reach – such as eBay, Amazon, and Google. However, remember that an Internet presence does not of itself create global trading conditions.

Failure to identify and concentrate on a focal point simply means that you'll lose out to those who do.

Culture Counts

You need to know and understand the particular locations in which you've decided to try and work. Doing so isn't as easy as it sounds. Many organisations have tried to set up activities in areas with high levels of unemployment and a readily available workforce, only to find that they haven't sufficiently tackled the cultural barriers. Understanding people's culture usually means having a physical presence in the particular location; and one of the early priorities after establishing a physical presence is to assess the key social and ethical (including religious) factors that dominate the ways in which people think and behave. For example:

- ✔ Many Western companies have established call centres in India, taking advantage of the high levels of education and low levels of wages. Many of these companies have been disappointed to find that Indian graduates (in common with their counterparts elsewhere in the world) are less than happy working in call centres, given any choice in the matter.

✔ Organisations seeking to establish themselves in France must understand the tightness and rigidity of the country's labour laws, the strict defence of the 35-hour working week, and (except in Paris and one or two other large cities) the more or less universal two-hour lunch-break!

It follows from this that one of the key outcomes of establishing a physical presence somewhere may be that you conclude that this is not the right place for you to be operating. This is a consequence of the decision to expand into new markets as well as to go global.

During the 1960s and 1970s, Japanese manufacturing companies such as Sharp, Sony, Nissan, and Toyota established manufacturing facilities in the UK, Western Europe, and North America on the basis that this was a long-term investment designed to bring enduring profitable performance to the companies, and in which the staff (and the communities in which they lived) were to have a genuine interest.

Accordingly, investment in production and service technology and the staff training required to make it work effectively was very high. This situation was underpinned by employment practices that included:

✔ The maximum possible stability and security of employment.

✔ High levels of wages in return for fully flexible working.

✔ Employee relations designed from the point of view of co-operation, active involvement, and mutual benefit – a partnership between company, employees and any recognised trade unions.

✔ Low levels of absenteeism, which were actively managed when they did arise.

These employment practices were underpinned by a full understanding of the social and cultural issues that were of value to the communities in which the companies were establishing themselves. And the results remain impressive – the Nissan factory in north-east England is the most productive in the world in terms of cars produced per employee.

Establishing Yourself

After you've decided to expand and go overseas, and have done all of the necessary groundwork, you have to decide how you're going to make your presence in your chosen location. You can do this by:

✔ Finding local partners.

✔ Deciding on a joint venture.

✔ Using agents and specialists.

✔ Merging with or acquiring a local provider.

Of course, you can also build your own facilities from scratch, but this does take time!

Local partners

Local partnering exists where the international organisation agrees to go into business with an indigenous organisation for a particular proposal or venture. Some countries insist on local partners being involved with multinational companies as a condition of entry. Do your homework and understand how the particular locality works in full detail before making any decisions.

Joint ventures

Joint ventures exist where two or more companies come together to pool their resources and expertise to develop a venture, project, products, services, or markets. The great advantage of being involved in joint ventures is that you get a good body of overseas experience very quickly without having to underwrite (insure) the risk of the venture in full. While at work in the joint venture, always make sure that you find out as much as possible about the particular location so that you're well placed to take advantage of any other opportunities as they arise.

Agents and specialists

If you simply want to export products and services to a particular locality, using an agent to act on your behalf may be possible. The advantage of this practice is that you don't have to invest heavily in establishing your own presence in the particular locality. The disadvantage is that you have to give up a large measure of control to the particular agent. You may also find that you have little influence over things like marketing, promotion. and distribution. You need to have full confidence in any agent who's acting on your behalf, and also ensure that you can get to see them whenever you need to do so (for example, if a sudden crisis occurs in the particular locality).

Signing on the dotted line

However you gain entry to an overseas location (by partnering, using an agent, merging, and so on), get the details in writing to ensure that your interests are as well protected as possible – and that also applies to any local partner or joint venture partner with whom you may be involved. Make sure that you understand the vagaries of the law in the locations in which you want to do business. Have a local lawyer acting on your behalf if you need to.

Written agreements should clearly specify and define the range of responsibilities apportioned to everyone involved, and where necessary (in joint ventures and local partnering agreements) where specific obligations and liabilities lie. You can't simply have the legal side of things defined in terms of your own country, and given that you don't want to be in dispute with foreign partners anyway, make sure that both parties' interests are fully protected in the locations where you're going to do business.

Mergers and acquisitions

Many Western companies have managed their expansion overseas through a process of merger and acquisition. The advantage of doing so is that the process is very quick, though it can be expensive. It does mean, however, that you acquire your own facilities. You can use the premises to both develop the business of the organisation that you've bought, and to bring in your own products and services.

Money Talks

Unfortunately, even with the largest and most powerful companies, many overseas ventures fail. You need to be able to support the financial cost of failures and errors, and to have contingency funds in place in case things do go wrong. Many people mistakenly think that if you get a large order from a foreign source, banks will be clamouring to give you money to buy the raw materials you need to fill the order. Sadly, nothing could be further from the truth. Export lenders, just like any other lenders, want to know that you have the resources to fill the orders. So do suppliers and distributors. Local partners and other members of joint ventures also need to know that you're going to be able to meet your obligations. So you need plenty of money to grow globally – the situation is as simple as that. At the very least, you have to be able to pay for creating and developing a presence in the new location, and giving it all of the support and resources required, including giving it sufficient resources to take advantage of any other opportunities that may become apparent after things are up and running.

You also have to be prepared to pay for developing your own reputation as a reliable deliverer of goods and services. You are, after all, entering someone else's field, and so existing players have the advantage of being known in the locality. Staff have to be paid and accommodated. Information systems have to be reliable and accessible. You'll have energy bills – heating, lighting, gas, electricity, and water. Transport and distribution all have to be paid for. Supply and distribution sides have to be underwritten. Security systems need to be in place and effective – and this includes the security of information, technology, and other electronic systems.

Acting global

When you consider how you're going to manage your new 'global' staff, you have a clear choice to make:

- ✔ **Act global – think global:** This means that you have sufficient confidence in the ways in which you do things to impose your own standards on the new location. In practice, Western companies and organisations can rarely do this in absolute terms, though some do clearly try. For example, the New Zealand dairy industry makes no concessions to its overseas markets – it simply exports what it sells to the domestic market, and has found profitable niches, especially in Great Britain. Western clothing and garment companies have been able to take advantage of their financial size and market influence to establish factory production activities in areas of cheap labour. Western banking and finance companies have taken advantage of high levels of indigenous technology and large-scale educated workforces to establish call centre operations and other customer service functions in India, central Europe, and South Africa.

- ✔ **Act global – think local:** This means that the strengths of the Western organisation are integrated with the local customs and culture of the new location, so that you can establish a fully productive relationship over the long term. For example, Nissan integrated its high production quality from Japan with the demands of north-east England for high and enduring levels of employment when it was establishing its UK factory. Honda at Swindon made a great feature of moving into a historic railway town when setting up in the UK. Eurotunnel, the channel tunnel operator, went to great lengths to establish close links with schools, colleges, and social groups in the south-east of England so that the project gained a high, immediate, and positive familiarity.

In an ideal world all this is what every business would strive for. However, some markets have only a limited useful life span; and some locations are subject to political changes and upheavals, not all of which may be of benefit to overseas operators.

Backers, financiers, and stockholders expect returns on investments, and enhanced values as the result of your overseas expansion. Customers and clients expect good products and services. They'll already be used to particular standards and quality of delivery from existing providers. If you want to take market share in the new location, you have to be prepared to invest up-front in making sure that customers and clients know what to expect from you.

You need to decide whether you're going to employ local staff or bring in your own (or a combination of both), and how much you're going to pay them. Consider:

- ✔ Are you going to pay your new staff the same rate as you pay your domestic/indigenous staff, regardless of location?
- ✔ Are you going to pay them a salary relative to wage rates in the new location?
- ✔ Are you going to pay them as much as possible – or as little as possible?

You need to arrive at an informed judgement – and you need to be able to deliver on it.

Selling to Another Country

Take the following example. You've just introduced a new machine that you spent four long years developing, patenting, and manufacturing. The machine is now ready for introduction into the domestic market. You get your first units into the market, and all of a sudden, people are offering to represent you in other countries, with big purchase orders in hand. You're very tempted to just grab these offers and run. But before you start planning where you're going to spend all your new-found money, you need to find out a few things about your foreign buyer. For instance, you need to understand the country's payment patterns and whether it has any creditor protection laws. You also need to investigate your customer's credit history. Providing a big purchase order is easy; making good on that order is another thing entirely.

If you extend credit to a company in another country, you are, for all intents and purposes, extending it to the country. Make sure that the country you pick is relatively stable and friendly to foreign companies. You can check out your foreign customer through your international bank, accounting firm, or most major credit reporting services. Most banks have their own credit reporting services or agencies, and the international central banking sector also provides references and assurances.

Keeping a beady eye on currency rates

The place where international sales become a virtual roulette game is in the area of currency rates. Fluctuating currency rates can both help and hurt you. At present, because of high oil prices and political uncertainty, currency exchange rates are particularly volatile all over the world. Exporters often make the mistake of believing that their money is at risk only in developing countries and unstable economies, but it can happen anywhere.

If you plan to extend terms to your customers over a long period of time, you probably want to take advantage of *currency hedging*, which means that you buy the right to lock in a predictable conversion rate. This is arranged either by your bank, or through a commercial finance house. The downside is that buying the hedge can cost a lot – up to 5 per cent per transaction.

Alternatively, you can set up a foreign bank account in the country in which you're doing business. Doing so can at least speed up the process of conversion and perhaps save you some money.

Of course, the best solution is to insist that payment is made in hard currency. That way, your customers assume the risk of currency fluctuations. Some customers may refuse, but remember, plenty of customers are out there, so stick to your guns!

Finding Partners with a Little Help

Fortunately, you don't have to think about going global completely on your own. Chambers of Commerce and Trade Federations have their own overseas contacts; and your bankers and other backers may also be able to help.

Part of the problem of going overseas is that you probably don't know anyone there, and they don't know you. So the first thing to do is to make sure that you get yourself known, and you can only do this by establishing a physical presence and getting out and about making contact with potential partners and venturers.

Embassies and Chambers of Trade in your preferred locations are always a useful starting point in putting you in touch with potential partners.

When you deal with potential partners, you must have people with you who can speak the language to the extent and expertise of being able to negotiate and deliver business deals. Unless you have fluent or bilingual native speakers in your domestic set up, you need to find interpreters immediately you set foot in the new location. You can find interpreters through your local embassy or trade mission, and through your own employer and trade federations.

You also need legal representations when dealing with potential partners, and again, local Embassies and Chambers of Trade are a useful starting point. Your own auditors or domestic lawyers may have contacts for you to try out.

When you've found the right business partners, you need to spend time getting to know and understand them. They'll see this partnership as a business venture in the same way as you, so you need to have in mind their interests as well as your own.

Chapter 4

Strategic Planning: Looking into the Crystal Ball

In This Chapter

▶ Getting to know your customers, the market, and the competition

▶ Doing strategic planning the right way

▶ Figuring out your company's strengths, weaknesses, opportunities, and threats

▶ Distinguishing between strategy and tactics

▶ Knowing when your strategy succeeds

*F*or decades, executives of large companies have met in back rooms or in expensive resort retreats miles from their corporate offices to strategise about their companies' futures. Although the strategies devised were often very creative, the executives rarely considered the fact that the environment they thought they knew might change overnight with the introduction of a new product or service from one of their competitors. In other words, the strategies rarely accounted for the possibility of a changing reality.

Forget this approach to strategy. This chapter explains how to approach strategy effectively, by thinking about what you can predict, and also considering what you can't predict.

Starting to Formulate Strategy

To start planning, you need to be able to answer clearly some basic questions:

- ✔ What products and services do you deliver, and what are you going to deliver, to whom, and where? How much are you going to charge for them?

- ✔ What size markets do you serve, and what size are you going to serve, and why? Where are the markets you're going to serve? Are there any markets you're not going to serve?

To answer these questions effectively, you have to be able to relate your own core purpose to the needs, wants, and demands of the markets, and to the actions and activities of competitors and alternative suppliers.

Essentially, the core of strategic planning comes down to the capability and willingness to choose a core or foundation position from which you'll conduct all of your activities. The core or foundation position requires that you choose one of the following as the basis for all your activities:

- ✔ **Cost advantage.** This means you seek to deliver everything to the best possible cost/value. This doesn't mean that you have to charge low prices for the products and services that you produce; it means that you can charge low prices for longer than anyone else if a price war occurs. In order to be able to deliver cost advantage effectively over the long term, you need to concentrate on the frontline, so that you deliver products and services to the maximum/optimum volume and quality possible.

- ✔ **Brand advantage.** Brand advantage means that your priority investment is in marketing, presentation, packaging, and image – concentrating on those benefits (real and perceived) and aspects of quality that are of value to your customers. Concentration on brand advantage usually means that you can charge high prices for your products and services – the top brands in all sectors are normally the most expensive (for example, Coca-Cola is more expensive than supermarket cola, and British Airways plane tickets are more expensive than Ryanair).

- ✔ **Something else.** If you don't choose to focus and strategise on cost advantage or brand advantage, then you must have something else. This 'something else' may be your concentration on a niche product or a narrow range of customers. Or it may be a distinctive and enduring working relationship between yourself and specific clients who have full confidence in you – regardless of whether you carry a branded reputation or deliver to the best possible cost advantage. Delivering 'something else' is difficult and needs full investment – if the 'something else' isn't delivered, customers will revert either to the brand advantage company or the cost advantage company.

Scanning the Business Environment

Don't make the mistake of thinking that strategic planning takes place only inside the organisation, preferably behind closed doors, in rooms with lots of coffee, Danish pastries, charts, spirited banter, and brainstorming. That image is only one way that strategic planning takes place, and it may not even be the most important way, as this chapter explains. A whole host of external environmental factors has a major impact on the planning you do for your business. Here's a look at three of the most important factors: customers, dynamic markets, and competition.

Do you really know your customers?

One of the constant themes in this book is the importance of knowing your customers and involving them in your business. Today, customers are jaded by a selection of products and services that overwhelm them with choices. In some markets, customers no longer rush to buy things in the sales, because a sale is always going on somewhere, every day of the week. Because customers have so many choices, they're more demanding. Levels of quality that were considered 'above and beyond' only a short time ago are now considered minimum quality standards. Today, you have to go far beyond those standards to grab your customers' attention.

At the same time, brand loyalty is declining. Businesses have to work much harder to keep their customers. Keeping customers is paramount because a customer becomes more valuable over time from repeat purchases and referrals.

The solution to planning in this new, very complex marketplace lies in building long-term customer relationships built on trust. You can't gain the trust of your customers if you don't interact with them. An excellent example of a company that is building that trust is UPS (United Parcel Service), the overnight shipper. UPS encourages its drivers to spend a few minutes talking to customers when they deliver packages, to get to know them. When you spend time with your customers, you discover more about what they need. Armed with this information, you can make the strategic planning process much easier and more accurate. (To discover some important tips for building long-term customer relationships, take a look at Chapter 15.)

The market is a bumpy ride

Market research has been the foundation of most strategic planning. That kind of information is typically too general to be of much use in specific markets. The information you really need for planning purposes comes directly from the customer. (Read the sidebar 'Delving into Coca-Cola's history books' for a classic case of the failure to listen to the customer.) Customers sometimes don't readily reveal what they really want. Often they give the easiest, most expedient answer to a question such as 'What do you think of this product?' No one wants to intentionally hurt someone's feelings, even if it is a big company like Coca-Cola. If you're not spending time out in the market listening to real people, you're taking a big chance that the information you're taking back to your company doesn't reflect the real feelings of the customer.

And the competition keeps changing, too

In the past, a business could relatively easily create a sustainable competitive advantage through such things as a unique market segment, lower costs, product/service differentiation, or superior execution. In today's fast-changing, global marketplace, staying ahead of the competition isn't that easy. Superiority in one or more of those areas can certainly get you started, but you won't be able to sustain it on those factors alone.

Delving into Coca-Cola's history books

Coca-Cola is a global brand, so when the Coca-Cola company decided to tweak its famous formula and introduce a beverage called New Coke, customers stepped up to complain. The interesting result was that Coca-Cola actually ended up enhancing the bond that people had with the original Coke, and saved face.

The story of New Coke begins with the advent of the cola wars dating back to the 1950s. At that time, Pepsi was defining Coke's image in the market by claiming that you got more for your money with Pepsi. This strategy introduced price as a competitive factor in the market. Pepsi's 'Pepsi Generation' ads then positioned Pepsi as exciting, youthful, and energetic, while Coke was pictured as stodgy and old. When the sugar crisis hit in 1975, the prices of both beverages went up, but when it was over, only Pepsi lowered its prices, which increased its competitive advantage yet again.

Pepsi introduced the Pepsi Challenge, which consisted of blind taste tests proving that customers preferred the taste of Pepsi. Coke ran campaign after campaign attacking Pepsi on every front, but it always came back to taste. The decision to come out with New Coke was based on a simple marketing question: What would you do if we gave you a product that tasted better than Pepsi but was a Coke; would

you like it? And, of course, the sample customers said yes, never having tasted the new product.

New Coke's introduction was a disaster that lasted just 77 days in 1985. Sergio Zyman, Coca-Cola's chief marketing officer at that time, asserts that New Coke happened because Coke didn't ask the customer the right question. Coca-Cola should have asked, 'If we took away Coca-Cola and gave you New Coke, would you accept it?' But Zyman turned a potential catastrophe into an enormous success. At the end of the 77 days, Coca-Cola reintroduced Classic Coke with a great fanfare and told its customers that it had made a mistake and wanted to correct it. As a result, Coca-Cola got free press on all the major networks in prime time and increased the loyalty of its customers to Coke.

Zyman believes that the most important basic question a good marketer must ask is 'why?' Zyman said, 'Why?' is a question that 'moves you from cognition to connection, from simply seeing what is happening to understanding the relationship of one event or trend to another.' This example serves to remind you to build interactive relationships with your customers so that you know at any moment where their tastes and preferences are.

Many businesses are now saying that you literally have to ignore the competition to gain a competitive advantage. The strategy of imitating your competition or one-upping them doesn't work as successfully as it used to. Today, one of the keys to standing out from the crowd is achieving operational excellence. In other words, you need to make sure that all your systems and operations are the best they can be and that they're fully integrated with your business strategies. Reaching those goals is going to take some planning from the bottom up, not the top down.

Planning Works – If You Do It Right

In practice, there's a lot less to planning than meets the eye! If you're clear about what you do, and what you're seeking to do, then the whole planning process becomes much simpler. In summary, you're addressing the following, points in terms of what you're good at, what's profitable, and what your company or organisation can sustain:

 ✔ What you need to deliver.

 ✔ What you can deliver.

 ✔ What you ought to deliver.

You need to plan both in terms of your own capability and capacity, and what the market demands and expects from you.

Doing your strategic planning correctly means that you accomplish the following goals. You'll:

 ✔ Provide information across the entire organisation so that everyone knows what's going to happen and where the priorities lie.

 ✔ Force management to look at the big picture in detail and answer the question: 'Where are we going?'

 ✔ Cause people to communicate about goals and the resources needed to achieve those goals.

 ✔ Create a sense of common focus and direction toward agreed-upon goals.

Here are some tips for avoiding most of the problems that poor strategic planning causes:

 ✔ When you have a plan in place, don't lock yourself into it. The environment in which your business operates changes almost daily. As a result, you have to keep your antennae out there listening for changes and be prepared to modify your plan to respond to those changes.

✔ Although your company's past performance plays an important role in your strategic planning, don't rely on it alone. Take this opportunity to try some creative and analytical thinking about what's possible for your business. Plan to do at least one radically new thing.

✔ Be sure to allocate resources to the radical new things that you're planning. Often companies base budgets on past performance. That approach may not be (and probably isn't) a good indicator of what you'll do in the future, particularly if you're planning to do something completely new. Be realistic about how much change will cost. (Chapter 13 covers budgets and financial planning.)

✔ You must turn your planning into behaviour. Saying that you want your company to increase sales by 50 per cent in the coming year is all well and good, but exactly how are you going to make that happen? Also, planners too often focus on structural changes and requirements, such as the plant and equipment, and never consider the human side of things – such as evaluation and reward systems, and management development. What are you specifically going to do to provide incentives for your employees?

Strategic Improvising

However good and effective your strategic planning processes are, strategic planning is never an end in itself. You have to be prepared to develop and improvise in response to opportunities and circumstances and above all, in response to changes in the market. You have to be able to use strategic planning as a continuous process as well as an organisational and managerial discipline. In this section we look at some of the key issues in strategic improvising.

Don't follow – lead

Doing business is a lot more difficult today than it used to be. You certainly can't rest on your laurels, especially when your competitors are waiting for the chance to puncture your happy balloon. That situation's what happened to Nintendo Entertainment Systems (NES), which at one time totally dominated the video-game market. NES, with its 8-bit system, was literally a household word, at least in homes with kids.

But then Sega introduced Genesis, the powerful 16-bit system that began eroding Nintendo's market share. Nintendo, not wanting to upset its current customers, delayed the introduction of a competitive machine. Subsequently, Sony introduced the Playstation series, and Microsoft introduced the X-Box series. From a position of total dominance, Nintendo found itself competing, and competing unsuccessfully, against powerful new players who had done their homework, planned in detail, and now had an enviable range of products available.

Nintendo certainly had plans, but it failed to keep its eyes on the market. It didn't recognise that those plans needed to change.

To make sure that your company is keeping its eyes on the market, you need to:

- ✔ Encourage everyone, from management to admin staff, to read trade journals for your industry. You can't stay competitive and meet the needs of your customers if your focus is completely inside the business.

- ✔ Attend trade association meetings and business conferences where you can network with others in your industry and get the latest information.

- ✔ Make sure that everyone stays close to the customers so that you're always up-to-date on their changing needs. You can do that by talking to customers on the phone, by bringing them to your company for a visit or tour, or by giving them access to your company via a Web site. (Read Chapter 16 for more about dealing with customers.)

Power to the people

Today's employees want the ability to make a difference in their organisation. They want to have the opportunity to grow and to develop their skills in a way that benefits their company. In a word, today's employees want *empowerment*. The traditional top-down style of strategic planning and management just doesn't work anymore. You need to give employees the opportunity to participate in the strategic planning for the future of the company. Their participation and drive will be important when you're ready to execute that plan and to make a big impact in your industry. Here's how you can get your employees involved in strategic planning:

- ✔ Have the various workgroups in your organisation meet individually to come up with at least one goal they want to achieve in the next six months. Also ask them to think of one or more goals they want to achieve in the next year.

- ✔ Ask each workgroup to meet with management to discuss these goals and to formulate strategies and tactics to achieve them.

✔ Management can then discuss with each team how the goals that each workgroup has developed will help the company meet its grand mission. In that way, all employees in the organisation understand that they're contributing an important piece to the jigsaw, and they're more likely to work harder to achieve their goals because they feel empowered.

✔ Finally, present the goals of each team to the entire organisation. Ideally, do this in direct presentations; otherwise communicate by email or teleconference. Doing so ensures that the goals of one team don't negatively affect the goals of another. This exercise is important for all employees because it enables them to clearly see that what they do affects everyone else and the company as a whole.

The bottom line is that as you begin to think about strategic planning for your organisation, think about it in terms of the changing environment in which your company operates. Don't plan so rigidly that you forget to change your plans before the environment changes and doing so is too late. Here's a checklist of questions to ask yourself to make sure that you're planning for change.

✔ What is the overriding mission for our company?

✔ Where is our source of competitive advantage?

✔ What goals do we have to reach to achieve our mission?

✔ What is our company doing to encourage everyone to keep abreast of what's happening in the industry?

✔ What are we doing to gather competitive intelligence so that we know what our competitors are doing?

✔ How are our employees at all levels of the organisation participating in our strategic planning process?

✔ In what ways are we staying close to our customers?

Swotting Up on Company Strengths and Weaknesses

One of the traditional jumping off points in the development of strategies is a SWOT analysis (shown in Figure 4-1). *SWOT* is an acronym that stands for strengths, weaknesses, opportunities, and threats. SWOT is a simple but effective guide for organising your thinking about your company and the environment in which it operates. Strengths and weaknesses are part of the *internal* analysis of your organisation. Opportunities and threats are part of the *external* analysis of the environment in which your company operates – in short, everything outside the organisation that might affect it.

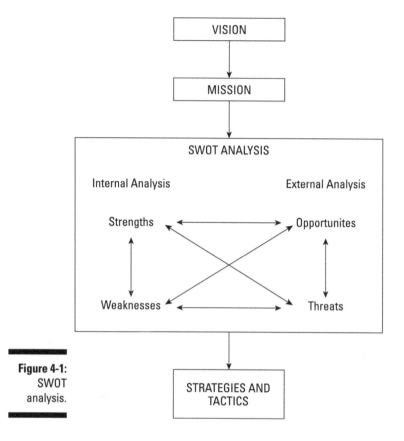

Figure 4-1:
SWOT
analysis.

To do your own SWOT analysis for your company, answer the following questions to see where your company stands.

1. What are my company's strengths?

2. What are my company's weaknesses?

3. What opportunities do we see for the future?

4. What are the threats that could prevent us from achieving our goals and how will we deal with those threats?

The following sections explore the interrelationships among the four components of a SWOT analysis.

Honing your company's strengths

Your company's strengths are its skills, capabilities, and core competencies that work together to help the company achieve its goals and objectives.

Examples of strengths are an extraordinary team that works well together, a breakthrough technology, or control of key distribution components. Successful companies like Intel capitalise on their strengths. Andy Grove, chairman and CEO of Intel Corporation, believes that one of Intel's strengths is its paranoia about the competition, which forces Intel to spend a huge amount of its revenue on R&D (research and development). Of course, that focus on R&D is what also gives Intel its 80 per cent market share.

One or more of your strengths may become your competitive advantage in the market. For example, suppose that your company is really good at coming up with innovative designs for new products. Focusing your efforts and resources on that strength to differentiate the company in the marketplace is probably in your best interest. Scattering your scarce resources over too many diverse capabilities only weakens your competitive stance. You can outsource your weaknesses to other companies and focus on what you do best.

Examining your company's weaknesses

CEOs can often more easily describe their strengths than their weaknesses – generally because they don't like to admit that they have any weaknesses. Weaknesses are those skills, capabilities, and competencies that your company lacks and that prevent you from achieving your goals and objectives. If your company doesn't have a critical skill or capability that it needs to achieve a particular goal, you have three choices:

✔ Modify the goal to something achievable with the skill set you have.

✔ Raise the capital needed to acquire the skill or capability you need through training or hiring.

✔ Find another company that has the core competency you need and outsource that need to them.

Suppose that you have a fast-food company that is known for its food and the ability to get it to the customer very quickly. Your weakness is administering the business side of the business – accounting, payroll, and so on. You can outsource those 'weaknesses' to a company that specialises in providing these services to businesses.

You must address your company's weaknesses so that it can rise to the level of performance it needs to meet its goals.

Thinking about your company's opportunities and threats

Opportunities are those things that help your business grow to new levels. Threats are barriers to growth. The classic books of Michael Porter on competitive strategy provide a framework for looking at the environmental factors that affect every business (*Competitive Strategy: Techniques for Analyzing Industries and Competitors*, and *Competitive Advantage: Creating and Sustaining Superior Performance*, both Free Press). These factors may sound like threats, but you can approach them as opportunities. When you see a way around a barrier or threat, it becomes an opportunity to move forward in the market. So each of the following needs to be identified, and you then need to think of ways in which with each you can address, tackle, respond to, or head it off. Here are Porter's five forces:

- **Barriers to entry in the industry:** Barriers include economies of scale, brand loyalty, capital requirements, switching costs (the costs buyers incur in time and money to retrain staff and learn a new product or relationship), access to distribution channels, proprietary factors (for example, technology owned by someone else), and government regulations. So if you're up against any of these, you need to establish your own strengths and pit them against what already exists in the market. This also applies to each of the following points – the remaining forces of competition.

- **Threat from substitute products:** These are products that may come from other industries but accomplish the same basic function as your product in a different way or at a different price.

- **Threat from buyers' bargaining power:** Volume buyers in an industry can force down prices.

- **Threat from suppliers' bargaining power:** Suppliers can exert pressure by threatening to raise prices or change quality or volume of supply.

- **Rivalry among existing industry firms:** A highly competitive industry drives down profits and prices. The airlines with their price wars are a good example of this tactic.

By looking at the industry from the Five Forces perspective, you can get a better sense of the opportunities and threats facing your business. Even when the environmental forces seem negative and threats appear to be more prevalent than the opportunities, your business can still do well. For example, Anita Roddick founded The Body Shop during the 1970s consumer recession – the last thing that anyone needed was a new cosmetics company, yet by providing a distinctive quality of service and nature of products, the company gained both a commercial foothold and an enduring reputation.

Putting your company through a post-SWOT test

After you complete the SWOT analysis, you can now ask yourself four very important questions – sort of a final exam.

✔ **Do you have the resources and capabilities necessary to take advantage of opportunities in the environment and neutralise threats?** Don't forget that the answer you give today may not be the same answer six months from now. The environment and its opportunities and threats are in a constant state of change.

✔ **How many competing firms already own the same valuable resources and competencies that your company has?** If several companies have the same resources you do, then they probably won't be a source of competitive advantage for you, although they will be a barrier to entry for a new company trying to compete with you. However, you need to find a competitive advantage that is unique to you.

✔ **If your company doesn't have a particular resource or capability, do you face a cost disadvantage in obtaining it?** If acquiring the rare resources and competencies you need costs you a lot, catching up to your competitor's advantage in that area may be more difficult and take longer. However, if you can find a good substitute, you may be able to achieve competitive equality.

✔ **Is your company organised to take full advantage of its resources and capabilities?** To take full advantage of what you have, you need to have a good support structure that consists of control systems, a formal reporting structure, compensation policies, and technology. This way, when you start to grow, your strategies won't fall apart.

The bottom line is, if you ensure that your company has strong resources and competencies, you can compete in nearly any environment, even if you appear to be facing few opportunities and many threats.

Strategy versus Tactics

Setting organisational goals is part of the planning process of any organisation. The traditional view of strategies versus tactics has been that *strategies* are broad goals set by top management to guide the growth of the company. *Tactics*, by contrast, are goals set by middle management to put strategies into action. That boundary between top management and middle management is quickly eroding in today's dynamic and complex marketplace. Today, strategy has seeped down into the lowest levels of management and supervision in the organisation, and at the same time, a CEO who doesn't understand tactics can't ensure that strategies are properly executed.

Organisational goals are vital because they:

✔ Give everyone a set of guidelines and a focus.

✔ Help motivate everyone to achieve.

✔ Provide a basis for measuring achievement.

The following sections take a look at the various categories of organisational goals.

Strategic goals

Strategic goals are generally developed by top management and focus on broad issues that affect the company overall. Some examples of strategic goals are:

✔ Growth

✔ Raising capital

✔ Marketing

✔ New product development

Increasingly, though, the responsibility for designing and implementing strategic goals is being shared with lower-level management and operations people – people closest to the market. In a time when market conditions fluctuate rapidly, relying on strategic plans and goals developed in the ivory towers of upper management, far removed from the street, is a very dangerous practice.

For example, product planners often have difficulty forecasting demand so that they can order the correct amount of raw material and schedule production efficiently. Some companies have formed departments of analysts to crank out copious volumes of numbers in an effort to correctly forecast needs. But the only thing you can ever be certain of is that the forecasts will always be off. Consequently, many companies are overstocked with costly supplies. Today, effective companies are approaching this problem not with forecasting tools but with more efficient and fast production times. They respond to actual market demand with rapid production. They order raw materials as needed and produce products as needed. So strategic planning for production is now done on the factory floor instead of in the executive penthouse.

Tactical goals

Tactical goals are those generally developed by middle managers. The purpose of tactical goals is to find ways to make strategies happen. Some examples of tactical goals are:

- ✔ Reaching customers
- ✔ Providing incentives for employees
- ✔ Raising capital

The metaphor most commonly used to describe tactics is that tactics are to the battle what strategy is to the war. Strategy is the big picture, while tactics are the steps to achieve the strategy. Where strategy is generally concerned with resources, market environment, and the mission of the company, tactics usually deal more with people and actions. In essence, tactics are about execution.

To effectively execute a tactical plan, you need to take the following actions:

- ✔ Look at all the possible alternatives before proceeding.
- ✔ Give all those involved in executing the tactical plan the resources and the level of authority they need to do their part.
- ✔ Make sure that effective modes of communication are in place to minimise conflict or overlap of activities.
- ✔ Continuously monitor progress to ensure that you're on target.

Sergio Zyman, Coca-Cola's chief marketing officer, had a strategy – to 'sell more products to more customers more often at higher prices.' However, his tactic for achieving his goal – introducing New Coke – didn't work (see the preceding sidebar 'Delving into Coca-Cola's history books'). But he still wanted to use the same strategy, so he had to find a new way to execute it; in short, a new tactic. Zyman once stopped all advertising in the Canadian market for an entire year and instead spent the money on new packaging. Zyman had found through his market research that Coke's generic style of packaging wasn't helping the product sell; in fact, it appeared that it was actually harming it. He believed that a better tactic was to use contour packaging to distinguish Coke from its competition. The result? This time the tactic was correct and achieved the desired strategy of selling more product.

Operational goals

Line managers typically create operational goals, which are designed to facilitate tactical steps. The steps are usually very narrow in focus and can be accomplished relatively quickly. Operational goals and plans come in many forms. To make it easy to see them all at a glance, look at Table 4-1 for an overview of common operational plans.

Table 4-1	Common Operational Plans
Type of Plan	*How It's Used*
One-time plans	Used to carry out an action that is not expected to be repeated.
Programmes	Programmes contain a large number of activities, such as a set of procedures for hiring and retaining technical employees.
Projects	A project is usually smaller and less complex than a programme. For example, a project can be the development of a staff handbook.
Standing plans	Used to manage activities that occur regularly over a longer period of time.
Policies	Policies are guidelines for how the organisation will respond in any particular situation, and they designate any exceptions to typical responses. For example, a policy might state that technical employees must have a college or university education.
Standard operating procedures	Standard operating procedures describe the steps that employees must follow in a particular situation. For example, a human resources manager might (1) check an applicant's CV for the requisite college or university education, (2) call the college or university to verify the information, and (3) mark the file that the candidate has met that requirement.
Rules and regulations	Rules and regulations take the decision-making out of the planning and execution process by stating emphatically what must be done. For example, the company may have a rule that the HR manager may override a requirement that applicants have a college or university education only if the manager secures the signature of the Chief Operating Officer. There is no decision-making power in this directive.

(continued)

Table 4-1 (continued)	
Type of Plan	**How It's Used**
Contingency plans	Contingency plans take into consideration what the company should do if the original plans cannot be realised due to some unforeseen change in the environment. Contingency plans generally answer 'what if' questions.

Planning to Restructure

One of the biggest trends in business over the past few years has been the notion of restructuring or redesigning every aspect of a business to reduce costs, to save time, or to provide better service. What's the reasoning behind restructuring? All systems – and that includes business organisations – are subject to *entropy*, a natural degradation that occurs over time. If your business strives to maintain its current status, ultimately it will begin consuming its own resources just to survive.

One of the best examples of the effects of entropy is what happened to the computer and software giant IBM. IBM's managers believed that the company's enormous success would last indefinitely if they just kept doing things the way they always had done. When the market suddenly changed, IBM was unprepared and dropped from its illustrious perch as the world's largest and most successful computer manufacturer. Microsoft, on the other hand, is an example of a large company that recognised – but almost too late – that the Internet was going to be a big thing. In a feat of re-engineering that should go down in the history books, Microsoft completely turned around and set its sights on this new frontier, changing its people, systems, and strategies to align itself toward the goal of having a significant presence in the Internet market.

The results of restructuring efforts have been mixed, but on balance, most of the effort has been in the area of cost cutting. Cost cutting is easier and less costly than finding new customers and new sources of revenue. Streamlining processes, increasing productivity, reducing labour, and eliminating jobs that don't provide value to the company have also all been successfully implemented with restructuring.

Despite this effort, the revenue results have been less than satisfactory. Few companies have been able to bring new products and services to the market quicker, and the reason has a lot to do with the fact that the focus has been on cutting costs. Cutting costs on the production of a particular product by

25 per cent is certainly better than not cutting costs at all. If you're cutting costs on a product that doesn't have much life left in it, however, you're shooting yourself in the foot. Putting time and resources into developing a new product that gives your company new life is a much better solution.

If restructuring is going to work, it usually has a better chance if the process occurs under conditions of urgency. An urgent need is more easily felt by everyone in the organisation, and the only way that restructuring can be successful is when everyone commits to it. The restructuring process has five components:

- Develop goals and a plan for restructuring your company.
- Ensure that top management conveys its total commitment to the effort.
- Make sure that everyone feels a sense of urgency.
- Start the structuring effort by looking at your company as if you were starting from scratch.
- Take perspectives from the top of the organisational chart and the bottom. Meet in the middle with a new perspective that is comprised of the best of both positions.

Any restructuring effort must begin with your customers. You need to ask them, 'How can we satisfy your needs?' Then begin to find and put into place procedures and systems designed to meet those needs.

How Do You Know When Your Strategy Succeeds?

When you turn goals into actions, you put them in a form that you can measure. In other words, you can ask, 'What did we set out to achieve? Did we achieve it; and if so, why? Did we fall short; and if so, why?'

Suppose that one of your operational objectives is to increase productivity in the packaging department. Will you reach your objective when one more box a day goes out? Or are 500 boxes more a day necessary to satisfy the objective? You need to state your objectives in measurable terms – for example, increase productivity in the packaging department by 50 per cent per day. With a clearly stated, measurable objective, you know when you've achieved it. Look at the following list of objectives and decide which ones are well written:

- To reduce our stocks by 25 per cent in six months.
- To increase sales this year.

✔ To reduce the employee turnover rate.

✔ To take on 20 new employees each month for the next six months.

✔ To beat our competitors.

The well-written objectives are 1 and 4 because they have clearly measurable objectives. You'll know when you've achieved them. To improve the other three objectives you can rewrite them as:

✔ To increase sales by 25 per cent by 31 December.

✔ To reduce employee turnover by 30 per cent in six months.

✔ To sell 25 per cent more product than our competitors by 31 December.

To produce effective objectives, you need to think about how you're going to measure progress and performance. Unfortunately, businesses typically have so many measures that sometimes they conflict with one another. Another frequent problem, particularly in businesses that are going through restructuring, is that, along with all the new measures, companies continue to use old measures that are usually out of date. For example, some companies are still creating measures around the drive to achieve economies of scale. Examples of economies of scale include the amount that production costs were reduced as the volume increased, or the savings in the costs of selling each unit as the result of increased volumes of sales. Although no one would argue the value of achieving economies of scale, the real competitive advantage for companies today centres on innovation, differentiation, low-cost leadership, and customer relationships. You need to measure your success in *those* areas.

Today, companies often have hundreds of measures, old and new, competing for the attention of the decision-makers. That so little is accomplished and that few people know what's important is hardly surprising. One large company in the video surveillance industry, with about 800 employees, gears all its measures towards one overriding goal – fanatical customer satisfaction. So the key measures are simple: 100 per cent on-time delivery, 100 per cent quality, 100 per cent customer satisfaction. And surprisingly enough, when the company doesn't reach its goals, it's only 0.03 per cent off target! The financial goals for the company come second to its customer goals, but logically, when customers' goals are met, so are the company's financial goals, off only by 0.03 per cent.

Juggling measures

Of course, you want to measure many aspects of your business, but remember that you can't measure them in a vacuum. Anything that happens in one area of your business has a measurable impact on at least one or more other areas. You need to know how to adjust for those effects. One team of management strategists uses the example of a company whose objective was to maintain enough stocks for one day's manufacturing only. Of course, this objective improves cash flow considerably, but it also requires the company to make some very fundamental (and potentially expensive) changes in the way it does business. Here's what that company needed to do to accomplish its objective:

- Reduce its manufacturing lead time.

- Put its parts on a just-in-time system. (For more information, see Chapter 19.)

- Design right the first time.

- Have processes for identifying design errors immediately, and remedying them.

- Invest in highly capable machine tools.

- Speed up machine set-up.

- Schedule machine usage more effectively.

- Purchase high-quality components.

- Reduce the number of parts.

- Design products that are easy to manufacture.

Focusing on critical points to achieve sustainability

Every successful business reaches a point where it is self-sustaining; that is, it can operate and grow without the need for outside capital. This point is called the *sustainability point*, which is often described as that point when a business breaks even on its cash flow. In other words, it takes in more cash than it spends. A very pleasant situation, indeed!

But how do you go about reaching the sustainability point? Every business has critical points that determine whether or not it is operating effectively. For example, in the hotel industry that figure is the occupancy rate. You can track a number of other measures, such as employee turnover, profit margins, and so on, and you'll certainly improve your business if you deal with them. But occupancy rate ultimately determines whether the hotel succeeds. So focus most of your efforts and resources on doing those things that will increase occupancy rate, because occupancy rate is what allows your business to become self-sustaining.

The critical point is different for each business, but you can find it by looking at the most vital aspect of your business. Whether the most vital aspect is the number of units sold or the number of customers on a daily basis, that figure is the most important measure of success in your business.

Each of the tasks in the preceding list can have its own measure of success. Don't forget that you must weigh the gains from reducing stocks against the costs of setting up the process and equipment that allows the reduction to occur. In short, measuring the various aspects of your business is a juggling act.

Measuring during and after operations

You can use four basic sets of measures to monitor progress toward your goals:

- ✔ **Leading measures** look at the immediate results of an operation and measure such things as defects, cycle time, throughput (how much is achieved), and break-even time. These measures give you a sense of the efficiency and effectiveness of the process itself.

- ✔ **Lagging measures** depict the results of completed operations over a period of time and include such things as earnings, cash flow, revenue, customer satisfaction, market share, and so on. These measures give you a sense of the effectiveness of the product/process as a whole.

- ✔ **Internal measures** gauge the effectiveness of the organisation itself and include such things as backlog, design costs, material costs, distribution costs, and end-product costs. But they also include non-cost-based measures, such as per cent of on-time delivery, number of new products, and design cycle time.

- ✔ **External measures** assess how the business performs in its environment, so they include such things as the business's performance relative to its competitors, suppliers, and the marketplace in general. They include cost-based measures, such as relative R&D expenditures and labour costs, and non-cost-based measures, such as number of repeat buyers and number of customer complaints.

When you use these measures make sure that they are as precise as possible. Imprecise measures mean that people can avoid tackling real problems if they choose to do so; if the measures are precise, they clearly show problems that have to be dealt with.

Strategic planning, if done effectively, can help ensure that your company channels all the energy being exerted by its business activities into a focused effort to meet the company's goals. It is a dynamic, living, flexible, ongoing process. Strategic planning always needs to be the means to an end, never the end itself.

Part II
Leading and Managing in the New World

'If you want to be part of our management team, you've got to be able to do this.'

In this part . . .

A working knowledge of the nuts and bolts of how to manage an organisation and the people within it is still a very important part of the business success equation. In this part, we consider the difference between managing and leading an organisation, and the latest trends in leadership. We look at how to best motivate and reward employees; how to recruit and retain the very best people; and how to organise them into effective teams. Finally, we look at the complex question of ethics in business and management.

Chapter 5

Managing Is Hard; Leading Is Even Harder

*N*o one ever said that managing employees was easy. If *you* have ever thought that managing people is a piece of cake, we know a psychiatrist who'd love to explore your delusion more deeply! Being a manager is one of the most difficult – and potentially one of the most rewarding – jobs that anyone can take on in an organisation.

People are incredibly complex, and to get their best work, day in and day out, you have to understand what motivates them and makes them tick. As the world of work has become faster, and as restructuring, re-engineering, and downsizing have flattened hierarchies and created a need for managers to share more and more of their traditional duties with frontline workers, managers have found their jobs to be more complicated than ever before.

Management used to be a fairly simple proposition. According to most management textbooks, all you had to do was master the four classic roles of management – planning, organising, leading, and controlling – and you were destined for success. Today, however, the profession of management is undergoing tremendous change. As a manager, you must know not only how to manage but also how to *lead*.

As we explain, managers and leaders are often two completely different kinds of people.

Managing people today is harder than ever before. But if you take the time to listen to your employees, respond to their needs, and set goals that bring out the best in them, your job is made much easier – and your organisation is much more effective.

Showing 'em who's Boss: What Managers Do

The very definition of *management* – getting work done through others, achieving results, and meeting targets – is deceptively simple. But, as every manager knows, management can be a very complicated, stressful, and sometimes traumatic and exhausting job.

Although many employees – software engineers, human resources co-ordinators, sales representatives, and the like – are specialists and able to focus their efforts on a fairly narrow range of responsibilities, companies expect managers to be generalists. Instead of knowing a lot about only a few topics, as a manager you need to know a little bit about everything that falls within the boundaries of your organisation.

During the course of your working day, you have to be able to shift focus from doing things that are planned, to meeting and resolving problems as they occur. Managers have to be flexible in outlook and this means being prepared to shuffle and change your working day, both in response to circumstances and also to ensure that the main work of the department of the organisation goes on whatever else occurs. Invariably, doing so means working with people, identifying and addressing their particular needs – and if an employee ever brings an issue to you, always remember that it is important to them, and so requires being treated with respect and immediacy.

Management, in traditional organisations, is split into three different levels, each with its own unique set of responsibilities and functions:

✔ **Top management:** The chairperson of the board, chief executive, top and senior functional managers, and other executives comprise an organisation's top management team. Top management usually creates an organisation's vision and key goals, communicates them to other managers and workers, and monitors the organisation's progress toward meeting them.

✔ **Middle management:** Department managers, project managers, brand managers, plant managers, and the many other kinds of managers who report to top management make up the middle management level. While top management's job is to develop an organisation's vision and key goals, middle management must create the plans, systems, and teams to achieve them. Middle managers generally report to top managers.

✔ **Supervisors:** Going by an amazing array of titles, supervisors are the employees in an organisation closest to frontline workers – and, therefore, often closest to the organisation's customers and clients. Supervisors execute the plans developed by middle managers and monitor worker performance on a day-to-day basis. Supervisors generally report to middle managers.

The good news is that this traditional model makes seeing where you reside on the corporate ladder easy. The bad news is that the model creates a very clear boundary – a wall, really – separating managers from workers, and different 'classes' of managers from one another. However, as we explain later in this chapter, the wall between managers and workers in many organisations is beginning to crumble – and has completely fallen apart in others. Today's workers are taking on roles that used to be reserved solely for managers. This shift in the traditional roles of managers and workers has led to incredible productivity gains in the companies that are employing them.

As all MBA students discover during the course of their studies, four traditional functions of management exist – planning, organising, leading, and controlling. In today's fast and furious world of business, these traditional roles are undergoing significant change, and successful managers are adapting to this new world of work.

Planning

Organisations need goals. Goals reflect what is most important to an organisation, and they make it easy for managers to prioritise work and the allocation of resources such as people, money, and equipment. Management's key jobs include developing organisational goals and then planning the strategies and tactics that the organisation will use to reach these goals.

An example of the planning function of management is when your company's management team flies to the Canary Islands to attend a week-long, offsite meeting. The goal: To create the organisation's five-year (long-range) plan. The problem with this situation is that it creates a form of corporate detachment – those who have gone to the Canary Islands invariably see themselves as being on a form of corporate holiday, and so little real work actually gets done. And it causes great resentment among those left behind.

Research has found that in most growing companies, regular planning falls by the wayside as managers end up spending most of their time either in meetings or else dealing with small everyday crises and problems. What results from this lack of planning is a ship without a rudder. Often, individual members of a management team actually have completely different goals for the same organisation!

Chapters 4, 13, and 17 cover the ins and outs of planning.

Organising

Organising is the allocation of resources such as people, money, and capital equipment to achieve an organisation's goals. Managers accomplish this task through organisational charts, staffing plans, and budgets. Managers sometimes spend endless hours developing new and exciting staffing and organisational configurations, only to amend them again in six months when things change.

When a management team returns from an offsite planning meeting, managers *organise* by drawing up a new organisation chart to implement the plans that they developed at the end of their week together. Doing so usually results in a grown-up game of musical chairs where everyone on the first floor moves to the second floor, and everyone on the second floor moves to the first floor. Of course, phone lines, computers, and e-mail usually take weeks or even months to catch up.

Today's organisations must be faster and more flexible than ever before. The days of the old-fashioned, rigid organisational chart – with its built-in bureaucracy and hierarchy – are fast disappearing in most organisations. In its place are organisations with self-managing work teams, cross-trained workers, virtual employees, flexible work schedules, ad hoc groups, and more. The key is the ability to adapt to a rapidly changing marketplace – and to do so quickly and completely.

Leading

Leading employees means motivating them and directing their efforts. Managers have a wide variety of positive motivational tools at their disposal, including communicating a vision, rewarding and recognising, encouraging, and personally thanking employees, as well as negative motivational tools such as disciplining, threatening, and coercing.

To continue our example, after the new organisation has been designed and implemented, managers must lead employees by selling them on how great things will be with the reorganisation. Managers go from division to division, department to department, and section to section to pitch their new plan. Initially, they encounter some resistance, but as these managers communicate a compelling vision of what the organisation can be, they do begin to change people's attitudes, and this is essential for any progress to be made. Implementing and driving change are hard enough without this kind of resistance.

Today, simply being a manager is not enough. Organisations also need their managers to be leaders – to inspire employees and to encourage them to give their very best every day of the week.

Exerting control

Control is the process of monitoring and evaluating activities to ensure that goals are achieved. To plan, organise, and lead isn't enough. For managers to be effective, they must also review periodically the organisation's progress toward achieving its goals. This review indicates whether plans and goals need to be updated, modified, or scrapped altogether; whether the organisation as designed is up to the task; whether the managers' efforts at leading employees are having the desired impact; and making sure that everyone is pulling their weight and staying on track.

As managers review weekly department financial reports, they quickly realise that the reorganisation is not having its desired effect. Sales are down and costs are up. Something has to be done – and soon. You need to review everything to see where the problems are – you have after all lost control of things that are vital to your success. And when you look at the results of your review, you need to use these as the basis for the actions that you're now going to take to get things back under control.

Although each of these four roles of managers is important to their overall success, *leading* employees is the one role that seemingly generates the most interest in organisations. What about leadership makes it different from management? Why is leadership so important to organisations today? Can managers learn to become better leaders? The next section answers these questions.

Defining the Differences between Managers and Leaders

Managers are responsible for making organisations work by leading the employees within the organisations. Good leadership is a skill that can turn an okay manager into a star. Employees want to work for strong leaders, and they consistently give their best efforts when they do.

What makes a leader? What subtle mix of tangible and intangible qualities sets someone apart from the rest of the pack and brings out the follower in the rest of us?

In general terms, leaders are:

- **Charismatic:** They attract people's interest.
- **Convincing:** They have the ability to sway people's opinions towards their own.
- **Credible:** They are honest and have integrity; people trust them.
- **Capable:** They are very good at what they do, and they inspire others to meet their high standards.
- **Visionary:** They can see a clear vision of the future and communicate it to others in compelling detail.
- **Focused:** They are supremely focused on attaining their vision.

The simple fact is that, when it comes to the workplace, managers are more effective when they are also good leaders. In an ideal world, the best managers are equally adept at both management skills and leadership skills.

Perhaps US Navy Admiral Grace Murray Hopper was right when she said, 'You manage things; you lead people.' *Management* focuses on things: Systems, processes, procedures, paperwork, and the rest of the matters that make businesses run. *Leadership* focuses on people: Inspiring, leading, convincing, motivating, and performing the rest of the duties that keep employees motivated and engaged in their jobs.

If you're strong at managing *things*, but not so good at leading *people*, focus on developing your leadership skills. You can learn to become a better leader. Roger Enrico, the former chairman and chief executive of PepsiCo, created an organisational leadership course for his aspiring managers. Called 'Executive Leadership: Building the Business', Enrico's course was conducted over a three-month period, and was compulsory for all those aspiring to top and senior positions. Those attending discovered how to improve their leadership skills by working through Enrico's five keys to leadership:

- Think in different terms. Leaders work on ideas that fuel growth in the future, not today.
- Develop a point of view and build a consensus for it.
- Put your ideas in front of people and get them to analyse, evaluate, and scrutinise them for the possibilities of success or otherwise.
- Make sure that everything stays co-ordinated and focused; don't consider things in isolation.
- Make it happen by communicating, communicating, communicating.

When leaders are at their best

In their book *The Leadership Challenge*, authors James Kouzes and Barry Posner found that successful leaders have five fundamental practices in common. These practices are:

Challenging processes. Leaders are not content with the status quo – they make things happen. Successful leaders don't wait for success to find them; they seek out success. They take the initiative, innovate, experiment, take risks, and push the limits of the organisation. In short, they challenge the process.

Inspiring a shared vision. Successful leaders have a clear and compelling vision of what an organisation could look like in the future, and they communicate this vision to all their employees. They inspire others to follow, and enlist them in their efforts.

Enabling others to act. Leaders cannot achieve success by themselves; they achieve success with the help of others. Leaders have to have followers. Great leaders don't simply assign work to their employees; they empower them with the authority to carry out their duties independently or in teams with a minimum of interference from management. Great leaders foster collaboration and they strengthen others.

Modelling the way. Successful leaders practise what they preach. If they tell employees that they want them to work longer and harder, they jump in first. The best leaders have clear values, and they exhibit them in everything that they do on the job. They plan a series of small wins to encourage employees and to raise morale.

Encouraging the heart. Everyone wants to be appreciated, respected, and recognised for their good work. According to Kouzes and Posner, successful leaders do exactly that – re-energising employee efforts and raising morale. Today's most successful leaders recognise and celebrate employee accomplishments.

Leaders are in demand in organisations today, not just within the ranks of management, but throughout the organisation. Fortunately you can become a better leader – and manager – by focusing on developing new leadership skills. Read books on the topic of leadership, including research studies and biographies. Observe how leaders whom you respect and admire lead others, and model yourself on them. Above all, keep striving to improve your leadership skills. Not only will *you* benefit – so will your employees.

Making Things Happen

Management consists of getting work done through others. That theory is all well and good, but exactly how do managers get workers to do the work that they want to achieve? A number of different ways exist, each with its own advantages, disadvantages, and limitations.

Power and influence

Five key sources of power exist in an organisation. Every one of us wields one or more of these sources of power within our own jobs, and they can change from situation to situation. *Power* gives us the ability to *influence* others to do what we ask of them.

You can use the following sources of power to get things done at work:

- **Personal power** comes from within yourself. This power springs from your personality, your charisma, the strength of your beliefs and convictions, and your ability to express them. For example, a hard-working front-line employee who inspires his colleagues to work harder by his example has personal power.

- **Relationship power** comes from the strength of your network of friends, contacts, and business associates. The phrase 'I've got friends in high places' sums this idea up. An example of relationship power in an organisation is the incredible power that assistants to CEOs and other top managers wield in their organisations. They often have as much power as – and sometimes more than – the executives to whom they report.

- **Position power** comes from your place within a company's hierarchy. A company's president has high position power. The post-room temp has low position power.

- **Knowledge power** comes from your experience, training, education, and expertise in your particular job, within your organisational unit, and in the organisation as a whole. This power includes technical prowess, as well as your ability to navigate the personalities of those you work with. Because computer networks – and their care and maintenance – have become extremely important in most organisations today, information technology professionals have very high knowledge power.

✔ **Task power** comes from the job itself. For example, in an advertising agency, account managers and executives who sell to new clients and who have a direct impact on bringing new money into the firm have higher task power than employees in the accounting department who actually send out invoices and collect payments.

Responsibility, authority, and accountability

Responsibility, authority, and accountability are extremely powerful forces in an organisation because they're the key ways that managers get work done through others.

✔ **Responsibility** signifies who in the organisation is accountable to complete a specific task or job. When you assign a task to an employee, also assign responsibility for its successful completion. Employees who are given responsibility for tasks are more likely to do them well and feel that they're a significant part of the organisation.

✔ **Authority** means that your organisation has formally granted you the power you need to do a specific job. When you delegate this power along with an assigned task, then you're delegating authority to the employee to complete the task.

✔ **Accountability** means answering for the results you accomplish – or don't accomplish – when you take on a task. When you assign a task to an employee, also assign accountability for whether the task is done correctly or not.

Delegation

No manager can do everything alone. Managers contribute most – multiplying the work they can accomplish many times – by delegating work, responsibility, and authority to employees. *Delegation* (assigning tasks to other people) is a great tool for you to increase the amount of work you can get done, achieving better results.

Why do so many managers have such a hard time delegating work to their employees? Fear causes part of the reluctance – fear that employees can't or won't do the work as well as the manager can. Some managers also feel that they're too busy to take the time to train employees to do a task well; therefore, simply tackling the job themselves is easier. And perhaps the desire to receive all the glory for completing important tasks contributes to some managers' reluctance to delegate (now, who could *that* be?) as well as guilt at overloading employees.

Delegation can be an incredibly effective tool to get work done through others if used correctly. Six steps for delegating the *right* way are:

1. **Communicate the task.** Describe exactly what you want done, when you want it done, and the end results you expect. Be clear and invite your employees to ask lots of questions until you're convinced they understand what you want done.

2. **Give a context for the task.** Most people want to know the reasons why they should do something. Explain to your employees why the task needs to be done, its importance in the overall scheme of things, and any possible complications that may arise during its performance. Again, invite questions and don't get defensive if your employees push you for answers.

3. **Determine standards.** We all need to know when we cross the finish line. Agree on the standards that you use to measure the success of a task's completion. These standards need to be realistic and attainable, and avoid changing them once performance has begun.

4. **Grant authority.** You must grant employees the authority necessary to complete the task without constant barriers and blockages from other employees.

5. **Provide support.** Determine the resources necessary for your employees to complete the task and then provide them. Successfully completing a task may require money, training, advice, and other resources.

6. **Get commitment.** Make sure that your employees have accepted the assignment. Confirm your expectations and your employees' understanding of the commitment to completing the task.

One of the biggest problems with delegation occurs when a manager delegates responsibility for a task, but not the authority and resources necessary to carry it out effectively. Inevitably, the task becomes much more difficult to carry out than it needs to be – perhaps impossible – and employees become frustrated and even angry. Don't forget that we all want happy employees. Happy employees lead to happy customers and clients. Be sure that when you delegate a task to an employee, you also give the employee the authority that goes along with it.

Goals

Goals do two things: They show you where you've been and where you're going. Managers and employees work together to develop personal goals to help employees attain the overall goals of the organisation. The acronym *SMART* signifies five traits that ensure goals are well designed – and well-designed goals are much more likely to have the outcomes you and your organisation desire. So make your goals:

- ✔ **Specific:** All goals need to be clear and unambiguous. Fuzzy goals lead to fuzzy outcomes.

- ✔ **Measurable:** Goals are useless if you can't measure them. If you can't measure an outcome, then you never know when your goal is achieved.

- ✔ **Attainable:** Nothing is more demoralising than being assigned goals that are impossible to attain. Be sure that you work with employees to develop realistic and attainable goals.

- ✔ **Relevant:** Don't waste your employees' time (or yours)! A good goal takes you and your employees closer to meeting the overall goals of the organisation.

- ✔ **Time-bound:** Be sure that your goals have beginnings and endings. The endpoints of goals should never be so far out that employees have no hope of attaining them. Developing lots of milestones along the way is better than creating only one or two end-all, be-all mega-goals with no ending.

Designing a Better Organisation

One of the four traditional roles of managers is that of an organiser. A manager must continuously improve systems and processes to make them more efficient, more effective, and less costly. Because the environment of business is always changing – new employees, new technology, new sources of supply, new competitors – managers always have to be alert to the need for restructuring their organisations to keep them competitive in the marketplace.

Building workforce structure

The very first step in organisational design is assigning specific employees to specific jobs, thus creating a *workforce structure*.

In a one-person organisation – say, a home-based public relations agency – only one person completes all the jobs that need to be done. The business owner types the letters, answers the phone, places advertisements, designs promotional materials for clients, writes press releases, schedules clients for media interviews and radio and television appearances, does the accounting, pays the bills, and even takes out the rubbish!

When the owner of the public relations agency takes on an employee, however, then he can make his operation more efficient through effective division of labour. The new employee can take on tasks that the owner isn't so good at or that require a lot of work but don't generate revenues – perhaps typing letters and answering phones. This way, the owner can concentrate his efforts on the things that he is best at and that have a better cash return on the investment of his time.

In his famous 1776 book on economics, *Wealth of Nations*, Adam Smith made a very clear case for the division of labour. As an example, he used the case of a pin-producing factory:

> 'One man draws out the wire, another straightens it, a third cuts it, a fourth points it, a fifth grinds it at the top for receiving the head; to make the head requires two or three distinct operations; to put it on is a peculiar business, to whiten the pins is another; it is even a trade by itself to put them into the paper; and the important business of making a pin is, in this manner, divided into about eighteen distinct operations, which, in some manufactories, are all performed by distinct hands, though in others the same man will sometimes perform two or three of them.'

According to Smith, through the division of labour, ten workers could produce approximately 48,000 pins a day, where a single person performing all these steps alone would be lucky to produce 20 pins in one day. Smith may have exaggerated his point just a bit, but it is essentially true: By assigning to individuals distinct, simplified tasks that are easily learned, productivity skyrockets.

When you assign a specific job to an employee, ensure that

- The duties of the job are clear and the boundaries are well defined.
- The job is not too complex or too simple for the particular employee.
- Employees are given the authority to execute their jobs without undue management interference.
- The job is kept interesting by varying tasks, goals, and approaches.
- Employees are well-trained to do their job.

Although the division of labour has a time-honoured place in modern business, today's most successful organisations are going a step farther – they are cross-training employees in the jobs of their colleagues. Employees who know one another's jobs are much more flexible, and the organisations they work for can be much more responsive to changing market conditions or to the challenges of competitors – and can simply fill in for an absent worker. Also, cross-trained employees often have higher morale than employees who aren't cross-trained because the varied tasks make their jobs more interesting.

Departments and divisions

In traditional organisations, after managers hand out individual jobs to employees, the managers then determine whether any jobs can be grouped together into logical divisions. So, for example, the managers group every employee assigned a sales-orientated task together with other sales-orientated employees to form a sales department. Employees who have an accounting function – whether payroll, accounts receivable, or accounts payable – are put together to form an accounting department. And so the process goes throughout the organisation.

Organisations today are driving for increasing output from existing resources. Consequently, many departments and divisions are now grouped into flexible and at least semi-autonomous work teams in which they set not only the ways of working, but also the daily and weekly output targets – subject only to delivering what is required for the organisation. Flexible work teams now comprise many functions within organisations, and some entrepreneurial-type businesses are not based on departments at all. Chapter 8 covers these new team-based organisations in detail.

Span of control

Span of control refers to the number of employees reporting to a particular supervisor or manager. A narrow span of control consists of only a few employees; a wide span of control includes many employees.

One of your authors, Peter, used to indirectly manage a staff of more than 200 employees working at some 45 locations nationwide. If each employee had reported directly to Peter, his task would have been almost impossible. But narrowing the span of control made Peter's job feasible. Only four employees reported directly to him – three project managers and an administrative assistant – and each of the project managers managed a group of ten or more site supervisors.

The tendency nowadays is to flatten organisations by widening the span of control and decreasing the layers of management (hierarchy), and by relying more on employee teams to take on many of the roles formerly performed only by managers. Widening the span of control means that:

- ✔ The flatter an organisation, the fewer layers of management. Less management leads to less bureaucracy and quicker decision-making.
- ✔ The fewer layers of management, the more money available to spend on other, productive activities.

Following Management Trends

Who says that you can't teach an old dog new tricks? The classic definition of management – plan, organise, lead, and control – has morphed into a new brand of management, infused with fresh leadership methods and approaches.

Many leadership trends and management fads come and go. However, some have endured the test of time; and some of the principles that underline the particular fads and trends remain constant. This section covers a few 'fads' that are still relevant today.

Total quality management

Total quality management (TQM) is a system of principles, tools, and practices to provide customer satisfaction. TQM helps you accomplish these goals by eliminating product and service defects, enhancing product design, speeding service, reducing costs, and improving the quality of work life by changing the culture of organisations.

TQM first captured the imagination of legions of managers in the early 1980s, and almost died an untimely death because most organisations applied its basic tenet of complete customer satisfaction inconsistently. They simply overlaid TQM on the organisation's current structure, instead of making the wholesale cultural changes needed to sustain it. However, TQM has made a come back as companies discover how to make it work.

Here are the six key elements of any successful TQM initiative:

- ✔ **Total commitment:** Everyone in an organisation – from the lowest-paid hourly worker to the chairperson of the board – must make a total commitment to TQM and make it a permanent part of the organisation's culture. Managers especially have the power to prioritise TQM within their organisations – or to kill it quickly. Without the active support and involvement of an organisation's management team, TQM is likely to live a very short life.

> ✔ **Employee empowerment:** Frontline employees generally know much more about the needs of clients and customers than their managers do. When employees have the authority they need to get their jobs done, they often do a better job more quickly than if managers interfere.

Deming's 14 points

The US statistician and consultant William Edwards Deming set out a philosophy of continuous improvement in a list of 14 points in his 1986 book, *Out of the Crisis*. Although Deming died in 1993, his legacy lives on in his 14 points and in the many companies that have adopted them. Pay particular attention to Point Seven!

1. Create constancy of purpose toward improvement of product and service, with the aim to become competitive, stay in business, and to provide jobs.

2. Adopt total quality in all activities as a new philosophy. Awaken to the challenges, learn responsibilities, and take on leadership for change.

3. Cease dependence on inspection to achieve quality. Eliminate the need for inspection on a mass basis by building quality into the product in the first place.

4. End the practice of awarding business (to suppliers, for example) on the basis of whoever is cheapest. Instead, minimise total cost.

5. Constantly improve the system of production and service, to improve quality and productivity, and thus constantly decrease costs.

6. Institute training on the job.

7. Institute leadership. The aim of leadership is to help people and machines do a better job. Leadership of management is in need of overhaul as well as leadership of production workers.

8. Drive out fear – fear of failure, of trying new things, of learning from failures as well as successes – so that everyone can work effectively for the company.

9. Break down barriers between departments. People in research, design, sales, and production must work as a team, to foresee problems of production and in use that may be encountered with the product or service.

10. Eliminate slogans, exhortations, and targets for the workforce asking for zero defects and new levels of productivity. Such exhortations only create adversarial relationships, because the bulk of the causes of low quality and low productivity belong to the system and so lie beyond the power of the workforce.

11. (a) Eliminate work standards (quotas) on the factory floor as the one driving force. Substitute leadership, and involvement, related to the quality as well as the volumes of output. (b) Eliminate management by objectives. Eliminate management by numerical goals. Substitute leadership.

12. (a) Remove barriers that rob the hourly worker of his right to pride of workmanship. The responsibility of supervisors must be changed from sheer numbers to quality. (b) Remove barriers that rob people in management and in engineering of their right to pride of workmanship. This means abolishing the annual or merit rating and of management by objectives.

13. Institute a vigorous programme of education and self-improvement.

14. Put everyone in the company to work to accomplish the transformation. The transformation is everybody's job.

✔ **Fact-based decision-making:** TQM requires you to make decisions based on quantitative data rather than hunches or 'feelings'. Adherents of TQM are very familiar with statistical approaches and methods such as flow-charts, cause-and-effect diagrams, scatter diagrams, and other quantitative methods of assessment.

✔ **Continuous improvement:** TQM encourages employees to be always on the lookout for improvements to organisational systems, processes, and procedures, and to make suggestions and take the initiative to effect changes. Quality is designed *into* products rather than inspected for at the end of the production line.

✔ **Customer focus:** Instead of the organisation deciding on standards for its products, TQM dictates that customers are the ones who drive standards. TQM also focuses on the satisfaction of all customers – including *internal* customers – and the development of strong, long-term partnerships with vendors not based solely on lowest price.

✔ **Integrating product and process:** When companies develop new products, they should also develop new work processes to go along with them. Not only does such an arrangement afford companies a distinct advantage over their competition, but these often proprietary processes create value for the companies as well.

TQM is alive and well, and can be very effective if you practise it along the above lines, and if everyone is involved. If you decide to go down the TQM route, get the process led by someone who knows what they're doing, and make sure that they concentrate on the results that you demand.

Six Sigma

Six Sigma originated at electronics manufacturer Motorola in the mid-1980s. It's a particularly rigorous training programme that gives managers specialised measurement and statistical analysis tools that they can use to reduce defects in products and processes and cut the costs of doing business. As with any management training programme, the purpose is to get those involved to think about and analyse every aspect of their business and its products and services in full detail. The main contribution of any approach based on measurement and statistical analysis is to provide absolute data that can then be used to identify where improvements need to be made – and the data is then used as a driving force for implementing those improvements. As long as data is gathered from every aspect of the organisation's activities and processes, and fully analysed, issues concerning each of the areas below can be identified and can lead to the following:

✔ Improved customer satisfaction

✔ Reduced cycle times

- ✔ Increased productivity

- ✔ Improved capacity and output

- ✔ Reduction in total defects

- ✔ Isolation and elimination of individual defects, process barriers, and blockages

- ✔ Increased product reliability

- ✔ Decreased work-in-progress

- ✔ Improved process flow

As with all approaches, making Six Sigma effective depends on total commitment to the approach, support from top management, and getting the resources necessary to do the job. Managers responsible for producing, analysing, and evaluating the data must be allowed to make recommendations and expect the recommendations to be implemented. You don't want experts to produce clear proposals for the future that can result in benefits for everyone – only to have them vetoed by top management on some grounds or other.

If you choose to go down the Six Sigma route, make sure that the person leading it is doing so in relation to the specific issues facing your company, and doesn't simply introduce an off-the-shelf package from a branded consultancy. If you choose to use an outside expert, make sure that you vet him or her before they start work.

Maintaining learning in your organisation

Learning organisations in which successes, failures and, most importantly, the reasons behind both are quickly communicated to all employees are critical to success in today's fast-paced, ever-changing business environment. A learning organisation is an organisation that has the ability to not only create knowledge but also to *learn*.

In his book *The Fifth Discipline*, Peter Senge named the following five learning disciplines as keys to building a learning organisation:

- ✔ **Systems thinking:** Changes in one part of an organisation send out ripples that affect other parts of the organisation. In an organisation, every person and every system share a connection with one another. Systems thinking trains you to look for these connections and to consider them when you take action.

- ✔ **Personal mastery:** Personal mastery means developing a high level of expertise in your craft or profession, primarily by making a commitment to lifelong learning. According to Senge, personal mastery is gained by continually clarifying and deepening your personal vision, focusing your energies, developing patience, and seeing things for what they truly are, and not what you'd like them to be.

✔ **Mental models:** Mental models are deeply ingrained assumptions and ways of thinking about how the world works. The key is learning how to recognise these mental models and then challenging their validity.

✔ **Shared vision:** A shared vision is a compelling picture of the future that inspires employees to work together to achieve it. Although an organisation's vision often comes from top management, this doesn't necessarily have to be the case. According to Senge, when given a choice, most people opt for pursuing a lofty goal, not only in times of crisis, but at all times.

✔ **Team learning:** Learning occurs much more rapidly in a team than it does for individuals on their own – a case of the whole adding up to more than its separate parts. Senge believes that teams, not individuals, are the fundamental learning unit in modern organisations. He says, 'unless teams can learn, the organisation cannot learn.'

The 'learning organisation' approach requires, in many cases, a fundamental change in attitude of those responsible for the direction of the organisation. The organisation gathers its strength from individual and collective learning and development, and this has to be given time to work. In particular, you need a high degree of investment in the staff, and you won't see the results overnight. If you're interested in the long-term future of the organisation and are prepared to invest in this approach, then it may well be effective. If you want instant results – then forget it!

Self-managing work teams

One of the strongest leadership trends today is the transfer of management responsibilities – and authority – to frontline employees. In the case of *self-managing work teams* – teams of workers that manage themselves – workers themselves are hiring and firing team members, putting together and executing plans and budgets, and independently running their operations. The result is improved efficiency and productivity and increased worker morale.

As with everything else, to be fully effective, self-managing teams have to be given sufficient resources and authority to carry out the job in the ways in which they see fit – and management must not then interfere in the ways in which the work is carried out. The best self-managing teams accept and discharge responsibility and accountability for everything from meeting production and service delivery schedules, to recruitment and selection, induction and orientation, and setting and maintaining schedules for the volume and quality of work required. Self-managing teams must still meet organisational, customer, and client targets. However, overall responsibility remains with company leadership and top management.

Work teams must manage themselves with integrity and positive responsibility – and not through bullying, victimisation, and coercion. Self-managing teams must not be allowed to either favour or freeze out particular employees for any reason – any operational, professional, occupational, or personal problems must be resolved strictly in accordance with employment law and organisational procedures.

As long as this environment represents the context in which self-managing teams are structured and implemented, they can be operationally successful. You can then apply the following principles to self-managing work teams:

- ✔ **Empower the team.** Give the team the authority to make decisions and then act on them.

- ✔ **Let the teams manage risk.** Give the team the ability to select the amount of risk that offers the highest likelihood of success.

- ✔ **Let the team control the budget.** Teams must make all decisions on project matters, including financial ones.

- ✔ **Recognise the phases that the team progresses through.** Be alert to signs that the team needs additional support or coaching from management.

- ✔ **Let the team be involved in the reward process.** Only team members know best what motivates them.

Chapter 8 addresses self-managing work teams in much greater detail.

Chapter 6

Carrots and Sticks: Motivation and Commitment

. . . .

In This Chapter

▶ Understanding what motivates employees

▶ Recognising and rewarding employees

▶ Building long-term employee–employer relationships

. . . .

*A*sk managers what their toughest job is and what answer do you think that you'll get? Working out a new operating budget for the upcoming fiscal year? No, probably not. Designing an assembly line for a new manufacturing plant in Manchester? No, not that either. Negotiating a new wage contract with the trade union? No, not even that (although that task's definitely no piece of cake).

The toughest – and in many ways the most important – job for most managers is keeping their employees motivated and productive.

If you've been in business for any length of time, you know that everyone is different. Some employees are highly motivated, bouncing from task to task as if the world might end tomorrow – getting things done and making things happen. Other employees don't seem to be motivated at all, barely doing the minimum required by their jobs – and sometimes not even doing that.

Of course, every manager would like to have a team filled with high achievers. Unfortunately, this situation is rarely the case. A few employees who need an extra bit of motivation are bound to be in the mix and motivating them is the real trick. How do you motivate employees who aren't motivated, and how do you keep employees who are motivated?

The answers to those questions are the very essence of carrots and sticks – the incentives and penalties of motivating employees.

Theories of Motivation

Understanding why people do what they do at work has been a source of endless speculation on the part of legions of business theorists and academics. And as any good MBA knows, many theories of motivation exist.

Two primary sources of motivation on the job exist:

- ✔ **Intrinsic motivation** comes from forces within an individual. Examples include the pride that comes from doing a job well, the satisfaction that you feel in beating a deadline, and the excitement that derives from being a part of a high-performing team.

- ✔ **Extrinsic motivation** comes from forces outside an individual. Positive examples (carrots) include receiving a cash bonus for doing a particularly good job on a project or being recognised by your boss in a staff meeting. Negative examples (sticks) include receiving a reprimand from your boss or getting fired.

Of these two sources of motivation, most people consider intrinsic motivation to be the strongest. If, for example, you absolutely *love* your job and feel the greatest satisfaction doing it (intrinsic motivation), a cash bonus or a pat on the back (extrinsic motivation) is going to have little or no impact on your job performance – certainly not in the long run. Similarly, if you absolutely *hate* your job, no amount of money or words of encouragement from your boss are going to make you like it better, or improve your performance over the long haul.

Therefore, matching employees to their jobs and setting realistic, attainable goals with them are absolutely critical. By doing so, you increase the power of the intrinsic motivation within each and every employee and rely less and less on extrinsic motivation – the carrots and sticks – to keep them engaged in their work.

In the immortal words of management theorist Frederick Herzberg, 'If you want someone to do a good job, give them a good job to do.'

Keep in mind that you can find no one right answer here. Each of the theories that follow has something to offer supervisors and managers who wish to apply them. Trying a *variety* of different approaches is the best idea; experimenting until you find the approach that works best in your particular situation.

The key is to keep trying until you hit upon an approach that works best for *each one* of your employees.

Content theories of motivation

Content theories focus on the specific factors that stimulate, direct, sustain, and stop behaviour in individuals. In essence, content theories of motivation answer the question: 'What specific employee needs cause motivation?'

Maslow's hierarchy of needs

Back in the 1940s, sociologist Abraham Maslow organised all human needs into five different levels – one on top of another – in the form of a pyramid (see Figure 6-1).

According to Maslow, humans strive to fulfil their lowest order (physiological) needs first. After the lowest-order needs are fulfilled, then they move up the pyramid to achieve the next level of needs (safety). And so on until they reach the top. Maslow's hierarchy of needs – from lowest order to highest – is as follows:

- **Physiological:** These are the very essentials of life: food, water, shelter, and sex. These needs are of the very highest priority because if they're left unfulfilled, the very survival of the individual – and of the species – is in immediate jeopardy.

- **Safety:** This factor includes security, protection from danger, a safe work environment, job security, and a stable (and ideally, increasing) income – and jobs that provide this are getting fewer and further between.

- **Social:** This is the need to have social interactions with others, to be a part of a group or team of individuals, and to experience friendship and love – as well as a productive, harmonious, and positive working relationship with your colleagues.

- **Esteem:** Esteem is the need that people have to feel good about themselves and the work they do. It drives their desire to perceive that their contributions are worthwhile and that they have the respect of others.

- **Self-actualisation:** This need derives directly from the human desire for a sense of purpose. As the highest-order need in Maslow's hierarchy, you can achieve it only after all your other needs are satisfied.

Maslow's hierarchy looks neat and tidy on paper. However, it's more complicated in practice. Above all, in a working environment, realising that everyone has self-actualisation needs, whatever their occupation or status, is essential. Those in top and senior management positions feel threatened at their physiological and safety levels when faced with organisational crises and potential redundancy.

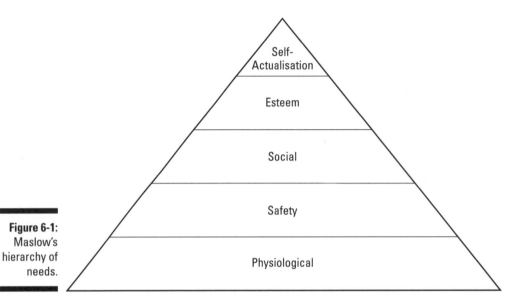

Figure 6-1:
Maslow's
hierarchy of
needs.

Self-Actualisation

Esteem

Social

Safety

Physiological

But, despite these complications, the application of Maslow's work to business *has* had a very positive influence on management practice, helping managers realise that workers aren't simply machines that can be turned on and off, but are people with needs and aspirations of their own. And this is something that managers even today sometimes seem to forget. So remember hierarchies of needs when it comes to leading and managing employees. Everyone seeks achievement and recognition – everyone has their own individual need for 'self actualisation', regardless of occupation.

Herzberg's two-factor theory

Management theorist Frederick Herzberg proposed a different approach to the theory of motivation, based on an extensive study of engineers and accountants in the 1950s. Herzberg determined that the factors that influence employee behaviour on the job can be classified as:

✔ **Maintenance factors:** These factors relate to the environment external to the job itself, and include salary, work environment, job security, company policies and administration, relationships with peers, and relationships with supervisors. They directly influence the level of an employee's *dissatisfaction* with his or her job. The absence of sufficient quality maintenance factors can lead to employee turnover, absenteeism, burnout, and even outright sabotage. When maintenance factors are available in sufficient quality and quantity, increasing their presence has little or no positive impact on employee motivation.

✔ **Motivational factors:** These factors relate to the job itself, and include personal responsibility, achievement, challenges, advancement, professional growth, recognition, and the interest level of the work itself. They directly influence the level of an employee's *satisfaction* with his or her job. When motivators are insufficient, employees become less motivated; as they increase, employees become more motivated.

Herzberg showed that job satisfaction and job dissatisfaction were rooted in two completely separate sets of factors. Before Herzberg, management theorists assumed that employees were, above all, motivated by money – and many managers today still think that's the case! A lack of money leads to dissatisfaction with one's job, but giving an employee professional growth in his or her job, recognition for a job well done, responsibility, and challenge leads to a satisfied and, therefore, a motivated employee.

As a result of Herzberg's work, managers found that they can increase employee motivation by increasing motivational factors, primarily by focusing on the structure of employee jobs – how work is arranged and the amount of control employees have over their work. And you can, too. Take a close look at the maintenance *and* motivational factors in your workplace. Are they sufficient to keep employees motivated and satisfied? If not, what can you do to improve them?

McGregor's Theory X and Theory Y

During the 1960s, psychologist Douglas McGregor's Theory X and Theory Y were very popular theories of motivation. Even today, hearing managers referred to as either Theory X or Theory Y type is common. In essence, Theory X and Theory Y describe two basic sets of assumptions that managers make about workers:

✔ **Theory X** managers assume that workers inherently dislike work, that they must be coerced, directed, and closely controlled to meet an organisation's goals. The average worker has little ambition, avoids responsibility, and seeks security above all else. And while you (of course!) have never thought that about any of your employees – many managers have, and many managers still do.

✔ **Theory Y** managers assume that workers inherently like work, that they exercise self-direction and self-control to achieve an organisation's goals. Under the right conditions, the average worker not only accepts responsibility but also seeks it out.

As you may imagine, if you are a Theory X manager, you're going to treat your employees completely differently to someone who's a Theory Y manager. A Theory X manager displays a task-orientated style focused on directing employees and coercing them to complete assigned tasks. On the other hand, a Theory Y manager displays a people-orientated style focused on building trust, empowerment, and autonomy.

Is one style better than the other? The answer to that question depends upon a few different factors. Clearly, when you have a new employee – one who is learning the ropes of a new job – then the Theory X, directive style of motivation is better. However, as an employee matures and is able to do the job without day-to-day supervision, then the Theory Y, supportive style is better. The best managers are able to adjust their style to match the needs of their employees.

Ouchi's Theory Z

During the 1980s, business professor William Ouchi developed a new motivation theory based on his study of the characteristics of Japanese business managers. Theory Z takes Theory Y one step further by determining that not only do employees desire responsibility, but organisations need to empower employees to participate in the kinds of decision making formerly reserved solely for managers.

Many managers weren't originally very excited about giving up power to their employees. In fact, some had to be dragged kicking and screaming to get with the programme. But apparently Ouchi had the right idea. *Self-managing work teams* – which give employees authority to manage themselves and their work without management interference – have taken the world of work by storm, and they're making organisations much faster and much more flexible, essential in a business world that's running on Internet time. Today, the Theory Z workplace is rapidly becoming the norm rather than the exception. For more on employee empowerment, check out Chapter 8.

Process theories of motivation

Process theories of motivation are different to content theories. Instead of focusing on employee needs, as content theories of motivation do, they focus on *how* behaviour is stimulated, directed, sustained, and stopped. In other words, process theories explain how motivation occurs.

Equity theory

According to social psychologist J. Stacy Adams, employees constantly compare the fairness of their work outcomes to the work outcomes of others in similar positions – both within and outside of their organisations. If you've ever talked to someone who didn't get a pay rise when a colleague did, you know exactly what we're talking about here. In general, employees are concerned not only about the absolute amount of an outcome – for example, the amount of a pay rise given with an annual performance appraisal – but also the amount relative to colleagues and peers in the industry.

The following model illustrates this relationship:

Employee's rewards	compared to	Other's rewards
Employee's efforts		Other's efforts

As long as the ratio of the employee's rewards to effort expended is close to the ratio of the other employee's rewards to effort expended, the first employee perceives equity and is satisfied. And everyone's ultimate goal is happy employees!

However, if the employee's ratio of rewards to effort expended is significantly less than the other employees, then the employee perceives a *negative* inequity and takes steps to restore equity. This situation isn't a good development. Some of these steps may include

✔ Decreasing the quality and quantity of work

✔ Asking for a transfer to another supervisor or department

✔ Leaving

Similarly, if the employee's ratio of rewards to effort expended is significantly greater than the other employee, then the employee perceives a *positive* inequity and takes the following steps to restore equity

✔ Increasing the quality and quantity of work

✔ Requesting more work

✔ Asking for more responsibility

In any situation, wise managers are sensitive to their employees and their perceptions of equity – and inequity – on the job. If employees are disgruntled, you can bet that they *always* have a reason. Your job is to work out what the reason is. If you want to get to the root of the problem, you need to talk to your employees about it and then see what you can do to remove the sources of perceptions of inequity.

Expectancy theory

Essentially, expectancy theories draw the relationship between:

✔ People's expectations of particular outcomes

✔ The efforts that they're prepared to put in assuming that the outcomes are available if they do put the efforts in

✔ The rewards that are available in relation to the efforts expended to achieve the expectations

This approach was developed in much more detail by Yale professor Victor Vroom in the 1960s. According to Vroom's expectancy theory, the probability of an employee's taking a specific action depends on (1) the strength of the expectation that the action leads to a given outcome, and (2) the attractiveness of that outcome to the employee. And, as you know, some outcomes are much more attractive than others!

Under expectancy theory, the motivational force (MF) within an employee is represented as

$$MF = Expectancy \times Instrumentality \times Valence$$

In the preceding formula, *Expectancy* is the belief that your effort results in the attainment of desired performance goals; *Instrumentality* is the relationship between what you expect and the amount of effort you're prepared to put in to meet your expectations. *Valence* is the value that you place on the expected reward.

Expectancy theory has been used to explain a variety of employee behaviours, including leadership effectiveness, turnover, absenteeism, career choice, and more. Expectancy theory can be a very effective tool to help managers understand why employees behave the way they do. For employees to be motivated, they must believe not only that they can achieve a desired level of performance but also that doing so leads to a desired reward. If either of those pieces is missing in your organisation, then employees aren't motivated to perform at the high level that you may expect of them.

Take a close look at your organisation and ask yourself these questions:

- ✔ Are goals realistic and achievable, or are they placed too high above your employees' ability to achieve them?
- ✔ Are rewards available for employees who achieve their goals?
- ✔ Do the employees themselves find the rewards desirable?

If you said no to any of these questions, then you can't expect employees to be motivated until you fix these broken links. So you need to get involved with your employees, talk to them, and find out where the problems might lie.

Behaviour modification

Behaviour modification states that external consequences determine an employee's behaviour. This theory is rooted in psychologist B.F. Skinner's pioneering work in *operant conditioning* (using consequences to modify behaviour). This application of Skinner's theory uses various methods of reinforcement to modify behaviour through that behaviour's consequences. *Reinforcement* means any stimulus that makes a behaviour more likely to occur.

Under behaviour modification, four different kinds of reinforcement exist, each with a different outcome:

- ✔ **Positive reinforcement** means strengthening a behaviour by applying a pleasant consequence. When an employee gets a word of congratulations from the boss for meeting a sales goal, the boss is employing positive reinforcement. As a result of this positive reinforcement, the employee is more likely to meet sales goals in the future.

- ✔ **Negative reinforcement** consists of strengthening a behaviour by removing an unpleasant consequence – also known as 'avoidance learning.' When employees show up for a staff meeting on time to avoid a reprimand from their supervisor, negative reinforcement has entered the picture.

- ✔ **Punishment** is weakening a behaviour by applying an unpleasant consequence. When an employee receives a reprimand for breaking a company policy, this is punishment. A reprimanded employee is less likely to break the company policy in the future. Most managers tend to focus more on these sticks of motivation rather than the carrots of positive reinforcement.

- ✔ **Extinction** refers to the weakening of behaviour with the application of a neutral consequence, or not following the behaviour with a pleasant consequence. For example, suppose that an employee puts in several weekends of extra effort to meet a customer deadline. If that employee's boss fails to reward or even acknowledge the behaviour, the employee is less likely to devote future weekends to meeting customer deadlines.

The frequency with which you reinforce behaviour influences the effectiveness of behaviour modification. *Continuous* reinforcement occurs when you reinforce behaviour after *every* correct response. When you reinforce a behaviour after some responses, but not after others, *partial* reinforcement develops.

Over time, partial reinforcement schedules are much more effective at causing desired behaviour than continuous schedules, which reward employees *every* time they perform the behaviour. They are also much more resistant to change or extinction. Why? When rewards are given on a continuous schedule, employees soon begin to take them for granted. The rewards therefore have a diminishing effect on behaviour.

When applying a partial reinforcement schedule, you have two major options:

- ✔ Vary the frequency of the reward according to the nature of the work being carried out and deliver the reward when it is completed. This is called a *ratio schedule*. The timing of reinforcement is irrelevant – completion is the key.

- ✔ Vary the frequency of the reward strictly according to time intervals. This is called an *interval schedule*. The number of responses that occur after the first correct response in an interval is irrelevant.

Whatever you do, make sure that everyone receives recognition and rewards for a job well done. Above all, you don't want to fall into the category of managers who take the view: 'If my staff don't hear from me, they know they're doing a good job.' The staff do not know this – they need to be told.

When giving rewards, make sure that you're consistent with everyone and everything. In particular, give small rewards – for example, a buffet lunch, trips to the theatre – for the small and regular achievements that constitute so much of what contributes to enduring success and progress. Make sure that everyone can participate, and make sure that you treat everyone equally, according to their contribution.

Above all, make sure that you're always visible, engaged, and involved. This is the greatest source of recognition and intrinsic reward for all staff; and no amount of letters, buffets, or tickets can ever substitute for personal recognition. Make sure that you're always fair and consistent. The minute that someone does not receive recognition when others have done so, motivation, commitment, and morale begin to fall. And this response doesn't only apply to the particular employee – others quickly realise that recognition is now not being given out where once it was.

Never over-reward for mediocre, average, or expected performance. While short-term incentives do work in particular sets of circumstances, they never act as long-term motivators – and if they're consistently delivered, people will quickly come to expect them as part of the norm, delivered anyway, rather than for exceptional or above average performance.

People expect rewards and recognition – so deliver them fairly and equitably at all times.

You Get What You Reward

We'll let you in on a little secret – a secret that can make your life as a supervisor or manager much easier, and the results of your employees much better. If you were enrolled in an MBA programme right now, you would have to pay thousands of pounds to learn this secret. But because you opted to buy this book instead, we give it to you for free.

You get what you reward.

If you reward people to achieve their goals, they'll do just that. Conversely, if you do *not* reward people to achieve their goals, they're less likely to do so. In fact, they may not even try to achieve them.

The good news about rewards – and the bad

The good news is that the most effective rewards cost little or no money. A study of 1,500 employees conducted by Dr Gerald Graham, management professor at Wichita State University, reported the following top five employee motivators:

- ✔ Spoken thanks from one's manager
- ✔ Written thanks from one's manager
- ✔ Promotion for performance
- ✔ Public praise
- ✔ Morale-building meetings

That rewards needn't be expensive is the good news. The bad news is that managers seldom reward their employees, and many don't bother at all. When Dr Graham asked the study group of 1,500 employees to report how often they received the top five employee motivators listed above, the results were shocking:

- ✔ 58 per cent seldom if ever received personal thanks from their managers.
- ✔ 76 per cent seldom if ever received written thanks from their managers.
- ✔ 78 per cent seldom if ever received promotions based on performance.
- ✔ 81 per cent seldom if ever received public praise in the workplace.
- ✔ 92 per cent seldom if ever participated in morale-building meetings.

Clearly a problem exists. Most managers seem to know that rewarding and recognising employees is a good thing to do – few would argue with that. But the reality is completely different. How can that be?

In his book *Understanding Organisations*, management guru Charles Handy states that 80 per cent of managers and supervisors see themselves as fully participative, easy to get hold of, and honest, open, and transparent in their dealings with their staff. However, the staff working for these managers see them in 80 per cent of cases as being remote, distant and aloof, difficult to get hold of, and less than transparent in their reward and recognition programmes. So make sure that you really do see yourself as others see you – ensure that you keep yourself visible, deal with staffing matters when they arise, and hand out praise and recognition when they're due.

Keys to effective rewards and recognition

Many managers think that they reward and recognise their employees adequately, when, in reality, they don't. What often happens is that, because a manager doesn't give a reward in an effective manner, the message is lost on the employee to whom it was directed. And, if the message is lost, then – as far as the employee is concerned – he or she has *not* been rewarded for his or her good work.

Four keys exist to make your employee rewards and recognition effective – regardless of what kinds of rewards and recognition you decide to apply in a specific situation:

✔ **The reward must specify the behaviour being rewarded.** When you reward an employee for landing a big new account, be sure that the reward is clearly linked to that behaviour. For example, make a big deal about the new account by presenting a bonus cheque to your employee in your weekly staff meeting. As a part of the presentation, be sure to explain that the employee is receiving the bonus for bringing in the new account and remind everyone that similar behaviour on their parts will bring a similar reward. By doing so, you reinforce the message that the other employees at the meeting can be rewarded in a similar way. Think about the impact you'll have if you print a story about the presentation along with a photograph in your company employee newsletter.

✔ **Give the reward sincerely.** Employees know when you're giving sincere thanks, and when you're faking it. The trouble is, if they sense that you aren't being sincere in your thanks, they discount it or – even worse – are insulted by it. Give rewards and recognition only when you feel that employees deserve it, but don't hesitate to do so when the situation merits.

✔ **Give the reward in a positive tone.** Good rewards and recognition are positive and uplifting. They highlight the behaviour that you want more of, and they inspire employees to strive to become even better in the future. A warning: Don't ever, *ever* immediately follow praise with a reprimand. You know, 'Thanks, Jaquinta, you handled that irate customer perfectly, but I'm really upset that you made five spelling errors in this report.' Not only does the employee immediately discount your praise, but your long-term relationship with the employee is diminished.

✔ **Give the reward as close to the event as possible.** To have maximum impact, give rewards immediately after the behaviour you want to reinforce. However, because that's not always possible, be sure that whatever the reward is – praise, cash, a gift certificate, a trip to Paris – it is given no more than a few days to a couple weeks after the event. At all costs, avoid relying only on an annual awards ceremony to hand out employee rewards and recognition. Unfortunately, for all their pomp and glory, much of the impact of employee rewards is lost when you give them out months after the behaviour you want to reinforce.

The best employee rewards and recognition programmes offer a mix of both informal and formal rewards, which we cover in the following sections.

Informal rewards and recognition

Informal rewards and recognition are just that – they're spontaneous, require little or no planning, and generally cost little or nothing. They can be incredibly effective because they demonstrate that someone in management (or the employee's peers, if one employee gives the reward to another) really cares about them – enough to take the time and effort to recognise the employee's good work.

Here are a few terrific examples of informal rewards and recognition in organisational settings:

✔ Store managers at the John Lewis partnership always make sure that their staff receive copies of any letters of congratulation on high quality service, whenever they are received; and they always pass on messages of verbal praise to the particular individual.

✔ University College London lists the achievements (work-related or otherwise) of all staff, and present and former students on its Web site.

✔ At Tait's Greetings' Cards, if a member of staff comes up with a design that's used commercially, their name goes on the card as the designer.

✔ At Dutton Engineering Ltd, if an employee comes up with a way in which the organisation can save money, they receive a cash bonus. In addition a small bonus is paid to every member of staff.

✔ At Compaq, the computer software and information systems company, all employees are allowed to propose their own schedules, hours, and patterns of work, dependent only upon their ability to deliver the results required on time and within budget.

Only your imagination limits informal rewards and recognition. So make it a part of your managerial task to let your imagination run free and find out what is of value to your employees. And using this knowledge as the basis, make sure that you use whatever you can to ensure the highest levels of motivation possible.

Formal rewards and recognition

Formal rewards and recognition programmes are the norm in most organisations, even those that have a strong culture of informal recognition. The recognition programmes are regular (weekly, monthly, or annual), subject to very specific criteria or rules, and often consist of something tangible, or of value. A few examples include:

- Employee-of-the-month awards
- Certificates of achievement
- Cash awards for cost savings
- Years-of-service pins, trophies, or cheques
- Stock options

A *well-designed* formal awards programme can be very effective. Note, however, the emphasis on the words *well-designed*. The best formal awards programmes incorporate all four keys to effective rewards and recognition, as noted earlier in this chapter.

When you structure a formal rewards and recognition programme, try to create a system that doesn't force employees to wait months after the fact to get their awards. You can create a formal system that rewards employees almost immediately after the behaviour you want to reinforce occurs. However, such a system requires that management make timeliness a priority, in addition to establishing policies and procedures that support quick action rather than hinder it.

No set of absolute rules exists for the creation of effective formal rewards and recognition programmes. Above all, concentrate on what employees like, and on rewarding the behaviours and activities that you want, and not those that you don't want. Additionally, make sure that you include the following when structuring formal awards:

- Peer involvement in designing and evaluating awards programmes, nominating individuals for awards, reviewing nominations, and recommending award amounts.
- On-the-spot awards because they're more timely and aren't based on appraisal ratings that have low credibility.

✔ Group/team awards where the predominant mode of getting the work done is through formal and informal teams.

✔ Standard formulas for determining awards budgets and individual award amounts.

✔ Prestigious honorary awards to recognise extraordinary professional or personal efforts that best represent the organisation's values and reflect great credit on the organisation, its mission, and its workforce.

✔ Public recognition to demonstrate management's support and confidence in the validity of the awards decisions and to reassure everyone that deserving employees will be rewarded for high performance.

Whatever your rewards system, always make sure that you think about the following points:

✔ Link performance recognition programmes and decisions to strategic plans, goals, and results.

✔ Establish balanced, flexible recognition programmes that feature a variety of group and individual awards, instead of focusing on one or two types of awards.

✔ Consider making more use of competitive and prestigious non-monetary (honorary) awards, with provisions for peer nomination and peer involvement in deciding award recipients.

✔ Improve publicity about individual award recipients and awards programme activity.

✔ Publish and disseminate to all organisation levels annual awards policies, expectations, and funding guidance for the year as soon as practicable at the beginning of each financial year.

✔ Consider employee concerns – including inconsistency in distribution, non-credible bases for awards, and awards given unfairly – when developing policies related to award practices and funding.

✔ Establish accountability systems to monitor adherence to awards policies and expectations, to spot problem trends, and to identify opportunities for programme improvement.

In a perfect world, perhaps rewarding and recognising employee effort wouldn't be necessary. If all employees were 100 per cent intrinsically motivated in their jobs (wouldn't *that* be nice!), no need would exist for the carrots of rewards and recognition. However, the world isn't perfect, and most managers will see immediate and positive results when they initiate a programme of regular and systematic rewards and recognition.

Cash and incentives

Who doesn't like an occasional cash bonus? Without a doubt, nothing is quite like having your boss hand you a cheque for doing something good at work. However, as good as cash feels when you get it – and spend it – it isn't always as effective at motivating employees in the long run as non-monetary rewards.

Studies show that non-monetary rewards have four major advantages over cash rewards:

- ✓ **Memory value:** The value of an honorary or informal recognition award, whether it's a plaque, a mug, or a similar item, lasts longer than cash because cash is spent and gone, whereas the recognition items remain on employees' desks or in their homes.

- ✓ **Trophy value:** Employees can show non-monetary awards to colleagues and friends as a trophy given in appreciation of good work. People don't generally display pay slips or bank statements.

- ✓ **Flexibility:** You can design the type of non-monetary recognition to emphasise particular organisational or team goals. For example, you could award a mug or a trophy with the company logo to a team that has accomplished a short-term goal on time. The award recognises good performance and promotes teamwork.

- ✓ **Cash awards cost more:** A study of private sector awards found that employers spent less money on non-monetary awards than cash awards. However, the survey also found that employers reported about the same level of performance improvement with cash and non-monetary awards and that the awards held approximately the same perceived value.

The message is clear: Cash is *not* the only thing that matters. Cash can be part of an effective rewards and recognition programme, but be sure to include a variety of non-cash rewards as well. Not only will your programme be more effective, but your budget will go a *lot* further!

Motivating Employees for the Long Term

For employee rewards and recognition to work over the long term instead of simply causing a short-term blip on management's radar, supervisors and managers have to create a recognition culture – a long-term strategy with long-term goals and long-term activity.

Creating an effective rewards and recognition programme needs exactly the same care and attention as every other managerial activity. One expert in the field, Bob Nelson, suggests several tips for developing effective recognition and reward programmes:

- **Focus on areas that have the most impact.** Goal-setting principles dictate that you need to focus on just a few goals to make the best progress possible. Select one or two objectives that will make the biggest difference to your group's success.

- **Involve your target employee group.** The best management is what you do *with* people, not *to* them. From the very start, involve those individuals you are most trying to motivate in the planning and implementation of your recognition programme.

- **Announce the programme with a fanfare.** A recognition programme should be fun and exciting – starting with how you announce the programme. If you'll be using merchandise incentives, for example, show pictures or have sample goods on hand.

- **Publicly track progress.** If you don't measure it, you can't manage it. If you do measure it and do it publicly, you increase the chances of employees paying attention to the desired performance on a daily basis.

- **Have lots of winners.** Because some of the best forms of recognition are free, why not do as much recognition as possible? Even simple recognition activities, such as spoken, written, or public thanks, can effectively obtain desired results.

- **Allow flexibility of rewards.** What motivates one person can vary widely from what motivates another, so allow individuals some choice of rewards whenever possible. For example, offer employees a choice of recognition activities, assignments, or merchandise.

- **Renew the programme as needed.** Even the best recognition programme eventually runs its course, often within just a few months. Build on the success of the programme, learn from your mistakes, and try something new to keep things fresh.

- **Link informal and formal rewards.** Get the best of both informal and formal rewards by combining their use.

- **Find ways to perpetuate new behaviours.** To sustain new levels of performance, other organisational systems need to reinforce the desired behaviour, and this includes recruitment and selection, communication, training, career development, merit pay, and promotion practices.

The best rewards and recognition Web sites

Motivating staff, and supporting your efforts with effective rewards and recognition programmes is never easy. However, you can always get help from the following sources:

Chartered Institute of Personnel and Development (CIPD): www.cipd.co.uk. The CIPD is the UK's foremost professional body dealing with all aspects of staff and human resource management. You can find a wealth of guidance on employee motivation, recognition, and reward on this Web site. If you have members of staff who belong to the CIPD, they can access all of this information for free.

Chartered Management Institute (CMI): www.managers.org.uk. The Chartered Management Institute is the professional body for everyone who holds a managerial position. You can find extremely useful information on all aspects of staff management and performance, freely available to everyone who is a member of the Chartered Management Institute.

Love2Reward: www.Love2reward.com. This is a very modern free site, that takes a full range of approaches and illustrates a wide and creative diversity to motivation and rewards.

Motivating employees is a continuous process. You can't simply thank your employee for doing a good job and then walk away – never to be seen or heard from again. Employees – even the best employees – need regular attention and feedback about how they're doing. Make sure that you spend at least as much time with your employees as you do with your clients, customers, and boss.

Chapter 7

Hiring and Firing: Getting and Keeping the Best Employees

In This Chapter

▶ Recruiting and selecting employees

▶ Disciplining and dismissing employees

▶ Understanding employee relations

▶ Understanding employment law

*E*very business in the world depends upon people to make it run and flourish. Businesses need more than buildings and stock stacked up to the rafters in countless warehouses in endless cities. Businesses need more than computers humming away as they direct the flow of bits and bytes over worldwide telecommunications networks. Without people to help oversee the buildings, manage the stock, and operate the computers, businesses can't exist.

Unsurprisingly, the better the quality of people in your organisation, the better the quality of the organisation itself. Quality people also result in better products and services. In this chapter, we focus on people. We explain how to find and employ the very best people for your company, how to monitor and correct performance, how to lay off employees when times get tough, and how to fire people. Finally, we briefly cover some of the most important legal issues in dealing with employees.

Attracting and Retaining the Best Employees

Creating the very best products and services requires having the very best employees available to produce them. And the most effective way to have the very best employees is to recruit that kind of person. Instead of taking on average employees and hoping that they develop into exceptional employees, why not take the time and effort to recruit the very finest employees right from the start?

Defining the job

Before you place an advertisement in the newspaper or post a job notice on the intranet, you must create the required job description. A job description explains the duties and responsibilities of a particular position and defines any special requirements or skills that the successful candidate needs. Always include some measure of flexibility to ensure space for growth and development, and the ability to meet changing organisation needs.

Here are some specific elements that every job description should contain, regardless of the position:

- ✔ **Job title:** This is the name of the job, for example Programmer/Analyst, Accountant, or Personal Assistant.

- ✔ **Department/division:** This element specifies the department or division in which the specific position is located, for example in the accounting department or the operations division.

- ✔ **Responsibilities:** The list of responsibilities isn't simply a one- or two-sentence summary of a job's most important duties; it includes every task of the position. Writing a complete description of a position's responsibilities is not a simple task. If you want a thorough job description, first ask your current employees exactly what they do – every single little thing. Then compare your employees' lists against what you think they should be doing. Compile your final list of responsibilities within this section of the job advert in a narrative/paragraph-type format or as a bulleted list.

- ✔ **Required skills/expertise:** Does a person need specific skills to do this job – perhaps experience with spreadsheet programs or the ability to build wooden forms for pouring concrete building foundations? This part of the job description needs to include the essential skills and expertise required.

- ✔ **Essential and desirable qualifications:** Some jobs require workers with specific qualifications in order to be able to practise; others require specific qualifications in order to be any good! Anyone doing secretarial work almost certainly requires keyboard qualifications; anyone required to do executive accounting work must have some form of accounting qualification. And if you need someone to do a lot of driving with their job, then check their driver's licence – don't take it for granted that they have one, or that it is clean.

Show me the money!

Many organisations now offer very complex reward packages to their staff – including company cars, further education, and nursery and crèche facilities. However, a survey carried out by the Internet recruitment agency Vault.com found that salary was still by far the most important consideration to the vast majority of people when considering whether to apply for a job. Here are the results of the survey question: 'Which part of the reward package at your job needs the most improvement?'

- ✔ Hours: 9.2 per cent
- ✔ Medical benefits: 11.6 per cent
- ✔ Salary: 48.8 per cent
- ✔ Share options: 17.6 per cent
- ✔ Holidays: 12.6 per cent

If you've never prepared job descriptions before or if you want an easier way to deal with them, then get help. The Chartered Institute of Personnel and Development (CIPD) can provide help with creating job descriptions (though you may have to pay a small fee for this service if none of your staff are members of the CIPD). After you've been advised on this, you'll always have a structure with which to work, and as you gain practice, you'll gain expertise.

Job descriptions must be written in ways that meet equal opportunities legislation and guidance. Unless specific qualities or qualifications are attached to the particular job, everyone must be given equal treatment when applying.

If you want to limit the field in any way, then you must be able to prove what is called a 'Genuine Occupational Qualification (GOQ). A GOQ is a specific element that precludes some people from applying for or being considered for the job, or which includes a specific sector of the community to the exclusion of others. The most usual grounds for a GOQ are:

- ✔ **Decency:** You can usually insist that a female member of staff look after the care needs of female clients in health or social care.

- ✔ **Cultural issues:** You can usually insist on staff accommodating certain specific cultural norms from a particular sector of the community.

- ✔ **Theatre presentation:** You can insist, for example, on employing a female to play female acting roles.

Paying your employees what they're worth

Your employees always deserve to be paid what they're worth. You can determine this worth by looking at the salaries of employees in similar positions in your geographic area and by determining the relative value of your employees' contributions to your organisation.

If you aren't offering pay rates and salaries that are competitive with other companies, you'll have a tough time attracting the best employees to your firm. Other elements of an overall reward package – such as health benefits, retirement plans, and share options – can also enter into a candidate's decision about whether to accept a job offer. Salary, however, is still the most important compensation consideration of all.

The first step in working out how much to pay your employees is to develop an overall rewards structure for your organisation that will become the foundation that helps to guide pay and salary decisions. One of your key goals is to ensure that the decisions you make are consistent from one employee to another. Few business issues have as direct, immediate, and personal an impact on employees as their salaries. If you're not clear about your pay and reward policies, you're asking for trouble. You need to be clear about what you're paying for, and why you've arrived at the balance of pay and salary with other benefits as the result. And you need to be able to provide detailed answers to the following questions:

- ✔ Are you going to make your basic salaries simply competitive with the going rate for employers in your area – or higher?

- ✔ Are you going to establish a structured pay scale for specific jobs in your company, or are you going to set salaries on an individual basis, based on the qualities and potential of the person filling the job?

- ✔ To what extent are the monetary rewards that you offer your employees going to take the form of salary, performance bonuses, and benefits?

- ✔ Are you going to base the salaries on how well people perform or on other factors, such as how long they stay with you or what credentials they bring to the job?

- ✔ Are you going to award bonuses on the basis of individual performance, tie bonuses to company results, or use a combination of both?

- ✔ Are you going to pay for loyalty, achievement, or output – or a combination?

- ✔ Are you going to take local factors into account and pay above or below the going rate for the particular job according to these factors?

- ✔ Are you going to balance the pay and rewards aspects with the fact that it's a good, worthwhile, and highly sought after job?

- ✔ Are you going to offer a structured career progression that people can understand and be comfortable with?

If you try to pay your employees badly for high levels of performance, they'll only put up with this situation until they can find other employment elsewhere.

After you've decided on your strategic approach to pay and reward, then all other decisions become much easier. For example, if you're going to base salaries on the going rates within your geographical area, then your first step is to do a wage survey to determine exactly what those going rates are for each position within your organisation. Wage information is available from a variety of sources, including the Internet, government employment offices, chambers of commerce, local business newspapers and magazines, and employment consulting firms.

However you decide to pay your employees, keep in mind that wages, salaries, bonuses, and benefits – and the fairness and consistency with which you determine them – have a direct and measurable effect on employee happiness and motivation. In turn, your employees' job satisfaction has a direct and measurable effect on customer satisfaction and, ultimately, revenues and profit. Also don't forget that if your competitors are offering better salary packages for the same jobs, your employees will almost certainly find out and be tempted to move to where the grass is greener.

The recruitment process

If you're serious about attracting the very best employees to work in your firm, the recruitment process is a lot of work. But the good news is that the rewards of making a good appointment are tremendous and long lasting. These rewards include:

- Increased productivity
- Improved morale
- Better customer satisfaction
- Increased revenues
- Increased profit

In the following sections, we explain the key steps in the recruitment process and offer advice on how to conduct them the right way, every time.

Finding the best of the best

Where do you go to find the very best employees? To some extent, the answer to that question depends on the kind of position you have to fill and the kind of people you're seeking. To increase the chances of getting your message in front of the right people, first decide what kind of person you're looking for and then decide the best method for communicating the opportunity to that person. Unfortunately, you may not be able to tell what method is best until you try recruiting your first employees. After you get a feel for what works, however, you can do more of that, and less of the methods that don't work as well.

You can choose from a variety of ways to advertise a job opportunity to the best candidates. Here are some of the most commonly used methods:

- **Newspaper advertisement:** This is probably the first place that most employers think of looking for new employees. But is placing an advertisement in your local newspaper the best way to find the people you're looking for? Possibly not. You have a chance that the best candidate for the job will see your advertisement. But you may miss many other terrific candidates, both locally and outside of your immediate geographic area because they simply don't buy the local newspaper. You can try a newspaper ad to see which candidates turn up, but if that doesn't do the trick for you, quickly move on to another method.

- **The Internet:** In the past few years, the World Wide Web has exploded as a resource for those seeking work and for those looking for staff. Hundreds of different Web sites cater for those seeking jobs. Many such Web sites are specific to different kinds of opportunities, such as information technology, purchasing, and sales. To get an idea of what's out there, carry out your own research. You'll soon find out which Web sites suit your needs best, and which do not. Two very good examples are www.jobsearch.co.uk and www.targetcareers. co.uk.

- **Executive search:** If you want to attract someone with specific expertise or experience, then one way to do so is to engage an executive search agency (headhunter) to produce a likely list of candidates and their profiles. Although this service costs money, you'll quickly get an idea of who's available, their level of experience, and how much you may have to pay them.

- **Business and personal networks:** We all have networks of contacts, both in our businesses and in our personal lives. Our friends and professional contacts can often be excellent sources of job candidates. People in your networks not only know about your business and the kind of people you're looking for but also are unlikely to send you candidates who would reflect badly on *them*. However, remember the warning about equality of treatment and opportunity in the previous section 'Defining the job'. If you offer plum positions to your friends, you are breaking the law – and will eventually be called to account.

✔ **Employment agencies:** Although you may be required to pay to use this resource, employment agencies (including temporary agencies, executive search firms, and so-called headhunting firms) can be terrific sources of job candidates. Plenty of employment agencies are always seeking to place staff, especially in urban areas, and those doing their job properly can quickly tell you whether they can help you.

✔ **Universities, colleges, and schools:** These are excellent sources of employees – provided that you understand that, while recent graduates are likely to have a high level of knowledge, and (hopefully!) boundless enthusiasm, they also need extensive induction, orientation, and settling in programmes to make sure that this knowledge and enthusiasm is made as effective as possible, as quickly as possible.

✔ **Inside your organisation:** One of the best sources of top-quality job candidates is within your own organisation. The beauty of internal candidates is that you can usually get very candid references on their job performance from their colleagues and past and present supervisors. Another plus is that internal candidates are already familiar with company policies and procedures. As a result, they can move into their new positions more quickly than someone from outside your firm. Don't overlook this rich resource of job candidates.

Recruiting is an uncertain game, even at the best of times. On the one hand, the larger your pool of candidates, the greater your chance of finding someone who is just right for you. However, this possibility has to be balanced against the fact that you can't interview hundreds of candidates for every available post. So you need to develop the expertise of defining your job requirements, while ensuring that these requirements are presented to the widest possible field of candidates in the given context.

Interviewing

Interviews are one of the most critical – and often among the most dreaded – parts of the recruitment process. For job candidates, they're an opportunity to answer detailed questions about their experience and to give their potential employer a glimpse of what kind of employee they'll be. For employers, interviews are a unique opportunity to ask questions that go beyond the one-sided marketing pitch of most applications, and to get a feel for how candidates will fit into an organisation.

Depending on the particular position you're seeking to fill, you may have hundreds of applications to sort through. Separate out your strongest candidates and reject any candidate who doesn't have the required qualifications, job skills, and experience. If an application is incomplete but otherwise strong, consider contacting the candidate to obtain the necessary information. Narrow down your selection to no more than five of the very best candidates; these are the people whom you are going to invite to interview for your position.

From the employer perspective, here are the three main reasons for interviewing job candidates:

✔ To get further in-depth information about a candidate's work skills and experience – straight from the job seeker's mouth. (This process gives you the opportunity to see whether what the candidate tells you is consistent with their application.)

✔ To assess the candidate's personality and to determine how that personality will fit into your existing work team.

✔ To try to assess a candidate's enthusiasm and intelligence, and to include in any structured interview anything else that you may wish to test, such as their ability to think and reason.

No one can guarantee that someone who shines during an interview will work out as a new employee. Every manager has tales of ace interviewees who got the job but didn't last long. However, a well-done interview can greatly increase your chances of landing the best candidate for the job. Here are some tips on conducting an interview:

✔ **Welcome the applicant and put them at ease.** Most job applicants are more than a little bit nervous when interviewing for a job, and with reason – job interviews often make or break candidates. Conduct the interview in a quiet office or conference room free of interruption from phones, computers, and other employees. Greet the candidate warmly, offer coffee, water, or a soft drink, and direct him or her to a seat. Instead of launching right into the interview, take a couple of minutes to break the ice and to take the edge off the interviewee's nervousness. Open the conversation by talking about neutral topics such as the weather or how difficult it can be to find your office. The point is to create as much rapport as you can in a few minutes. This small talk allows the candidate to focus more on your questions than on their nervousness.

✔ **Summarise the position.** Take a minute or two to give the candidate a brief summary of the position. Include details of job responsibilities, how the job fits into the organisation, reporting relationships, and expected customer interactions.

✔ **Ask a variety of questions.** Have a structured set of questions to ask everyone, and make sure that you cover all the essential ground. You need to address the following questions:

  • Why are you here?

  • What can you do for us?

  • What do you expect us to do for you?

  • What kind of person are you?

  • Can we afford you?

Ask questions that explore each of these areas (don't be as blunt as this, though!), and carefully note your candidate's answers. If you don't get the answer you're looking for or if the candidate seems to be evasive on a particular point, don't hesitate to push until you get a satisfactory response.

✓ **Probe the candidate's strengths and weaknesses.** You probably picked up on a candidate's strengths and weaknesses when you assessed the application before the interview. Probe your candidate further about those strengths and weaknesses on the application, as well as any others that become apparent during the interview.

✓ **Conclude the interview on an upbeat note.** Ask your candidate whether he or she has any other information to offer that you should consider in your decision process. Then give the candidate a chance to explain that information. Ask if the candidate has any questions for you, and answer them fully. Thank the candidate for their interest in the job (no matter how well or how poorly the interview went) and give the person some idea when you'll be making a decision about additional rounds of interviews. Do *not* make any sort of promises such as, 'You're definitely the best candidate – we'll be making you an offer soon.' Not only are you setting yourself up for real trouble if you don't follow through on your promises, but the next candidate you interview may be even better than the last.

Take plenty of notes during your interviews. Better still, prepare an interview form in advance to guide you through your questions and to allow you to jot down notes on your candidates' responses. This advice is especially important if you have a lot of candidates to interview or if you won't have a chance to review the candidates' performance immediately after the interviews.

Checking references

Although many employers are understandably wary about providing reference information about former employees (many employers have been sued for giving bad references), checking them out is still very much worth your time. You just never know what kind of information is going to turn up in your investigation. You may uncover information that can have great bearing on whether you extend a job offer to a candidate.

Most people still check references. However, remember that excellent past performance is no guarantee of excellent future performance; likewise, poor past performance doesn't mean that the person will perform poorly for you also. References are simply one more piece of information in the selection process and have to be assessed fully as such.

Here are some of the best places to dig deeper to find out how your candidate might really work out in the new job:

- ✔ Current and former supervisors
- ✔ Current and former customers and clients
- ✔ Colleges, universities, and other schools
- ✔ Networks of common acquaintances, such as industry associations or professional groups

If in doubt, have the best candidates back for second or third interviews, and restructure the next round of interviews so that you can probe the areas that you still need to explore. This process seems expensive and time-consuming, but, when you compare it to the cost of appointing a bad candidate, it's time and resources well spent.

Ranking your candidates

After you've completed your interviews and conducted your reference checks, rank each of your candidates against one another. The easiest way to do so is to put the name of each candidate along the left side of a piece of paper and list your recruitment criteria along the top of the page. You create a grid like the one in Table 7-1, which shows a hypothetical group of three candidates.

Knowing interview taboo

Equality of opportunity and equality of treatment legislation require that every candidate is given an equal chance at interview and other parts of the selection process. The overall purpose is to ensure that you get the best possible candidate for the job. In particular, you may not discriminate on any of the following grounds at the selection process unless there is a 'Genuine Occupational Qualification' (see the earlier section 'Defining the job') that permits you to target persons of a specific gender or ethnic origin. So, at interview, never ask any questions that relate to any of the following:

- ✔ Race or ethnic origin
- ✔ Gender or gender preference

- ✔ Marital status
- ✔ Religious beliefs
- ✔ Arrest and conviction record (unless directly related to the job requirements; for example, you may ask about any motoring convictions if the post is a driving job)
- ✔ Age
- ✔ Disability (although you can of course ask if the candidate has any special needs, or needs help getting into the building for interview)

If you become aware of any interviewer asking questions along these lines, then put a stop to it immediately.

Table 7-1:	Candidate Ranking Worksheet			
	Customer Service Skills (A)	Help Desk Experience (B)	References (C)	Total Points (A+B+C)
Maria	1	2	1	4
Tom	3	1	2	6
Sally	2	3	3	8

Rank each employee on each of the recruitment criteria. In our example, Maria was ranked number one for customer service skills, while Sandeep was ranked second and Tom third. Go through each of your recruitment criteria (you may have many more items than our simple example does) and assign rankings in this way. Finally, after you've ranked all the candidates, add up the totals for each employee and note it on the worksheet. The candidate with the lowest score is the best for you. In the example, it's Maria.

Now, at last, you can make your job offer. If for some reason your top candidate declines the offer, then you can go to the next-ranked candidate on your worksheet. Or you can restart the whole recruitment process all over again.

Whatever you decide, guard against allowing desperation to rule your recruitment decisions. Leaving a position unfilled is usually better than taking on an inferior candidate. If your first round of recruiting and interviews doesn't bring you the right candidates for the job, then by all means try it again. Interviewing more candidates is far less painful than dismissing someone who doesn't work out the way you hoped.

Induction

The first few days and weeks of work for your new employee can be both exciting and disorientating. No matter how much experience a new employee may have under their belt, starting a new job to some extent means starting from scratch. And when you add in a new office, new colleagues, and entirely new relationships, policies, and procedures to sort out, you have a recipe for instant confusion.

Fortunately, you can help make your new employee's transition into your organisation relatively painless and quick. Here are some tips on how to make your new employee's first day at work one that is productive and that helps ease the transition:

- **Make them feel welcome.** Set aside plenty of time for your new employee. Be sure that others who'll supervise or be supervised by the new employee also allot some time for the new starter. Nothing is worse for a new employee than to be shoved aside for hours (or days, or weeks) because no one can spare a few hours of time to help welcome a new member of the team.

- **Provide a sense of place and belonging.** Be sure that the new employee's office or workstation is ready to move into straight away. Stock it with a full complement of office essentials (paper clips, pens, pencils, paper, stapler, and so on) and make sure that phones and computers are properly hooked up and immediately available.

- **Introduce your new employee to the team.** Take the time to introduce them to their new colleagues. You can do this by escorting the person around your offices to meet people on an informal basis. As another option, you can schedule an informal get-together early in the day or over lunch so that your work unit or department can get to know the new employee.

- **Don't drown your new employee in forms and paperwork.** Although new-starter paperwork is a necessary evil, take care of only the essentials on the first day. Give the new employee a week to complete the rest of the forms and turn them in.

- **Make the first day enjoyable.** Above all, make sure that your new employee's first day is enjoyable and positive – one that starts off on the right foot with your organisation. The employee will have plenty of time down the road for the job to get serious, so you don't need to rush it now.

You only have one chance to make a first impression. Take the time to ensure that the first impression of your organisation is one of truly caring about the new employee's well-being. Don't let that impression end after the first day of work; renew it every day with *all* your employees through your own actions.

Discipline and Dismissal

Sometimes, no matter what you do to try to work with an employee or to help them achieve an acceptable standard of performance, all your efforts fail. You may be left with no choice but to remove your employee from their job. Firing an employee is certainly the toughest job by far for any manager or supervisor – and a job that no one looks forward to (unless you're a sadist). The pain of dismissing an employee is felt not only by the employee but also by the entire organisation, especially by colleagues and the employee's supervisor or manager.

Dismissal should *always* be the last resort in any organisation. Before you ever get to that point, do whatever you can to help the employee get back on track and become a productive member of your team. In some cases, disciplining the employee through written or spoken warnings is all the wake-up call that the employee needs. In other cases, you may be able to transfer the employee to another job or to another department. In fact, always explore the possibility of a transfer if the employee shows the potential to become a productive member of the organisation, but in a different position.

In the sections that follow, we take a close look at how to discipline and dismiss employees.

Discipline

If employees aren't performing up to the standards you have mutually agreed, then you must take action and not ignore the problem. Here are the two key reasons for disciplining employees:

- ✔ **Misconduct:** Every organisation has policies and procedures that employees are supposed to follow. Breaking certain policies and procedures may have only a minor impact on the organisation (for example, taking two reams of paper from the supply cabinet when you're supposed to take only one ream at a time). But other infractions, including stealing from colleagues, lying to your boss, and making fraudulent travel expense claims, are very serious.

- ✔ **Performance:** Every employee is expected to achieve a certain level of performance. Whether it's producing 50 widgets an hour, selling £50,000 worth of products a month, or answering the telephone before the third ring 90 per cent of the time, everyone has minimum standards to meet on the job. Falling below these minimum standards repeatedly or for a prolonged period of time usually triggers the disciplinary process.

The term *discipline* applies to a very wide range of activities meant to provide feedback to employees about deficiencies in their conduct or performance. Employers generally provide such feedback in the hope that employees will change their behaviour so that a supervisor or manager doesn't need to take further action. The most commonly accepted discipline in use today is called *progressive discipline*, meaning that feedback becomes progressively more serious for repeated or major performance lapses or cases of misconduct.

All organisations must have disciplinary procedures that meet the minimum standards laid down by the Advisory, Conciliation and Arbitration Service (ACAS). ACAS is the UK statutory body responsible for establishing, maintaining, and ensuring the highest possible standards of employment practice and the promotion of effective employee relations. Disciplinary procedures must:

- Be in writing
- Specify to whom they apply
- Be freely available to all staff
- State the conditions under which they are to be applied
- Specify the penalties for serious and gross misconduct, and give examples of each

Disciplinary procedures must have a series of warnings. You must give at least two warnings before you contemplate dismissal; and many organisations have three. Procedures must allow for employees facing discipline to be represented and/or accompanied. Procedures must allow for the case against an employee to be stated clearly, and for the employee to respond. You must allow for the employee to *appeal* (contest any finding) at each stage.

When undertaking disciplinary action, you must always ask employees for an explanation of their conduct and/or performance, and you need to listen carefully to this explanation before applying any sanction. Sanctions may include warnings, suspensions, and notes on file; and for gross misconduct, the normal penalty is dismissal. But you must follow procedures, and you must listen to explanations – or you'll automatically be found to have acted unfairly.

Of course, you hope to avoid recourse to serious disciplinary action, and in the vast majority of cases, a quick word in the employee's ear is enough to remedy poor or unacceptable behaviour and/or performance. However, when you apply a disciplinary procedure, you need to record the whole process in each case. If you issue warnings to employees, you must retain a copy on file. Such warnings must state what the disciplinary matter is, how it is to be remedied, and by when. You must review matters when the particular deadline arrives. Make sure the written warnings state how long they will remain on the individual's file before you delete them.

You *must* follow procedures at all times when disciplining employees. Failure to do so means that you put yourself in the danger of being accused of unfairly applying the sanction; and if you're dismissing, failure to follow procedures normally results in you being found guilty of unfairly dismissing.

Suspension

Where a disciplinary case is complex, or where an individual is facing serious allegations, you may need to suspend the employee from work. Suspension is normally on full pay – always remember that the individual is innocent until proven guilty. Where an employee is suspended, use the period of suspension to carry out a full and thorough investigation as quickly as possible, so that the matter doesn't drag on.

After the investigation is carried out to your satisfaction, invite the individual in with their representative, present the case against them, and ask for their explanation. Employees are entitled to have a representative with them at all stages. The representative may be from a recognised trade union, or else a work colleague.

You must listen to the explanation before you come to any conclusion or pass judgement. If you come to a conclusion before you've listened to the explanation, you'll normally be found to have acted unfairly.

Equality of treatment

You must treat all employees equally when facing the same or similar offences or issues. Treating people differently for similar offences on the grounds of their occupation, status, length of service, or hours of work is unfair (and against the law). The only exception to this situation is where a new employee is working a probationary period. Even in these cases, you must give the employee the opportunity to state their case in advance of any decision to end their employment after the probationary period finishes.

When disciplining employees – especially if the discipline escalates beyond a single warning – make sure that you notify your own manager and the human resources department of the problem, and the actions you're taking to solve it. Not only do they need to know what's going on, but they can also offer you their support and assistance during the process. In many cases, HR will by now be directly involved anyway.

Dismissal

Dismissal should take place only after you give employees ample opportunities to improve their performance or behaviour and they fail to do so; or when an offence constitutes serious or gross misconduct and merits immediate or summary dismissal. *Summary dismissal* means that the person is to be dismissed immediately the case against them is proven. Here are some examples of serious or gross misconduct meriting summary dismissal:

- Using or selling illegal drugs at work
- Stealing from colleagues or from the organisation
- Fraud
- Breaking confidentiality concerning the organisation and/or members of staff

- Gross insubordination
- Extreme violation of safety rules
- Misrepresentation on a job application
- Bullying, victimisation, discrimination, and harassment
- Vandalism and violence

Even when you discipline someone for one of the preceding offences, you must follow procedures. Employees facing such allegations must be allowed to state their case and to respond to any allegations. They are allowed the right of representation and to appeal against any sentence.

Before you dismiss

Firing an employee is bound to unleash all kinds of hurt and resentment on the part of the dismissed employee and can even land you in court or at a tribunal. For these reasons, be sure that your action meets the following criteria before you dismiss an employee:

- **Documentation:** If you're planning to dismiss an employee for performance shortcomings, make sure that you have written proof of those shortcomings and that they're supportable from the evidence. Documentation can be anything from a supervisor's written notes in a daily planner to time cards showing that an employee is habitually late – all the way up to falsified expense reports or other documents. When you make the decision as to what kind of documentation will be most appropriate for a particular situation, first ask yourself this question: Would the documentation convince a court or a tribunal that dismissing your employee was justified?

- **Fair warning:** Fair play says that employees with performance problems should be given fair warning of the consequences of continued problems. If you plan to dismiss your employee for performance shortcomings, be sure that you give them fair warning. However, serious misconduct can be grounds for immediate dismissal and doesn't necessarily require advance warning – though you must still follow procedures when such a case arises.

- **Response time:** Along with giving employees fair warning that their jobs are in jeopardy if improvement isn't soon forthcoming, you must also give them sufficient time to improve. You can reasonably expect an employee's performance to improve after a couple of weeks to a month.

- **Reasonableness:** The ultimate punishment of dismissal should be reasonable and appropriate for whatever offence led up to it. Firing an employee for being five minutes late to work once or twice isn't reasonable. Firing an employee for being consistently two hours late for several weeks or more – with no change in behaviour even after repeated oral and written warnings – is reasonable, provided that you've followed procedures and asked for an explanation.

✔ **Appeals:** All disciplinary and dismissal procedures must have an appeals process. When you've made a particular decision, you must allow any appeal as quickly as possible so that the matter is resolved promptly and effectively – this is in both your interests and those of the employee.

Dismissing an employee

Dismissing an employee is one of the most unpleasant tasks of being an employer or manager. Nevertheless, if you have to do it, do it effectively and professionally. Here are some ways of helping you through the process:

1. **Meet with the employee in a private location.** Never make an example of an employee in front of everyone, and use a private office where you won't be disturbed. This is a professional and business meeting, so lay down a form of agenda and structure in advance. Arrange to meet with the employee and their representative; and have someone accompanying you also, ideally someone from HR.

2. **Tell the employee that you are dismissing them.** Be straightforward and direct. Tell them why they are being dismissed, and when they have to leave. Ask about any mitigating circumstances, and if the employee does raise genuine concerns, then you need to take time out to review your decision. However, if you've followed procedures, and exhausted the appeals processes, then only some radically new information should have any effect on the process.

3. **Explain why the individual is being dismissed.** Give the reasons for dismissal in concise and precise terms. Provide a written version – and this written version must match what you stated verbally.

4. **Announce the date of departure.** After you announce and finalise the date of departure, you and your organisation have obligations to ensure that the employee is paid up in full, and that they receive all necessary documentation that they need. In particular, notify HR, payroll, and your own manager.

5. **Engage any final arrangements.** Make sure that the employee knows the procedures for clearing their desk and for removing their own personal effects. If they want to say goodbye to colleagues, then allow them to do so. If the employee wants to have a reference from you, make sure that the terms of the reference are agreed at this point.

Dismissing someone is neither easy nor enjoyable. Always conduct yourself professionally when dismissing someone, and never shirk your duty. When you do have to face unpleasant situations, make sure that you do so fully effectively – apart from anything else, this sets an example to everyone in the organisation of the standards and demeanour of conduct that you set for yourself.

Obeying the Long Arm of the Law

If you discover anything from running or managing a business, it is that you have to comply with a huge range of UK and EU (European Union) laws in terms of employment practice.

Be sure that you are closely familiar with the key employment laws that affect the way that you run or manage your business. If you don't comply with the law, on any matter to do with employment, you can be prosecuted, taken to tribunal, or have to answer to the offices of ACAS. Larger organisations have human resources departments and experts to deal with these matters, but don't use that as an excuse for not knowing the basics. You must know what you can and cannot do, and you must see that others stick within these boundaries. The following areas are of particular importance:

- ✔ **Equal pay.** Everyone has the right to receive the same pay and other terms of employment as an employee of the opposite sex doing the same or similar work, or carrying out equivalent work of equal value.

- ✔ **Minimum wages.** Minimum levels of pay are laid down by the government, and reviewed every year. Employees must receive at least the minimum wage, regardless of occupation, status, length of service, or hours worked. Know the specific provisions for those aged between 16–18, and for those aged 18 and over.

- ✔ **Discrimination.** By law you must not discriminate against anyone on grounds of: Sex/gender; race/ethnic origin; religion; membership of a trade union/refusal to belong to a trade union; age; or registered disability. If you have allegations of discrimination made against you, normally you have to answer the case in full, and prove that you did not discriminate. So make sure that your employment practices preclude the possibility of this happening under any circumstances whatsoever! Discriminating against people on the grounds of spent convictions for offences previously committed is also illegal; though many exceptions to this exist, and you need to deal with each case on its merits. As with all employment practice, the best source of advice is ACAS. Go to www.acas.org.uk and follow the links to discrimination.

- ✔ **Trade union membership.** Anyone may belong to the trade union of their choice; and anyone may refuse to belong to any trade union at all. However, organisations and employers can state clearly the particular trade unions that they recognise. Some employers take the view that recognising trade unions makes for simplified and effective employee relations; others take the opposite view. Whichever view you take, it needs to be an active management decision. Where trade unions are not recognised, managers need to ensure that they remove all of the reasons why employees would want to join a trade union, such as poor pay or bad working conditions.

✔ **Transfers of undertakings.** If your business is bought, sold, or acquired, or if it changes its status or activities, all employees must be transferred to the new ownership or directorate on their existing terms of employment. In particular, you may not conduct redundancies and lay-offs with a view to making one part of your business more attractive to potential buyers or acquirers.

✔ **Redundancy.** Redundancies occur where there's no more work for employees to carry out. You must have redundancy procedures in place that show who is at risk of redundancy, and the circumstances in which you'd conduct redundancies. The guiding principle is 'last in, first out' – and if you don't want to follow this, you must produce alternative criteria that are fair and just to all concerned.

✔ **Working hours.** You're not permitted to ask an employee to work more than 48 hours a week, except with their actively expressed consent. If someone refuses to work more than 48 hours a week, they may not be victimised or discriminated against on any grounds whatsoever.

✔ **Right to consultation.** The EU Acquired Rights Directive states that employees must be consulted and informed on any business decision that actively affects their future. All organisations of 500 employees or more must have a forum for consultation; and all organisations with 1,000 employees or more must have a European Works' Council at which employee representatives may raise any matter at all for debate and discussion. In particular, all employees must be consulted on: The possibility or threat of redundancies; changes in working times and practices; changes in working hours; changes in technology usage; and material changes in occupation. All of these may arise as the result of legitimate and essential business decisions, but employees must still be consulted.

✔ **Pregnancy and maternity.** All employees becoming pregnant must be given full statutory rights to attend medical institutions in any matter regarding their pregnancy, regardless of length of service or hours worked. Employees who give birth within one year of starting employment receive maternity leave of six months; and this is extended up to one year after 52 weeks or more of continuous service. The father may also take paternity leave of up to four weeks at any time during the first year of a child's life.

✔ **Contracts of employment.** You must issue contracts of employment, stating the main conditions under which work is carried out, to all employees. If, for some reason, you can't issue a contract of employment, a contract *de facto* (one in which the custom, practice, and habits of the previous 13 weeks form the actual contract) is deemed to exist after 13 weeks' continuous employment. Contracts specify: Hours worked; duties carried out; disciplinary procedures; wages and salary; other benefits; and the conditions under which the contract may be changed (such as pay rises).

European Union employment law

European Union employment law is broadly superior to that of the UK. Any case that goes through the UK tribunal and court system and reaches the European Court of Justice is judged by European standards as the final conclusion to the matter in hand. The particular priority of European Union employment law is the strengthening and upholding of individual and collective rights in all aspects of life – and this includes employment. EU employment law is mainly concerned with:

✔ Freedom of movement for workers and self-employed persons across the European Union

✔ Protection of employment and remuneration (pay)

✔ Adequate and continual vocational training

✔ Freedom of association, especially the right to join trade unions and associations, or the right not to join trade unions and associations

✔ Consultation with and participation of employees on all major workplace issues

✔ Adequate health and safety at work

✔ Specific protection for stated groups of employees, especially children and young persons, elderly persons, and disabled persons

✔ Equal treatment for everyone regardless of race, gender, ethnic origin, or nationality

Although this list is by no means an in-depth guide to employment law, it does provide the main areas of concern that all managers need to know and understand. Additional guidance is available on each area from ACAS. Employers' associations and trade federations are also excellent sources of information. Many large organisations have expert employee relations' departments, including legal experts; and most smaller organisations have an employment lawyer available at the end of the phone. So don't hesitate to use a lawyer if you need to.

Chapter 8

One for All and All for One: Teamwork and Employee Empowerment

*E*ffective teams really work. The simple fact is that no one person can be an expert at everything. And you can't expect one person to get everything done in an organisation. Teams allow employees with a variety of skills and experience to combine their talents to find and implement solutions that would be impossible for one person alone to do. Thus teams can leverage their talents to create an outcome much greater than the sum of its parts.

Teamwork can make a tremendous difference in the way employees work together, and that difference can positively affect the quality of products, services, and customer satisfaction. When employees work *with* instead of *against* one another, the result is a much more effective and efficient organisation. Teamwork can lead to quicker decision-making, less wasted time, and a reduction in expenses. And everyone benefits.

In this chapter, we take a close look at how companies use teams to improve products and services while creating happy customers in the process. We also find out about empowering employees – a very important part of successful team processes – and about how to set and monitor goals. Finally, we explore business meetings and discover how to make them better.

Pulling Together: Teamwork

Employee teams have become one of the most popular ways for organisations to get their work done. No matter which type of organisation you work for – whether private or public, large or small – chances are, you've been part of a team.

Reaping the benefits of teamwork

Teams are now a prominent part of organisations because of the flattening of organisational hierarchies – through the elimination of layers of management – and an increasing need for organisations to be fast and flexible in the marketplace. In the past, middle managers made most of the operational decisions in most organisations.

In many cases, middle-management has been replaced by self-managing teams in which those directly responsible for the work make all the key decisions, including recruitment and selection, pay rates, performance targets, and research and development.

Many such teams have shown real, quantifiable results. Here are some examples:

- ✔ Nissan UK was able to remove the whole of its quality control function by having the car production teams handle any customer complaints or queries about specific models produced. This led to a 75 per cent reduction in customer complaints and queries over the first two years of its operation.

- ✔ Harvest Time Restaurants removed the jobs of restaurant manager and deputy manager. Chefs and kitchen staff became responsible for design and structure of menus, ordering food and other ingredients, and ensuring that supplies were managed to minimise waste. The head waiter and other waiting staff working in the restaurants became responsible for budgeting, cashing up, and reconciling the day's takings. Each restaurant team reported to a regional manager; otherwise they were fully autonomous.

- ✔ The cabin crew teams working for British Airways are fully and extensively trained in all aspects of cabin crew work, including first-aid and security practice, before they're allowed on the airliners. Crew members choose specific tasks on the flights on which they work on the basis of length of service. Individuals know and understand both the job that they have to carry out, and also the basis on which it has been allocated. This has led, for many years, to the airline receiving numerous awards for excellent customer service.

Clearly, the potential benefits of teams are enormous. Another benefit is a saving in overheads if teams can work without traditional hierarchical supervision.

Analysing different kinds of teams

All kinds of teams are at work in organisations today. Although management may delegate formal teams of employees to address specific issues or challenges, informal teams of employees form and disband all the time.

Here's a look at the most common types of teams.

Formal teams

Formal teams are generally the most visible ones within most organisations. Management sanctions these teams, which are often launched with a great fanfare. Although formal teams hold great promise in getting useful things done in organisations, they can do their best work only with a minimum of interference by management.

Formal teams include:

- ✔ **Command teams:** These teams are comprised of a manager or supervisor and all of their employees. Sales teams, management teams, and executive teams are examples of command teams.

- ✔ **Committees:** Committees are teams of employees pulled together to solve an ongoing or long-term organisational problem or to achieve some sort of specific organisational goal. Committees may exist for years, with membership changing as employees come and go. Safety committees, employee morale committees, and investment committees are common examples of committees.

- ✔ **Task forces:** Task forces are teams of employees who must quickly solve organisational problems or respond to opportunities. Task forces usually have very specific goals and strict deadlines. Task forces work intensively: They 'blitz' problems, providing a huge range of information very quickly, from which the company can take a quick, effective, and informed decision.

- ✔ **Project teams:** Project teams are teams of employees (and often teams of employees from other organisations) who work on specific projects and ventures, such as technology installation, premises development, or new product and service initiatives. Project teams have mixes of distinctive expertise so that, at given times, one person's specialism is the absolute priority. Project teams require full mutual confidence and respect, and ways of working that allow for the integration of what are often very diverse and distinctive activities.

✔ **Research teams:** Research teams work on new developments, and new products, projects, and services. Research teams may work to a relatively limited brief, requiring them only to produce inventions for example; or they may work to a broader brief, requiring them to produce products and services that are demonstrably capable of being developed and marketed effectively.

✔ **Work improvement and quality improvement teams:** Work improvement and quality improvement teams are brought together to work on specific aspects of work activities and processes, and the quality and durability of products and services. They may tackle specific problems; or they may go back to the drawing board and try to reconstruct and redesign processes, products, and services so as to eliminate any existing defects or faults.

Informal teams

Informal teams are the most common teams of all. By nature, they're not sanctioned by an organisation's management, but they often hold a power that far exceeds their apparent authority.

Examples of informal teams include groups of employees who share a table every day at lunch. They are the lunch shifts of fast-food workers who are pulled together by a common bond of working in a particularly hectic environment day after day. They are the accounting assistants who chat with each other as they process invoices to be paid.

Here are a couple of benefits offered by informal teams:

✔ Informal teams provide employees with channels of communication outside of the organisation's sanctioned, formal channels.

✔ Informal teams allow employees to let off steam about issues of concern with others in their peer group.

Although informal teams are, by definition, not a part of a company's formal structure, they are an important part of every organisation. In fact, they're often an organisation's backbone, its continuity, and its memory. Successful managers know the importance of informal teams, and they're mindful of their power when they make decisions that affect the organisation.

Self-managing teams

Perhaps the most revolutionary of teams, self-managing teams of workers have replaced traditional managers in many organisations. Self-managing teams are, as their title suggests, teams of workers that are granted the authority to manage themselves. Instead of a supervisor or manager calling the shots, self-managing teams decide what needs to be done and then work out the best way to do it.

To work effectively, self-managing teams have to truly be free of the interference of supervisors and managers. Although supervisors and managers can set overall goals, self-managing teams need to be granted the authority to make the decisions that determine how they'll achieve these goals.

Any organisation – but especially large public bodies and medium and large domestic and multinational organisations – can employ self-managing teams. The kind of organisation or its size doesn't matter – what's important is the willingness of managers to give up some of their decision-making authority to workers, as well as the willingness of workers to accept the responsibilities that go along with authority.

Examples of self-managing teams that work include the following:

- ✔ Self-managing teams at the Morgan Motor Company take charge of all activities, including ordering parts for stock and production, the scheduling and allocation of work, and delivery of the finished product on time. The work is fully flexible, and everyone is prepared and willing to carry out every task.

- ✔ Self-managing work teams at Airbus Industries are presently engaged in the process of designing the Airbus long-range, low-fuel consumption airliner. The deadline that they're working to is five years before the airliner goes into full production – half the normal lead time.

Successful self-managing teams have:

- ✔ High levels of autonomy and the ability to self-manage and self-organise without becoming arrogant or inward-looking.

- ✔ Clear and unambiguous performance targets, which are related to the overall purpose of the organisation and are capable of being achieved.

- ✔ Full responsibility for all aspects of production, service delivery and output processes, quality assurance, and customer relations and complaints.

- ✔ Team-based reward systems available and payable to everyone who contributes, based on salary percentages rather than occupation.

- ✔ A positive culture and set of shared values, allowing for growth and development, and with the attention on problem-solving rather than problem avoidance.

- ✔ Open and professional relationships, based on full mutual respect and understanding.

- ✔ The capability to raise problems and issues as soon as they become apparent. The best teams have discussion forums that allow for everything to be aired fully and openly, and resolved in the interests of the team and organisation, rather than according to the whims of individuals.

> ✔ Easy access to managerial support, and administrative and back-up staff, so that problems beyond the scope of the team can be easily remedied. Access to managerial staff is particularly important when having to face issues outside the remit or authority of the particular team.

In most organisations, self-managing teams are the way forward. Companies can no longer afford to have managers make all the decisions. For organisations to be competitive in today's fast and furious global marketplace, the responsibility and authority for decision-making have to be pushed as far down into the organisation as possible, where it is closest to customers and their needs.

Climbing the ladder of team growth

Teams don't simply happen. Teams evolve, becoming stronger and more effective over time. If you've spent any amount of time in teams, you've probably experienced the different stages of team growth. At the beginning, team members are tentative, and little real work gets done. By the end, however, the team is extremely cohesive and productive.

Here are the four stages of team growth:

> ✔ **Stage 1: Forming.** During the first stage of team growth, known as forming, members of the team get to know one another while cautiously testing the boundaries of the team and its leadership. Participants are generally energised and excited by the prospect of getting things done, but they're a bit nervous about how the team will go forward. In this stage, the team actually accomplishes very little.

> ✔ **Stage 2: Storming.** The second stage of team growth, storming, is marked by a kind of panic among team members as they begin to realise the difficulty of the tasks they need to accomplish. Participants become impatient about the lack of progress in the first stage of team growth. They react by arguing with one another, questioning the team's leadership, and choosing sides. In this stage, progress toward accomplishing the team's goals is minimal. However, team members are learning more about – and becoming more comfortable with – one another.

> ✔ **Stage 3: Norming.** The third stage of team growth is called norming. During this period, team members finally begin to accept the team and follow the team's ground rules. Members establish roles and start supporting each other in their efforts. The fear encountered in the storming stage of team growth disappears and is replaced by a belief that the team will accomplish its goals.

✔ **Stage 4: Performing.** In the fourth, or performing, stage of team growth, team members are fully comfortable in their relationships with one another. They begin to have insights into the behaviour and thought processes of their team-mates. Team members are happy with the team's substantial progress toward goals, and work at peak efficiency. The team is truly performing as a team: Every member supports every other member, and the team pulls together to create an entity that can achieve more together than any one person can do alone.

The following stages also occur in the effective development of teams:

✔ **Rejuvenating.** All teams need rejuvenating from time to time. This may come about as the result of taking on fresh people with fresh talents, ideas, and input; or it may result from sending people on training and development courses. No team can afford to stagnate, and all teams must be exposed to fresh ideas along the way.

✔ **Reforming.** Re-formation is necessary when, for whatever reason, teams fail to perform. It may be that the original brief was weak, or that insufficient time was taken at the forming, storming, and norming stages. Re-forming is a crucial intervention for those with ultimate managerial responsibility. Unsuccessful, inert, or under-performing teams need to be made to work. Re-formation usually means going back to the drawing board, and getting everybody fired up with enthusiasm all over again.

✔ **Disbanding.** Ultimately, all teams have a finite useful life and eventually, the work of the team comes to an end. Make sure that you celebrate the work of the team before the individual members move on. If you allow people to simply drift away, then the impact of the team (however great it may have been) is soon lost. So celebrate the achievements before moving on!

Empowering Employees

Employee empowerment is an enduring business and management buzz-phrase. While everyone was talking about the power of empowerment, however, few companies were actually putting their words into action. For those who did act, the result was an unleashing of employee energy unmatched in the history of business. A wealth of evidence demonstrates that, after the interest of employees is engaged, they'll act on their own initiative and in the organisation's best interests.

Here are some examples of empowered employees in action:

- ✔ At Domino's Pizza, a caretaker in a central distribution centre became a hero when he fielded an after-hours call from a busy store that had run out of pepperoni. The empowered employee threw a box of pepperoni in the back of a company-owned truck and drove across London to make his delivery to a grateful branch manager.

- ✔ When an item is missing a price tag, cashiers at Alldays retail stores are empowered to ask customers whether they know the price. If the price seems reasonable, the cashier can enter it into the till without first getting management approval.

- ✔ Customer service representatives at Halifax Plc. can waive customer late fees and make decisions to increase customers' credit limits immediately, all at their own discretion.

You have to take several steps to give your employees the authority to make decisions that have an impact on their work lives. Here are five easy tips for empowering your employees:

- ✔ Clearly define your employees' responsibilities and be sure that they understand them, as well as understand your expectations of performance.

- ✔ Give your employees the complete authority necessary to successfully undertake all their responsibilities.

- ✔ Treat your employees with respect at all times. Trust them implicitly.

- ✔ Be sure that your employees have the training necessary to successfully undertake their responsibilities.

- ✔ Err on the side of giving your employees too much information rather than not enough.

Employee empowerment is much more than a management buzzword or fad; it's a concept that will separate the firms that thrive in the future from those that fail. Empowering employees allows organisations to tap into the almost boundless energy and talents contained within every employee. The power is there – don't let it go to waste!

Setting Goals and Tracking Progress

We all need goals in our lives to provide direction and movement. Without goals, we're not motivated to do anything in particular with our lives, both at the office and away, so we often don't bother. With goals, however, we give our lives direction and focus as we strive to achieve them. The best goals direct employee and team effort towards the tasks and behaviours that are most important to an organisation's long-term success. Goals also clearly indicate when an employee or team has achieved them.

Words of wisdom on employee involvement

Andy Grove, the former chairman of, and now senior advisor to, global computer chip-maker Intel Corporation, is a big believer in the power of employee involvement and initiative. He sees this power as part of his policy of 'organised common sense'. Here are his nine tips for encouraging employee involvement and initiative on the job:

✔ Motivation comes from within. The most a manager can do is create an environment in which motivated people can flourish.

✔ Good coaches take no personal credit for the success of the team. They have played the game and understand it completely and are tough enough to get the very best performance the team can give.

✔ Think about what you have to do today to solve – and avoid – tomorrow's problems.

✔ Do everything within your power to provide colleagues with the best possible service.

✔ Time is your one finite resource; remember that when you say yes to one thing, you'll have to say no to something else.

✔ Schedule one hour every day to deal with the inevitable interruptions in a planned, organised manner.

✔ Performance reviews are absolutely necessary.

✔ To gather information about a corporate division or department, go on an unannounced visit and observe what's going on.

✔ If an employee isn't doing their job, the only two possible explanations are that the employee either can't do it or won't do it. To determine the reason, apply the following test: If the person's life depended on doing the work, could the employee do it? If the answer is yes, the problem is motivational. If the answer is no, the problem is a lack of ability.

Setting goals is a necessary part of doing business. Whether the goals are strategic, tactical, or operational, they're central to an organisation's planning process, and they're the way that work gets done. (For an in-depth look at planning and the role of strategic, tactical, and operational goals, refer to Chapter 4.)

Unfortunately, many managers shy away from setting goals with their employees, doing so only when forced to by company planning or performance review processes. And when managers do finally get around to it, the goals set are often flawed in some way, or are dictated to employees without employee involvement in creating them.

Setting goals with your employees doesn't have to be a complicated process. In fact, the best goals are often short, concise, and to the point. Employees are more likely to accomplish their goals if they can easily understand them and if they have no more than two or three goals at a time.

To ensure that the things you and your employees agree to get done, you have to monitor and track task performance during the course of completion.

Here are the two most common ways to keep track of employee performance:

✔ **Milestones.** You can break every project into a series of individual tasks, the completion of which comprises the achievement of the intended project goals. Here, for example, are the milestones for production of a company newsletter:

- Interview five employees from several different divisions: 1st February.

- Write articles and submit to editor: 15th February.

- Type up newsletter and check for typographical errors: 1st March.

- Drop newsletter off at printer: 15th March.

- Pick up newsletter from printer and distribute to all employees: 1st April.

By breaking a project down into its individual tasks, you can easily track employee performance and ensure that the project is on schedule. Close monitoring of the project milestones helps prevent any unfortunate surprises along the way.

✔ **Charts and graphs.** As projects become more complex, using a graphical format to chart milestones can be extremely useful. When monitoring project performance, a picture really does tell a thousand words. A variety of different graphing options are available to you, such as:

- **Gantt charts:** Also known as bar charts, Gantt charts are the most commonly used method for monitoring project completion graphically.

- **Flow charts:** Some projects, especially complex ones that involve a sequential flow of actions, require more than simple Gantt charts to keep track of performance. By following the longest path in terms of operations (activities or tasks), you can determine the *critical path* of the project which determines the overall duration of a project plan. The critical path generally represents the shortest time in which a project can be completed.

- **Software:** Software programs are useful and valuable for employees or managers who can't get into particular locations to see current Gantt charts and flow charts. ProjectPLUS and PERTPLUS are standard programs that deliver excellent and constant results, and as long as they're kept up-to-date on the computer network, they deliver exactly the same results as charts, and they also identify potential problem areas and blockages.

Charts, graphs, and software really do make project monitoring much easier than eyeballing pages of text. With just a glance, you can quickly assess project progress and pick out problem areas that may require more management attention.

Making Meetings Useful

Almost every business, whether it has only 2 employees or 2,000, has meetings as a regular part of getting things done. Although employees can communicate with one another in an organisation in many different ways, meetings – if they're conducted the right way – can be incredibly effective and efficient.

Meetings are not only one of the most important ways for employees to communicate within organisations, they're also the way that teams get their work done. Although individual team members work on tasks outside of meetings, team meetings give members the opportunity to come together to determine the team's goals, its plans for achieving its goals, and who will do what – and *when*.

In this section, we take a close look at what makes meetings tick and find out how to conduct better business meetings.

The good news (and the bad) about meetings

We've all probably experienced both good and bad meetings. What makes some meetings terrific, while others are simply useless?

Employees benefit in several ways when a meeting is well run. Here's the good news about well-run business meetings:

- ✔ **Meetings are empowering.** Meetings provide a forum for employees throughout an organisation to have their voices heard – no matter what their position in the hierarchy or their seniority or experience (or lack of). Employees can even call their own meetings if they want to. They don't need to wait around for someone else to do it.

- ✔ **Meetings are a great way to communicate.** When a message needs to reach a large number of people at the same time, meetings are a great way to accomplish that task. Meetings where the chairperson or CEO explains their vision of the future can be extremely inspirational and can galvanise an entire group of people to take action to achieve the vision. Smaller meetings can be particularly effective when you want to solicit employee ideas and to focus employee efforts on developing solutions to problems.

✔ **Meetings develop work skills and leadership.** Becoming a full and active participant in meetings requires employees to develop their work skills and to become leaders. As they're assigned tasks in meetings, complete them, and report their progress and results in follow-up meetings, employees work with others in teams and under deadlines. Meetings also give employees a chance to present their results in front of others, thus boosting their self-confidence.

✔ **Meetings are morale boosting.** Employees want to know what's going on in their organisation, and they want to feel that they're an important part of the organisation's present, as well as its future. In the best organisations management regularly involves employees by providing extensive financial updates and other information in meetings. The result is an engaged, motivated workforce that gives its very best effort every day of the week.

Unfortunately, we also have some bad news about many meetings. Here's the negative side of meetings:

✔ **Meetings may not have focus.** If you've ever been a part of a meeting that wandered all over the place, from topic to topic, with little or no focus, then you know exactly what we're talking about. The trouble with meetings without focus is that they rarely achieve the goals that are the reason for calling them in the first place.

✔ **Companies have too many meetings.** One of the biggest complaints about meetings is that teams or organisations have too many of them. When meetings aren't working effectively in an organisation, then you're probably having too many of them. The key is to have fewer meetings and to make those you do have more efficient and more effective.

✔ **Attendees may be unprepared.** Unprepared attendees are unproductive attendees. And unproductive attendees do little to help you accomplish the goals you have set for your organisation or work unit.

✔ **Most meeting time is wasted.** Unfortunately, this bad news is really true. Research shows that, on average, fully 53 per cent of all meeting time is wasted. For most organisations, this percentage can amount to thousands of hours of wasted time a year. And the larger the organisation, the more time that is wasted in meetings.

Although this bad news may seem bleak, there *is* hope. For each of these problems, and for the many other kinds of problems that often plague business meetings, solutions are available. You simply need to be open to changing the way that meetings are conducted in your organisation. You may even need to take on a leadership role, if necessary, to make your meetings work better.

Improving your meetings

Everyone has suffered through far too many meetings that took up far too much time and accomplished far too little. Unfortunately, this sad state of affairs has happened so often to most of us that we may find ourselves becoming numb to the fact that our meetings aren't as good as they should be – and could be, if we just had some way to fix them.

Help is at hand! You *can* make your meetings better, and you don't have to tolerate meetings that accomplish little or nothing. Here are some time-tested techniques to ensure better business meetings:

- **Be prepared.** Meetings are work, so, just as in any other work activity, the better prepared you are for them, the better the results you can expect. For example, suppose that the topic of the meeting is the next fiscal year's budget. In that case, dig up your budget for this fiscal year and become totally familiar with it. You may want to review any budget reports you've received. That way, you can use your knowledge of the results of the previous budget process to talk intelligently about next year's budget.

- **Have an agenda.** An *agenda* – a list of the topics you want to cover during the course of a meeting – can play a critical role in the success of any meeting. Be sure to distribute the agenda and any pre-work in advance. By distributing the agenda and pre-work before the meeting, participants can prepare for the meeting ahead of time. As a result, employees can be immediately engaged in the business of the meeting, and they'll waste far less time throughout the meeting.

- **Start on time and end on time.** In these days of faster and more flexible organisations, everyone always has plenty of work on the to-do list. Announce the length of the meeting and then stick to it, and fewer participants will keep looking at their watches, and more participants will take an active role in your meetings. If the meeting does look as if it's going to overrun, the chairperson needs to take a quick and informed decision as to whether or not things are going to be resolved as the result of an extra few minutes, or whether it will be necessary to wrap things up on time and then call a further meeting in the future.

- **Have fewer (but better) meetings.** Call a meeting only when it is absolutely necessary. Before you call a meeting, ask yourself whether you can achieve your goal in some other way, perhaps through a one-to-one discussion with someone in your organisation, a telephone conference call, or a simple e-mail exchange. As you reduce the number of meetings you have, be sure to improve their quality.

✔ **Include, rather than exclude.** Meetings are only as good as the ideas that the participants bring forward. Great ideas can come from anyone in an organisation, not only its managers. So make sure that everyone gets to have their say. Welcoming ideas encourages full participation, which is excellent for collective morale.

✔ **Maintain the focus.** Meetings can easily get off track and stay off track. And the result is meetings that don't achieve their goals. Meeting leaders and participants must actively work to keep meetings focused on the agenda items. Whenever things start to drift, bring them back. If someone is wandering off the point, or getting on to their favourite subject, bring them back down to earth. And make sure that everyone has the opportunity to contribute clearly and concisely.

✔ **Clarify action points.** If the meeting is to result in action points, make sure that everyone knows what they have to do, and by when, and always follow this up with a written reminder. Make sure that people do deliver what they have promised, otherwise they won't take the next round of meetings on the subject seriously.

✔ **Get feedback.** Every meeting always has room for improvement. Solicit feedback from meeting attendees on how the meeting was useful for them – and how it wasn't. Was the meeting too long? Did one person dominate the discussion? Were attendees unprepared? Were the items on the agenda unclear? Whatever the problems, you can't fix them if you don't know about them. You can use a simple form to solicit feedback, or you can informally speak with attendees after the meeting to get their input.

Chapter 9

Behaving Yourself: Ethics and Standards

. . . .

In This Chapter

▶ Discovering the relationship between ethics and successful business

▶ Setting and maintaining high standards

▶ Dealing with ethical problems

▶ Implementing codes of conduct

. . . .

*P*eople have debated the relationship between ethics, business, and management for a long time, but the relationship is quite simple and straightforward. *Whatever you do in business, do it right, and do it to the best of your ability.* You need suppliers to provide to you, staff to work for you, and customers to buy and use your products and services, and you cannot expect any of this if you're dishonest or duplicitous, if you cut corners, or if you fail to deliver what you promise.

If you compound poor behaviour by understating or overstating your accounts, your ability to deliver, or otherwise fail to keep your promises, people will lose confidence in you, and go elsewhere.

Of course, behind this simplicity lies a great deal of managerial responsibility, and not a little expertise. You need to understand where your full range of responsibilities lies, and you need to commit to meeting them at all times. Consider the following:

- ✔ If you ever do something wrong, you will get caught.

- ✔ Losing a good reputation is a lot easier than earning one.

- ✔ One bad action can undo generations of excellent work.

In this chapter, we look at where the main responsibilities of ethics and standards lie, and at the actions you need to take to ensure that you don't become the next corporate victim of scandal or incompetence.

Ethics and Business Do Mix!

Ethics are simply the standards that you set for yourself, and the codes of conduct by which you operate in your dealings with customers, suppliers, shareholders, and staff. These standards include the following:

- ✔ What you consider to be right and wrong in absolute terms.
- ✔ The desired ends and outcomes you seek to achieve, and the ways and means by which you achieve them.
- ✔ The nature of working, professional, and personal relationships that you foster in your organisation.
- ✔ The quality of working life in your organisation.
- ✔ Your organisation's compliance with the law.
- ✔ The way you work within social, cultural, religious, and other constraints.

At the core of your ethical approach to standards is your attitude to:

- ✔ The extent to which everyone benefits from your business or organisation; or the extent to which particular groups benefit at the expense of others.
- ✔ Ordinary common decency – the humanity in your business operations.
- ✔ Staff, customers, suppliers, and backers.
- ✔ The communities and locations in which your organisation conducts its operations.
- ✔ Specific issues such as the environment, waste disposal, pollution, and energy consumption.
- ✔ Operational factors specific to your business such as the extent to which noise, heating, and lighting cause pollution and environmental blight.

Each of the above attitudes informs and underpins the ways in which you behave towards everyone with whom you come into contact. These attitudes are a reflection of the reputation that your business or organisation enjoys in the community, and the basis on which this reputation is built.

The key ethical priority and responsibility is to ensure that your organisation survives and continues to be profitable and effective. Staff require long-term working relationships, and a pension at the end of their working lives; suppliers need to know that you'll need to do regular business with them; customers expect your products and services over the long term; backers and financiers want you to pay their dividends when required. You're much more likely to be able to do all of this if you set high standards of integrity, conduct, behaviour, and performance – and stick to them.

Active responsibility

You need to become *actively responsible* for everything that goes on – and accountable if it all goes wrong. Active responsibility means setting and maintaining your own standards, and not allowing standards to emerge from what others want. If you don't take this attitude, you lay yourself wide open to any shortcomings inherent in the standards that others set for themselves, and their approach to business.

iSoft, the information systems software company, took on the design, implementation, delivery, upgrade, and servicing of the information systems for the whole of the UK National Health Service (NHS). Originally priced at £900 million, the contract value rose to £6.2 billion over seven years. Deadlines were routinely missed. Design and delivery specifications and schedules were ignored. No clear management or organisational structure was in place, so nobody took responsibility for any of these outcomes. The financial position steadily became worse, not better – in spite of the NHS simply paying what iSoft demanded. The situation became even worse when iSoft made clear that it had overstated its resource and asset base at the outset, and it couldn't support £6.2 billion worth of work – after all, this is nearly 7 times the original value.

So responsibilities on all sides were neither acknowledged nor managed because no one took active responsibility for the project. The result remains a service that is neither fully functional nor operational, in spite of the fact that iSoft agreed to do the work, and the NHS agreed to pay.

Acting ethically isn't always easy. At times you have to take some awkward decisions. You may have to conduct lay-offs, or outsource some work to other companies and organisations. For members of staff directly affected, the decision is wrong and traumatic, but it is right for the greater good – the long-term survival of the organisation as a whole.

As a manager or entrepreneur, you may be asked or told to do things by your backers or superiors that go against your own better judgement or sense of what is right. You're then faced – in your own eyes at least – with having to do what you see as the wrong thing.

In order to get staff to accept and discharge their responsibilities, and to take an attitude of overall active responsibility, they have to know and understand what you expect of them. You must be aware of everything that can, and will, go wrong if you don't set and enforce standards. As well as business responsibilities, you have to make sure that everyone discharges their duties, responsibilities and actions, especially in the areas of staff relations and business dealings. As manager, business owner, entrepreneur, or MBA student, you need to do the following:

- Set standards and enforce them.
- Deal with bullying, victimisation, discrimination, and harassment.

> ✔ Deal with theft and fraud.
>
> ✔ Establish codes of conduct.

The following sections delve deeper into these issues.

Setting Standards and Enforcing Them

Employees take their lead from you. If you say what you mean, mean what you say, and do what you say, people can trust you and may emulate your behaviour in their own actions at work.

If you say one thing and then do another, employees, suppliers, and customers will note and follow your actions, not your words. If you use duplicitous or imprecise language, people will always look for hidden meanings – and they'll usually find them.

Following the golden rule

The golden rule is: *Do as you would be done by*. Doing so means treating others – your employees, suppliers, and customers – as you would expect to be treated. Treat people badly, and you can expect the same poor treatment in return. Treat people with respect, and you'll get respect back. (Have you ever noticed how hard it is to resist returning a broad smile?)

If you set your own standards following the golden rule, you have little to worry about. However, you do need to worry if you ever forget the golden rule. For example:

> ✔ A UN-based diplomat working at the centre of the terrorist scares of 2006 complained long and loud when he wasn't allowed to board a flight because he didn't have the right documentation. He compounded his own folly by then showing his UN credentials to the check-in staff and aggressively asking: 'Don't you know how important I am?'
>
> ✔ A regional director of one of the world's largest car companies received over-the-counter compensation from an airline because his flight was cancelled. He went into a policy meeting a day later and decided to suppress acknowledgement of a potentially serious mechanical fault on one of the company's off-road models. The result was that the company eventually had to recall half a million models from customers and show-rooms to put right the fault.

> ✔ A UK primary healthcare trust opened a new maternity unit at one of its hospitals. Costing £10 million, the unit included all the latest equipment and technology. However, the hospital's chief executive, whose wife had just given birth to their first child, refused to sanction a steam-clean and sterilisation of the new unit, which would have cost £13,000. Within a week, the bacteria MRSA was discovered in the new maternity unit.

In each of these cases, those involved had expected certain standards of treatment, but were not prepared to give them in return. If you behave in this manner people may think that you lack integrity, and may even believe that you're dishonest.

Scenting the whiff of scandal

If you don't set and enforce standards, and if you don't do as you would be done by, how far are you prepared to let standards slide?

Standards and language

If you're ever in any doubt over the relationship between the standards that you wish to set, and the language that you use, consider your own immediate response to the following universal business phrases:

✔ 'We have no plans for redundancies or lay-offs.'

✔ 'We are doing everything that we can.'

✔ 'Work smarter, not harder.'

The first is dishonest (if you really are planning redundancies in future), the second is imprecise, the third is a broad and useless cliché. So make up your mind never to be dishonest, imprecise, or use useless clichés. If you need to discuss any of the above issues, then make the language precise, open, and direct.

And consider the following example: Eurocom, a broadband provider, bought landline capacity at wholesale prices from British Telecom (BT).

It then sold this capacity on to customers at very attractive consumer prices. For an up-front payment of £100 you'd have unlimited broadband access for two years. After three months, the service suddenly ceased. Customers of Eurocom rang the customer helpline and received the following recorded message: 'We are very sorry that you are experiencing difficulties with your broadband service. This is due to circumstances outside of our control. We aim to restore the service as soon as possible. In the meantime, we are considering legal action against BT for cancelling the service.'

Initially the message is sound and reassuring. However, look closely at the language used and you can see that Eurocom is not committing itself to anything. In addition, anyone who rang BT to find out what was going on was told in very straightforward terms that Eurocom had been cut off because it had not paid its own bills.

You don't have to run your business like a prison camp or military headquarters. But you do need to know where the divide lies between:

- ✔ Joking and abuse
- ✔ Argument and conflict
- ✔ Legitimate expense and waste

After you cross the divide from, say, joking to abuse, getting high standards back is very hard. You need to tackle activities and behaviour that you know to be wrong immediately, before they become acceptable in the eyes of your staff. And it is a very short step from this situation to serious problems and scandals.

For example:

- ✔ Nick Leeson, a financial trader who ruined Barings Bank, was never properly supervised the whole time that he was at first borrowing the company's money to try to make up his trading losses, and then when he crossed the divide into more fraudulent transactions.

- ✔ A financial services practice paid £1.3 million to a female city trader for serious sexual assault which, when it was notified, was described as 'horseplay' by the senior partner who assaulted her.

- ✔ The accountancy firm Arthur Andersen signed off the accounts of the energy company Enron for each of the three years before Enron collapsed, on the basis of assurances from top management, rather than the evidence of the figures. Arthur Andersen was fully aware of how the finances were being addressed and the amount of money that was being placed elsewhere, but accepted the company's assurances that everything would work out in the end.

Make up your mind that nothing similar is going to happen to you – and stick to your standards and principles. In truth, everyone knows when they've crossed the divide; and anyone who doesn't know the fundamental difference between right and wrong should not be in a leadership position – or on an MBA course.

You get what you reward – and punish

Getting what you reward is a constant refrain throughout this book! But this concept is vitally important to business leaders. Be sure to know and understand just how critical your approach to rewards and punishment is in setting and maintaining the standards that you require.

If you say you reward output, but actually reward compliance, you'll get compliance. If you say you reward participation, but actually reward bullying, you'll get bullying. If you say you reward excellent work, but actually reward corner-cutters, people will cut corners. And so on. So be absolutely certain on exactly what you reward, or else face the consequences.

The same goes for punishments. If you punish people for lateness, they'll turn up on time. By the same token, if you punish people for raising legitimate concerns or grievances, they won't raise them (and you may eventually get prosecuted through the courts and tribunals).

Banishing Bullying, Discrimination, and Harassment

Bullying, victimisation, discrimination, and harassment at work are all against the law, as well as being morally reprehensible. However, these are awkward problems that nobody likes to face. When a member of staff comes to a manager to make allegations of this nature against a colleague, the common response is: 'Aren't you over-reacting just a little bit?'

Unfortunately, the answer is invariably *no*. Up to 250,000 cases of bullying and discrimination are notified to trades unions, employers' associations, and the tribunal system each year. A study carried out by the Trades Union Congress (TUC) in 2005 found that 50 per cent of all UK employees had experienced some form of bullying, victimisation, discrimination, or harassment over the course of their working life.

Cases that reach the tribunals or courts are normally heard in public, so, even if no one is prosecuted, your reputation is going to suffer. And in bullying and discrimination cases, courts and tribunals can impose unlimited fines and damages. So part of your job as manager is to see that legal action doesn't happen because it's very expensive. And part of your responsibility as a human being, as well as a manager, is to see that bullying or discrimination don't happen – because they are despicable behaviour. If you're still in any doubt, think about how you would react if you were bullied or victimised.

If you're accused of bullying, you need to:

✔ Take a long hard look at yourself and your behaviour. If you're being a bully, stop – immediately.

✔ If you're not being a bully, ask yourself why the accusation is being made, and get to the bottom of the matter immediately.

✔ If the accusation is malicious, be very clear that you're going to have to counter it in unequivocal terms, and address the falsehood.

Cracking Down on Theft and Fraud

The financial scandals of recent years – Enron, Shell, BCCI, Guinness, Barings – all received extensive and detailed coverage in the media, and all produced the same response from the directors and managers of other companies and organisations: 'It couldn't happen here.'

Unfortunately, theft and fraud can happen anywhere; indeed, some say that theft at least, does happen everywhere. Using the firm's telephone to make a quick call home or using your company computer to book a holiday on the Internet is still theft. Between that and theft on the scale of BCCI or Enron, lies the thin red line that divides what you will and won't tolerate. Make clear to everyone where the dividing line lies, and make sure that everyone stays on the right side of it. Publish rules and guidelines for consultation, ensure that everyone knows and understands them – and always stick to them.

Theft and fraud arise from corporate and managerial inertia or ineptitude. Consider the following:

- ✔ An overtly successful computer hardware manufacturing company has been told repeatedly by its auditors that up to 20 per cent of its products are being 'lost' or 'damaged' either at the factory or in transit. Yet the company won't sanction a full audit, because if it did, it would know and understand the real scale of the problem and would therefore have to do something about it.

- ✔ Until recently, the purchasing manager of a specialist aerospace firm and the sales manager whose firm supplied some of the key components had a fraudulent business relationship. Both managers structured their contracts so as to maximise the operational bonus that each received from their own employer. When the matter came to light, no action was taken on either side because neither company wanted to acknowledge that a trading relationship of many years standing was in fact dishonest. The fraud had been easy to operate because the purchasing manager's bonus was calculated on the discount that he received from suppliers; and the sales manager's bonus was calculated on the volume of components sold.

Creating Codes of Conduct

To set and enforce standards, and to prevent bullying, victimisation, discrimination, harassment, theft, and fraud, you need to have effective codes of conduct. A *code of conduct* is a set of rules, principles, and guidance that state how people are to behave, how people must not behave, and the consequences or sanctions that apply for particular transgressions.

Ensure your codes of conduct are:

- ✔ Clear and easy to read and understand
- ✔ Made available to everyone
- ✔ Integrated within discipline, grievance, and dispute procedures
- ✔ Integrated into risk management policies to avoid physical accidents

Ensure that all codes of conduct treat people equally. Setting and maintaining standards and using codes of conduct are only effective if you apply them universally. Indeed, universal application itself is ethical, while uneven application is not – treating people differently for the same transgression is fundamentally dishonest and (normally) illegal.

You also have to make sure that people know and understand that you enforce the codes of conduct. If someone who has stolen £20,000 from the organisation is allowed to keep their job, then you need to make clear to everyone what the mitigating circumstances are, otherwise you've simply destroyed your own standards and the operation of the codes of conduct that underpin them. If you promote a bully, you need to be able to explain why to everyone else (above all, to the bully's victims). Always relate codes of conduct to disciplinary procedures. Where proven, summary dismissal must always be the normal penalty for offences such as stealing or bullying.

Leading from the top

Creating and following a code of conduct comes from the top of the organisation. You cannot expect people lower down the company to conduct themselves to high standards of integrity and commitment if those at the top are dishonest or sloppy; indeed, if you do so, you may be contravening equality of treatment laws and regulations.

Set and practise standards from the top down. Make sure that following codes of conduct are included in the training programmes of every manager or supervisor, both in the ways in which managers conduct themselves, and the ways in which they behave towards staff, customers, and suppliers.

The inquiry into the 'Herald of Free Enterprise' ferry disaster (the English Channel ferry that capsized, killing 193 passengers) found that the company operating the ferry was 'infected throughout with the disease of sloppiness'. Management was accused of 'staggering complacency'. The father of one of the victims stated: 'Everyone on the ship behaved as they believed they should. They took their lead from top management.'

Saturday night's the night for fighting

The deputy branch manager of a high street retail bank was arrested for his involvement in a night-club brawl. The fight was on a Saturday night, so plainly not during working hours. The deputy branch manager turned up for work the following Monday, having been released on police bail. However, when the case was reported in the local paper the following weekend, and covered on BBC regional television, the bank dismissed him. The deputy branch manager successfully took the bank to employment tribunal, winning £5,000 in compensation. The bank preferred to lose the case and pay the compensation rather than take back the former employee. Since then the bank has had no reported trouble among its 93,000 retail branch staff.

Following through on your code of conduct sets a strong example to all employees.

Your staff handbook needs to include all of the codes of conduct that directly relate to staff management and performance: Discipline and grievances; selection for redundancies; health and safety at work; and ensuring professional relationships between staff. You also need codes of conduct relating to risk management to ensure that the potential for theft, fraud, and accidents is kept to an absolute minimum.

Reinforce your codes of conduct by letting people know what happens when real situations arise, and how you have dealt with them (see the sidebar 'Saturday night's the night for fighting' for an example). You're showing that not only do you have standards of practice and behaviour, and codes of conduct to support them, but also that you're going to use – and enforce – them whenever necessary.

Benefiting from an ethical approach

Setting and enforcing an ethical code of conduct has many benefits. Your staff have full confidence in you because they know where they stand. This confidence filters into dealings with customers, suppliers, and backers. You gain a local professional and occupational reputation for being a good employer. You always have an honest answer for everything that comes your way – and if you don't, you either hand the matter to someone who does, or else find out yourself and get back with a proper answer.

You build a reputation for knowing how to deal with serious problems, and being effective in resolving them. Again, this leads to staff having full confidence in you; and again, it builds your reputation as an excellent employer. And excellent employers attract excellent staff!

Ethics and the Law

Setting absolute standards of behaviour and conduct is one of the main foundations on which profitable and effective performance is based. Remember that you also have to operate within the law.

If and when you face employment law issues, get all the guidance that you can from the Advisory, Conciliation and Arbitration Service (ACAS). *Small Business Employment Law For Dummies* by Liz Barclay (Wiley) is also an excellent place to start.

Businesses have a fundamental requirement to comply with company, business, product, service, and employment law. Not to do so is itself unethical, and, your company loses reputation and confidence if it becomes known or perceived to have a cavalier attitude to any aspect of the laws and directives that ultimately govern its activities and operations.

Merely complying with the law is seldom enough. You have to be prepared to set your own standards within (and normally above) the constraints of the law. Consider the following:

- ✔ Mere compliance with the law won't prevent you from getting a bad reputation. Oil companies dumping effluent in the Niger Delta; clothing companies employing children in south-east Asia to manufacture their garments; and mining companies employing staff at unprotected rock faces all comply with the law. But they are neither ethical nor desirable employers. You cannot abdicate responsibility or accountability merely by stating, 'We comply with the law.'

- ✔ If you do cut corners, you'll normally be caught, and the fact that your auditors or inspectors have found nothing wrong for years won't save you from even one mistake, whatever assurances you've given them (see the previous Enron example).

The state of company law in the UK at the moment is such that, if someone chooses to prosecute you, the courts and legal system will normally allow a case to go ahead, provided that some evidence is produced that can be substantiated. Where cases relate to standards of corporate conduct, equality of treatment, or bullying and victimisation, then you may effectively have to prove yourself innocent. While this is a departure from the normal principle of 'innocent until proven guilty', if you set your standards high enough in the first place, and enforce them, you won't be faced with these problems.

Part III

Money: What You Don't Know Will Hurt You

'Look, Mr Brinkley, you don't fool me —
you don't have a proper accountant in
this company do you?'

In this part . . .

*U*nderstanding where a business's money comes from – and where it goes – is an important skill for anyone in business or management. In this part, we present the basics of accounting as well as looking at the most important and widely used financial statements. We decipher the mysteries of financial analysis. We also look at the wider question of finance; and we consider the whys and wherefores of having people invest in you and your organisation.

Chapter 10

Basic Economics

· ·

In This Chapter

▶ Looking at conflicting economic theories

▶ Dealing with fundamental economic questions

▶ Discovering key economic concepts

▶ Looking at entrepreneurial, organisational, and managerial inventions

· ·

*E*conomics is the study of how society decides what, how, and for whom to produce goods and services, and how it prioritises, allocates, and charges for those resources. So economics, the actions taken in the name of economics, and economic forces affect the daily lives of everyone, everywhere in the world.

In this chapter, we talk about the fundamental principles of economics, and how organisational, managerial, and entrepreneurial actions influence economics. Understanding how these actions and initiatives affect the prospects of organisation success, patterns of consumption, and changes in markets is essential for any budding MBA. This chapter also looks at different economists who often disagree, especially when looking at the impact of organisational, entrepreneurial, and managerial actions on the economy as a whole.

Why Adam Smith Knew What He Was Talking About

In 1776, Adam Smith wrote *The Wealth of Nations*, a book that marked the beginning of modern economics. In it, he wrestled with a paradox: 'How is it that water, which is so very useful that life is impossible without it, has such a low price – while diamonds, which are quite unnecessary, have such a high price?' We are grappling with this same issue over 225 years later as we struggle to understand the valuations on some highly specialist organisations. A company producing a product that everyone uses may have a very low valuation, and a company producing something that only a relatively small percentage of the country uses has a stratospheric valuation. Why?

Water isn't really a scarce item relative to diamonds, so it costs more to get more diamonds than it does to get more water, which is consequently less expensive because it's more available. Smith didn't have the economic tools about supply and demand to arrive at that conclusion, but he did recognise that *value in use* isn't the same as *value in exchange*. What this means is that you can't usually price an item higher simply because it is more useful. In fact, quite the opposite is true. A product's highest price is determined by its *marginal utility*, which is the value of its usage to individual customers.

So if you apply Adam Smith's paradox, water has a relatively low price because it's everywhere and it's so useful. Diamonds, on the other hand, have a relatively high price because they're scarce by comparison and not a necessity – they have a very high marginal utility.

You can take four rules away from this discussion:

- ✔ If your company produces products that are very useful, they'll become commodities, and the price will come down. As a result, you must sell in large volumes to make a profit. For example, Intel's microprocessor chips come down in price very quickly after they first hit the market as the latest technology. Within a few months, they become the standard and are sold in large volumes at a very low cost.

- ✔ If your company produces products that are limited in their use and availability, the price will go up. That means you'll probably sell few products, but you'll make more money on each product. Mercedes intentionally produced its CLK car in short supply to keep the value up. Some customers paid as much as £5,000 over the *manufacturer's suggested retail price* (MSRP).

- ✔ You can take managerial action to try to influence the price and/or value of products, services, and commodities. However, if these products, services, and/or commodities are high on the list of consumer essentials, your actions will have limited effects on consumption. Using Adam Smith's water example, people have turned water from a commodity into a product by putting a price on it. However, this has had only a limited effect on consumption. Because people need water to survive, they have had to pay the higher prices, rather than reduce consumption.

- ✔ You can influence product and service values by ascribing perceived utility and benefits to a product as well as a core usage. People buy diamonds for their loved ones as a mark of enduring love. These perceived benefits have been delivered as the result of extensive marketing, promotional, and branding activities, quite apart from the intrinsic worth and value of the diamonds themselves.

Classic versus neo-classic

Today we understand that entrepreneurs play a critical role in the economy, but economists didn't always believe that. Adam Smith was really the first to define 'capitalist' as an owner-manager who brought together land, labour, and capital to form a successful enterprise and make profits. Over the next 100 years, people began to argue furiously about Smith's theories and to add to and subtract from them with their own theories.

In the late 1800s, economists such as Leon Walras and Alfred Marshall developed models by using new-found tools provided by mathematician Sir Isaac Newton. These neo-classic models ignored the entrepreneur and focused on perfectly competitive markets with lots of buyers and sellers who make sure that supply equals demand and creates that nirvana called equilibrium. *Equilibrium* in economic terms simply means that the supply of goods produced equals the demand by customers. Today, the only place where this type of near-perfection exists is in *commodity markets*, where buyers and sellers actually meet on the trading floor to buy and sell.

For this type of perfect market to exist, several things need to be in place:

✔ Every buyer and seller must have information about all the transactions that happen.

✔ No one buyer or seller can influence the market.

✔ The market determines prices.

✔ Products and services need to be fundamentally alike so that the only difference among them is price.

This type of market, essentially a commodity market, is predictable, distributes income fairly equally, and has long been the primary model of commodity-based economics. The *neo-classic theory* is compatible with large corporations and economies of scale, which means that as the size of a company increases it can produce its products more cheaply because it can buy raw materials in larger quantities and can more efficiently use its plant and equipment. But this neo-classic theory has had its legions of critics because it doesn't account for entrepreneurship, opportunity, and market entry, each of which disrupt this market equilibrium by causing new demand that didn't exist previously.

Size does not of itself create wealth or value. If you're a large organisation producing what are essentially commodity products and services, you have to do one of the following:

✔ Increase your product and service range, so that your existing customers and clients buy more from you, but without expanding your fixed cost base.

✔ Find new customers for your existing products and services by speeding up your production processes, again without increasing your fixed cost base.

✔ Cut costs, so as to try to ensure that you deliver the same quality and volume of products and services more efficiently.

Smaller companies producing scarcer and higher value products and services have higher production costs, and yet can make more money per item by charging premium prices.

Smaller companies are more likely to have the flexibility and responsiveness to be able to change quickly to meet alterations in customer and market demand, though many large organisations are beginning to wake up to this too.

The Austrian point of view

At the end of the 19th century, the classical economists, primarily from the Austrian school, tried to get over the fact that the neo-classic economists were ignoring entrepreneurs. Joseph Schumpeter, often called the father of entrepreneurship as we know it today, said that there is no such thing as equilibrium between supply and demand, and that markets are actually chaotic. Schumpeter referred to entrepreneurship as 'creative destruction', because the innovations of entrepreneurs destroy old markets and build new wealth.

And the winner is . . .

One of the more important moments in economic theory occurred in 1979 when economist David Birch published the results of his research on all US firms from 1969 to 1976. His findings were astounding. He found that small firms (100 or fewer employees) created 81 per cent of net new jobs in the United States.

This discovery meant that small businesses, not big corporations, were driving the US economy. Shocked by the finding, mainstream economists were quick to say that it was nonsense. But when Birch's study was replicated, these economists found that his conclusions were correct! And whenever and wherever the research has been repeated, the conclusions have remained constant.

This finding confirms that a critical part of understanding economics today is about understanding entrepreneurship and how entrepreneurs affect the economy.

Answering Fundamental Economic Questions

Economics deals with three fundamental problem areas for any society:

- ✔ What should we produce and how much?
- ✔ How should we produce these goods and with what resources?
- ✔ For whom should we produce these goods?

Every business deals with these questions, often in different ways. They form the basis on which you start and run a business. The answers to these questions are guided by some fundamental principles, which we look at in the next two sections.

The law of scarcity: You can't have it all

When you consider the three economic questions asked in the preceding section, the economic principle in play is the *law of scarcity*, meaning that whatever needs to be done is carried out with finite and therefore limited resources. And because resources are ultimately limited and finite, they therefore carry their own value – and cost. This principle applies because economic organisations wouldn't have to answer these three questions if they had unlimited resources. Because they don't have unlimited resources, they have to allocate their scarce resources between necessities and luxuries; and they have to prioritise their activities.

Your business is an economic organisation that must make decisions about scarce resources. Which products to produce, how to produce them, and for whom are central questions that you have to answer before you can successfully negotiate the marketplace. You answer the three questions by answering the following:

- ✔ Who are our customers?
- ✔ What do they want from us?
- ✔ How much are they prepared to pay?

Your customers tell you what to produce, when to produce it, and how to get the products to them. In addition, your suppliers and others in your industry can help you decide the most cost-effective means to produce the product.

The law of diminishing returns

The *law of diminishing returns* describes how much extra return you get on your output as you add extra units of input, whether finance, staff, or raw materials. For example, if you have a factory that produces widgets, as you add labour to the production process, your ability to produce more goods increases to the point at which capacity or near capacity is reached; but after that, the rate of increase decreases or diminishes. So, if you have two people who do 100 per cent of the work and the factory is working at near capacity, then on average each person will do 50 per cent of the work. If you add a third member of staff, then the average output per member of staff is reduced to 33 per cent.

You need to know and understand this because you need to be able to work out the point at which you are the most productive. That point determines when you achieve the biggest gains for your efforts, investment and resources allocation.

Delving into Some Key Economic Concepts

All western economies, including the United Kingdom, are *mixed*, which means that they combine the freedom to engage in particular activities with some restraints on how you have to organise and manage your affairs. Working in a mixed economy essentially means taking on board the following:

- ✔ **Regulation:** Business activity is limited, governed by laws that affect your freedom to charge the prices you want, pay wages, package and present your products and services, and dispose of waste and effluent. You have to conduct each of these activities in accordance with regulations, and these regulations raise, not lower, the charges present. You must also conduct your activities in a healthy and safe manner at all times.

- ✔ **Profit:** You must ultimately operate at a profit. You are not allowed to give away your products and services with the express aim of driving out the competition and creating a monopoly. And you're not allowed to charge pure market prices for commodities such as water, gas, electricity, and fuel; these prices are regulated and limited by government watchdogs because they're deemed essentials of life.

✔ **Sectoral economics:** All business sectors have their own particular mixes of economics, and you need to understand these, in whichever sector you happen to find yourself. To give two examples:

- Companies involved in civil engineering receive payments at relatively irregular intervals; but when payments do come in, they're very large. Civil engineering sectoral economics means that cash flow for regular payments out has to be managed, either through retaining profits, or else having an overdraft – and each of these activities affects 'pure' profits.

- Pharmaceutical companies charge for research costs in advance of introducing new drugs. Pharmaceutical companies are allowed to do this by custom and practice, and by the charges that they make for new drugs to national health services and private healthcare companies. Therefore, while many proprietary drugs and pharmaceuticals do seem expensive when sold to the public, a proportion of the price charged is paying for the research that was required to bring them to market in the first place.

What you're free to do

As business owners, you're free to do certain things. These economic concepts include free enterprise, freedom of choice, and freedom to compete.

Free enterprise

You are free to own resources, and to control how you use those resources. You are also free to employ others, if you can afford and choose to do so. For example, you can use technology to improve efficiency so that you can make a profit. You can use computerised production machines to produce your products, thereby improving the efficiency of your processes. An environment in which you can make decisions about how to run your business and compete in the market is called a *competitive marketplace* or *free enterprise system.*

Freedom of choice

Freedom of choice means that you have the right to decide how to spend your money. Your choice of what to buy is called demand, and that demand affects the supply of whatever it is that you want to buy. Naturally, supply and demand also affect price. Too much of something brings the price down, and too little makes the price go up.

Of course, the one thing no one has any choice about is paying taxes and meeting other statutory obligations. Those taxes support the many services that our society requires: roads, the army, government services, the health service, schools, and so on.

Freedom to compete

Competition arises when two or more businesses are selling the same or similar products or services and competing for the same customers or consumers. Typically, higher quality or a lower price wins out. But where price is the primary competing factor, the best entrepreneurs and managers create additional value through services or additional products that their competitors don't have. To compete effectively in a free market economy, you must do the following:

- ✔ Provide customers with products and services that meet their needs and wants.

- ✔ Differentiate your products and services from your competitors by offering additional value, such as great customer service.

- ✔ Stay close to your customers and even closer to your competitors.

The rollercoaster of economic cycles

The economy is not really in equilibrium for very long. It is subject to many changes in the form of *business cycles*. If the economy is in a period of prosperity and inflation of prices and incomes, these will eventually taper off, and a contraction will take place, during which activity slows down. If the contraction lasts long enough, the economy will slide into a recession or collapse into a slump, called a depression. Emergence from a slump or depression is called recovery.

Inflation

Inflation is simply upward pressure on prices. During times of high inflation, your money purchases less in terms of goods and services. During times of inflation, not all prices rise, but on average they do. So, if you get a 3 per cent pay rise and the price of the goods and services you buy goes up by 7 per cent, you won't be able to buy as much with the same money.

Three different scenarios cause inflation:

- ✔ **Demand-pull inflation.** Too much demand and too little supply means that prices rise. This type of inflation often happens when the government cuts taxes (which isn't often) or consumers save less.

- ✔ **Cost-push inflation.** This type of inflation occurs when production costs skyrocket. Manufacturers usually push the costs along to the customer in the form of higher prices. Of course, then workers demand higher wages so that they can pay for these higher prices. As a result, unemployment is typically high because the higher costs are not driven by demand, so companies aren't taking people on.

✔ **Government-led inflation.** Government interventions in the form of placing taxes and statutory charges on things like energy prices, road and rail transport, telecommunications, and waste disposal, add costs that are outside the control of buyers, sellers, producers, or distributors. Strictly, this is a form of cost-push inflation; however, the costs are imposed from outside, rather than occurring as the result of market activity. Raising interest rates additionally causes money to be taken out of the consumer side of the equation, thus reducing demand – but still putting up costs.

Recession/depression

When the economy doesn't grow for a period of at least six months, it is said to be in a *recession*. Both the 1980s and the 1990s started with recessions. During a recession, people typically cut their spending, a behaviour that, in turn, causes the recession to get worse because it slows down the economy even more.

A very bad recession can turn into a *depression*, which is when many businesses fail, prices drop, and supply exceeds demand.

Preparing for changes in the economy

How does a business prepare for change in the economy? Here are some tips:

✔ Stay aware of what's going on in the world by reading newspapers and surfing the Web. The following Web sites are good places to start:

- The BBC (www.bbc.co.uk)

- The Financial Times (www.ft.com)

- The Department of Trade and Industry (www.dti.gov.uk)

✔ Watch for *leading* and *key indicators*, statistics and other figures, which are the main indicators of how well or otherwise your company, organisation, or sector is doing. Make contacts with your own trade federations and employers' associations, and make sure that they supply you with up-to-the-minute and detailed information wherever possible.

✔ Stay as liquid as possible, meaning that you have cash to expand in good times and a cushion to help you survive the bad times.

Measuring the health of the economy

Economists regularly measure the health of the economy during the year. What they find determines everything from whether the Bank of England raises interest rates to whether you get a pay rise. Here's a look at some of the more common indicators of economic health.

Gross Domestic Product

The *Gross Domestic Product* (GDP) is the total monetary value of all goods and services produced in the UK. It is essentially a record of how much workers produced for consumers to purchase – the cost of living. GDP only looks at new goods, for example new cars.

Gross National Product

The *Gross National Product* (GNP) is the same as the GDP except that it includes all transactions including the sale and purchase of used and second-hand goods and services. GNP also includes property sales and purchases in the UK, and money spent on public services.

Retail Price Index

The *Retail Price Index* (RPI) represents the change in price of a specific group of goods and services over time. This group of goods and services is simply called the *basket of goods*, and it includes items in such categories as food, housing, transportation, clothing, entertainment, medicines, and personal care. The RPI is a reflection of inflation, though not a direct measure of inflation.

When inflation goes up by a certain percentage, it is more often than not a change in the price of things people typically buy. As a manager or business owner, you need to be aware of changes in the RPI because eventually these will work their way through to you, and affect not only your costs and charges, but also the costs of living of everyone who works for you, and this in turn is likely to lead to demands for pay rises and reviews.

Income

Income is a way of measuring how much money is available for individuals and businesses to spend. National income includes such things as wages and salaries, self-employed income, rental income, corporate profits, and interest on savings and investments.

Economists are most interested in disposable and personal income. *Personal income* is all income received before taxes are paid, while *disposable income* is that income left over after taxes.

Unemployment

The unemployment rate reflects the number of people out of work and seeking employment, and the number of people out of work with no prospect of employment. If the figure is low, everyone is happy, but if the figure is high or rising, people start to get nervous about their own jobs. This is because high and rising unemployment lead to losses of confidence, business uncertainties, recruitment freezes, and delays in investment; and this in turn puts further pressures on companies and organisations to cut costs and jobs still further. Both the United Kingdom and the European Union take the issue of unemployment very seriously. Of particular concern at present is the large number of people out of work in the new accession states (such as Latvia, Lithuania, and Poland); and also the large pockets of unemployment that remain in the older member states, especially in the Rhinelands of Germany, and the north-east and north-west of England.

Balance of trade

In the measuring of the current global economy, you hear a lot about things like *balance of trade* because nearly every business is affected by global conditions. The difference between the value of our exports to other countries and our imports from other countries is termed the *balance of trade*. In an ideal situation, countries want to bring in more money from exports than they spend on imports. This situation is considered a positive balance of trade. If, on the other hand, a country spends more for imports than it takes in from exports, it has a *trade deficit*.

National debt

In common with many western governments, the UK government operates at a deficit – which means that it has a *national debt*. The country uses deficit financing to underwrite and pay for many of its core programmes, including expanding healthcare, and providing education and social security. In recent years, the UK government has engaged in private finance initiatives, and public–private partnerships, in which the cost of building new public facilities is transferred to the private sector, and then the rental charges are repaid from current income (such as taxation). Such initiatives tend to be engaged when the taxation burden is as high as it should be, and this reinforces any conclusion or perception that the health of the economy is very brittle.

In each case, however, the government incurs a debt at the point of expenditure. At present, the UK runs a national debt of something over £1 trillion.

Economics and Entrepreneurship

If you decide to start up your own business, you eventually contribute to the growth of the national economy – if you are successful! After you have established yourself, you create and support employment, even if it is only through the hiring of one or two part-time staff or subcontractors.

In the UK, 95 per cent of all new start-ups fail in the first two years of their operation. So to give yourself a good chance, go into it with your eyes open, remembering that you have to have customers and clients prepared to spend money with you in volumes that will make your business sustainable.

What kind of business do you want to be?

Plenty of opportunities are around to start up your own business. Look at the following economic categories to see which you fall into – and to be aware of some of the main risks and constraints involved!

Economic core: If you want to be one of the crowd

Most start-up businesses fall into the economic core category. They don't innovate much, and consequently, they grow little. These small businesses essentially provide a job for the owner and an income for the owner's family.

Ambitious: If you want to stand out from the crowd

Ambitious firms usually benefit from very high rates of innovation. These companies find one unique thing that sets them apart from the crowd and allows them to grow. However, to continue to grow in a sustained manner, they must continue to innovate.

Glamorous: If you like lots of publicity

The glamorous category includes a very special and rare form of business. For the most part, these businesses are technology-based businesses that attract media attention. However, even the most profligate of investors have now realised that Internet and telecommunications, and even football club start-ups have to be sustained through the sale of real products and services to real customers – otherwise they fail!

Fashion and fad: Profile – and substance

The fashionable and faddish category of new business start-up includes outsourcing and overseas ventures, as well as Internet, telecommunications, and other technology inventions. Many entrepreneurs have set up fashion-able nightclubs and restaurants, especially in big cities. Only a few of these survive longer than a year or two in the form in which they were originally conceived. If you go into a fashionable or faddish line, remember that after the publicity all dies down, you still have to sustain business volumes.

Genuine invention: If you're truly lucky!

Genuine inventions are indeed rare. And the most sustainable of these inven-tions are usually pretty dull products and services – the cat's eye on roads; the Tetra Brik packaging system; milk pasteurisation. If you make such an invention, you are very fortunate; nevertheless, you may still have great difficulties in securing start-up finance, however much benefit to society you may ultimately bring.

Social: If you want to give something back

Social entrepreneurship is growing in the UK at present. It probably has its roots in the foundation of cosmetics company The Body Shop, in which a social element, especially in employment practice and the relationships with third world suppliers, was introduced and sustained. Since then, these principles have been adapted to ensure that employment based on the creation and delivery of commercially viable products and services has been extended to disadvantaged groups, such as the disabled, and those from deprived urban and rural areas.

Opportunistic: If place and product come together

Opportunistic entrepreneurship simply means that you're lucky enough to be in the right place at the right time, and able to take advantage of a particular opportunity. For example, Michael O'Leary was seeking to expand Ryanair but had to make very hard choices about how to pay for his airliner fleet. Due to the loss of confidence in flying after the 2001 World Trade Centre attack, the opportunity simply fell into his lap and he was able to order an airliner fleet at knock-down prices. He was able to include replacement, service, and after-care packages in the price because of the prevailing trading conditions.

Something else: Convenience – or what?

'Something else' is where you bring your own particular strength to the business that you propose to start-up. If your customers are presently well served by high-quality, high-brand offerings, or low-cost, good value offerings, you have to bring something else. What you bring is very much down to you! Perhaps you offer your own personal reputation, demeanour, or character, and build that into something that is sustainable from a business point of view.

Constrained growth: If you don't have enough money or you're afraid of failure

Some glamorous firms started as constrained growth firms, usually because they didn't have enough capital to support growth. When revenues don't come in fast enough to allow the company to put some of its money into more innovation, the company's growth is slowed. Growth is very expensive. If you want to understand how much money it takes to grow, take a look at Chapter 13.

Believe it or not, some business owners are afraid of growth, or afraid of losing control during growth, so they put controls on growth or refuse to do what's necessary to get help to grow. For example, an inventor who doesn't understand business (and this is sometimes even true for businesspeople!) refusing to give up any equity in their company in order to get an investor to take the risk and supply the capital necessary to grow isn't uncommon. This attitude has killed heaps of potentially great deals and great companies.

In some cases, business owners have trouble finding growth funding because no one is interested in what they're trying to do. Maybe they're manufacturing an innovative product with lots of potential, but to the investor, their business is just not as sexy as that dot com company that's losing £100 million a year. As well as the finances, you have to take into account people's behaviour and perceptions – and personal preferences.

Riding the Waves: Making Predictions

Although innovation has always been a key factor in economic success, the ability to sustain constant innovation in a rapidly changing and turbulent world is a new challenge for most businesses. Innovation is only one of the many issues facing economists today, in a world that doesn't look a whole lot like anything that's come before.

A major constraint on your predictive powers

No one has ever been able to successfully predict economic growth into any time in the future beyond perhaps the next few days. The main part of the problem is that no one can be certain what actions governments are going to take to enhance or restrain economic growth from one day to the next; and even if you knew that, what of actions taken elsewhere in the world? Or by the major financial institutions of the world – such as the World Bank, or the International Monetary Fund? Or by governments of emerging economies such as India and China?

The other part of the problem is that no one can even predict what productivity will be at any point in the future, and productivity is a key part of economic growth. If everyone agrees that the output of an economy is based on its input, it would make sense that if you double the input, you would get double the output. Right? And if that worked, you could double it again and quadruple your output. Right? Wrong! The law of diminishing returns says that, beyond a certain point, successive additions of input produce less and less output.

Can you still catch the fifth wave?

Joseph Schumpeter was the Austrian maverick who challenged the classical economists and said that *creative destruction* (the need to break up the existing ways of doing things as a fundamental part of developing things for the future) is part of a healthy economy. He was also one of the first to recognise that the economy has *waves* of business cycles, each driven by a different industry. Look at Figure 10-1 to see an example of Schumpeter's Waves.

As you can see from Figure 10-1, a long period of upswing in the cycle starts when a breakthrough set of innovations is introduced. For example, in the late 18th century, water power, textiles, and iron were the predominant innovators; in the 19th century, the innovations were the steam engine, railroads, and steel; by the 20th century, electricity, chemicals, and the internal combustion engine were the innovations of the age. Notice that as each innovation was replaced by a new set of disrupting innovations, growth in the previous sectors died. Notice also that as economies move through the cycles, the length of each time period for major innovations lessens somewhat. Today the world is in the midst of the fifth wave, led by semiconductors, fibre optics, genetics, and software. Actually, this wave may even be approaching its maturity, because it started in the late 1980s. The major companies in these fifth wave industries (for example, Microsoft, Intel, Nissan, Sony, and Toyota) are already established, profitable, and effective. And it is more or less certain that wireless communications, mass global transportation, and anything that doesn't depend on oil for its energy, are part of the next wave.

However, you can still find opportunities in the current wave. Opportunities always appear in any economic period. The important thing to remember is to *be aware and prepare*!

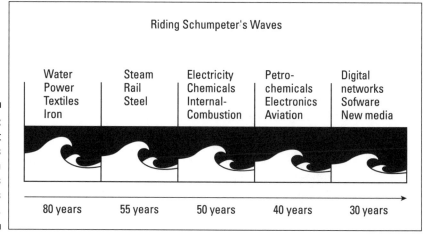

Figure 10-1:
Different industries drive an economy's business cycles.

Riding Schumpeter's Waves

| Water Power Textiles Iron | Steam Rail Steel | Electricity Chemicals Internal-Combustion | Petro-chemicals Electronics Aviation | Digital networks Sofware New media |

| 80 years | 55 years | 50 years | 40 years | 30 years |

Chapter 11

All You Ever Wanted to Know about Accounting

In This Chapter

▶ Understanding the basics of accounting

▶ Creating budgets

▶ Monitoring financial results

*I*f you've ever played in a competitive sporting match – whether it's football, cricket, tennis, badminton, or hockey – you know the importance of keeping the score. An individual or team score instantly tells you three things:

✔ During the course of competition, who is ahead and by how much.

✔ At the end of competition, who won and by how much.

✔ How well you did in relation to everyone else.

Business works in much the same way. However, instead of recording the number of goals, points, or runs scored, business tracks money. Accounting is the process of tracking money in a company.

An accounting system shows how much money has come into a company and how much has gone out (preferably your company has more coming in than going out!). It shows how much cash you have in your bank account, how much money you owe to other companies and individuals, and how much money others owe you. An accounting system shows the value of the products that you keep on hand to sell to customers, and it shows the money that you pay to employees in the form of salary and benefits. And, perhaps most importantly, an accounting system shows the money that's left over at the end of each month – your company's profit.

Going Back to Basics

In business, as in sport, you have winners and losers. Although some businesses make lots of money and thrive, others lose lots of money and die. A third kind of business (such as the Internet start-up Amazon.com) loses lots of money for years but still has a stock market value of billions of pounds. (You can read more about understanding stocks and bonds in Chapter 14.)

For the most part, winning and losing in the world of business is determined on the basis of financial measures. The most important financial measures are undoubtedly sales (revenue) and profit. _Sales_ represents the total amount of money that flows into a company as a result of selling a company's goods and services. _Profit_ represents the money that is left over after a company's expenses (payroll, benefits, cost of goods sold, rent, telephones, and so on) have been subtracted from its revenues.

However, before we get too deep into the nuts and bolts of accounting systems, we start at the beginning by discussing the accounting cycle.

The accounting cycle

The entire accounting process – from beginning to end – is called the _accounting cycle_. The accounting cycle has three parts:

- ✔ **Transaction:** A transaction is something your business does that generates a financial impact that's recorded in the accounting system. An example of a transaction is if a member of your sales staff sells a three-year subscription to _Bon Appétit_ magazine to a customer and the cheque for £110 arrives and is deposited in the company's bank account. Similarly, when your company makes a payment to Joe's House of Cheese for supplying food for a company party, that also creates a transaction.

- ✔ **Cash book:** As each transaction occurs, it is put into a cash book. A cash book is nothing more than a general file to temporarily hold transactions until they're classified by transaction type.

- ✔ **Ledger:** On a regular basis – daily, weekly, monthly, or other frequency – transactions in the cash book are classified by type and moved into individual accounts called ledgers. Individual ledgers include such accounts as payroll, travel, and sales.

After transactions have been put into their ledgers, managers have access to a wide variety of reports that summarise transactions and their effect on the business. These reports, which include the income statement, balance sheet, statement of cash flow, and much more, are detailed in Chapter 12.

The accounting equation

The accounting equation is the foundation of the science of accounting:

Assets = Liabilities + Share Capital

Here's a look at each part of the accounting equation and how it affects an organisation's finances.

Assets

Assets are generally anything in a business that has some sort of financial value and can be converted to cash. The products you have stocked in your warehouse are assets, as is the cash in your cash register.

Assets come in two different forms, current and fixed. These forms represent how quickly the assets can be converted into cash.

Current assets are assets that you can convert to cash within one year. These assets include money that arrived in the post today, invoices for a month's worth of consulting services, or the computers for sale on your showroom floor. Assets that you can quickly convert into cash are also known as *liquid* assets; the speed by which assets can be converted to cash is called *liquidity*.

Fixed assets are assets that take more than a year to be converted to cash. Fixed assets include the custom-built industrial milling machine that only three companies in the world have any use for, the building that houses your headquarters, and everything that you otherwise own to make your business fully effective.

When organisations indicate 'sales of assets' in their accounts, what they're actually stating is that they're selling off something that they no longer need or want – they're selling off *liabilities*. Companies and organisations that do this find that the price that they can command in these circumstances invariably goes down because potential purchasers quickly understand that the selling company needs to get rid of something.

Here's a list of the most common kinds of business assets – both current and fixed.

- ✔ **Cash:** Cash includes good old-fashioned money and money equivalents such as cheques, money orders, marketable securities, bank deposits, and foreign currency (if applicable).

- ✔ **Accounts receivable:** *Accounts receivable* represents the money that your clients and customers owe you for purchasing your products or services. When you allow a customer to buy your goods today and pay for them later, you are creating a receivable. If you work strictly on a cash basis (ice cream van, ticket agency, e-commerce site), then you won't have any receivables, and this item is always zero.

✔ **Stock:** Stock comprises the finished products that you purchase or manufacture to sell to customers, as well as raw materials, work in process, and supplies used in operations. If you run a grocery shop, then your stock is everything on display for sale in your shop – the carrots, the tubs of margarine, and the boxes of cakes.

✔ **Prepaid expenses:** When you pay for a product or service in advance, you create an asset known as a *prepaid expense*. Examples of prepaid expenses include a prepaid maintenance contract on a computer system, an insurance policy with a one-year term paid in advance, and an agreement for security alarm monitoring paid in advance on a quarterly basis.

✔ **Equipment:** Equipment is the wide variety of property that your organisation purchases to carry out its operations. Examples include desks, chairs, computers, electronic testing gear, and forklifts.

✔ **Property:** Property includes assets such as the land, buildings, and facilities that your company owns and occupies. Some companies have little or no property assets, while others have huge property portfolios.

Liabilities

Liabilities are money owed to others outside your organisation. They are the bills that you owe to the company that delivers your office supplies, the payments you owe on the construction loan that financed your warehouse expansion, and the mortgage on your corporate headquarters building.

Like assets, liabilities also come in two forms, current and long-term, each representing the amount of time to repay the obligation.

Current liabilities are liabilities that you repay within one year. This includes the money for next month's salaries, other short-term bill payments, and short-term loans from the bank. *Long-term liabilities* are liabilities that you repay in a period longer than one year. This includes the payments on the company delivery van, the mortgage on the company's depot, and dividends to preference shareholders. A *preference shareholder* is a shareholder who is entitled to assured and sometimes preferential dividend rates when dividends are being assessed.

Here's a list of the most common business liabilities:

✔ **Accounts payable:** Accounts payable are the obligations owed to the many individuals and organisations that have provided goods and services to your company. Examples include money owed to your computer network consultant, your local utility company, and an external advertising agency that your marketing department uses for ad campaigns.

- ✔ **Loan notes and debentures:** Loan notes and debentures represent loans made to your company by individuals or by organisations such as banks. They can be anything from an IOU to a multi-million-pound loan secured from a large bank.

- ✔ **Accrued expenses:** Sometimes a company incurs an expense but doesn't need to immediately reimburse individuals and organisations that are owed the money. Examples include future wages to be paid to employees, interest due on loans, and utility bills.

- ✔ **Bonds payable:** When companies issue *bonds* to raise money to finance large projects, then they incur obligations to pay back the individuals and organisations that purchase them. A bond is a specific amount of money raised from individuals or organisations for a fixed period of time and a guaranteed rate of interest.

- ✔ **Mortgages payable:** When companies purchase property, they often do so by taking out a *mortgage* – a long-term loan, secured by the property itself – on it. Mortgages payable represent the mortgages that an organisation has on all its properties.

- ✔ **Obsolete technology, equipment, premises, and expertise:** These are all liabilities because they no longer do the job that was intended, and so they have to be divested. This can be expensive either in terms of paying to have technology and equipment taken away, or else (in the case of staff), having to make redundancy payments.

Share capital

Share capital is the money that's left over when you take all of a company's assets and subtract all of its liabilities. Share capital represents the owners' direct investment in the firm, or the owners' claims on the company's assets. Another way of expressing a company's share capital is its net worth. *Net worth* is simply a snapshot of your company's financial health for a particular period of time.

Here are the two types of share capital:

- ✔ **Paid-up shares:** Paid-up shares represent the money that people invest in a company. When companies such as British Airways, British Telecom, or Google offer to sell shares to investors, the investors are providing paid-up shareholdings to the companies.

- ✔ **Retained earnings and profits:** These are a company's earnings and profits that are held within the company to be re-invested and not paid out to shareholders as dividends.

Although paid-up share capital is generally positive, it can become negative when the company takes on large amounts of debt, for example to acquire another company.

Double-entry bookkeeping

The accounting equation is like any other equation; a change to one side of the equation results in a change in the other side. Therefore, every financial transaction results in not one, but two entries to your accounting records.

Remember, the accounting equation says that:

Assets = Liabilities + Share Capital

So, for example, when Big Beef Steakhouses buy a large volume of beef to serve to customers, here's how the accounting equation is affected. In this example, assume that Big Beef Steakhouses starts with assets (stock) of £1,000, liabilities (accounts payable) of £500, and share capital of £500, like so:

Assets = Liabilities + Share Capital

£1000 = £500 + £500

(Stock) (Accounts payable)

When Big Beef Steakhouses purchase their beef from the meat market for £100 and the meat market agrees to invoice them for it, they acquire an asset (stock – literally raw material). They also take on a liability of £100, the money owed to the meat market (accounts payable). After this transaction, the accounting equation now looks like this:

Assets = Liabilities + Share Capital

£1100 = £600 + £500

(Stock) (Accounts payable)

As you can see, Big Beef Steakhouses added £100 worth of stock to their assets, but they simultaneously added a payable of £100 to their liabilities. The share capital didn't change. Every transaction on one side of the accounting equation results in a transaction on the other side of the accounting equation.

A small business might process relatively few transactions a day, making its accounting system pretty simple. An accounting system for a very large business that does millions of pounds of business a day is quite complex. In either case, accounting systems – and the computers that run them and the people who run the computers – are always vitally important, regardless of the size of the business.

Stock

Stock includes the finished products that you purchase or manufacture to sell to customers, as well as raw materials, work in process, and supplies used in operations. Although the nature of stock may seem simple on the surface, the way its value is handled by your accounting system is actually quite complex.

Businesses have two major ways of accounting for the value of stock:

- **FIFO (first in, first out):** Under this method of stock accounting, the stock that a company purchased first is the stock that it sells first to customers. When prices are rising (when *aren't* they rising?), the FIFO method results in a higher income figure as stock is sold off to customers than does the LIFO method, because it was most likely purchased at a lower original price than later stock purchases.

- **LIFO (last in, first out):** Under this method of stock accounting, the stock that a company purchased last is the stock that it sells first to customers. When prices are rising, the LIFO method results in a lower income figure as stock is sold off to customers than does the LIFO method, because the more recent purchases of stock most likely mean that purchase prices were higher, and so the sell-on margin is lower than FIFO.

If you want to enhance your total asset values, then you can use stock values to contribute to this by using FIFO. This may be important when seeking to enhance the value of an organisation – for example, when you're seeking to raise funds. On the other hand, if your organisation is operating right at the margin, then one way of reducing liabilities is to reduce stock value. In this case, you'd use LIFO.

Depreciation

Fixed assets have finite lifetimes. No asset lasts forever (especially if it has *anything* to do with technology). A computer may have a useful lifetime of 4 or 5 years, a steel mill may have a lifetime of 50 or 60 years. As you use assets over the course of their lifetimes, they gradually wear out or become obsolete. So, in the case of a steel mill with a 60-year lifetime, the mill doesn't retain 100 per cent of its value through year 59 and then suddenly lose all its value on the first day of its 60th year. Instead, this fixed asset steadily loses value as it experiences normal wear and tear over time.

Depreciation represents this loss of value of a fixed asset and is a method of allocating the cost of the asset over its useful lifetime.

You can choose from many different methods for calculating depreciation, some better than others. Here's a look at some of the most common methods.

Straight-line

Straight-line depreciation is the simplest method of depreciating an asset. In the straight-line method, you simply divide the cost of the asset by its expected lifetime in years. Table 11-1 shows the straight-line depreciation of a £2,500 computer that has an expected lifetime of five years.

Table 11-1	Straight-line Depreciation	
Year	Depreciation Expense	Cumulative Depreciation
1	£500	£500
2	£500	£1,000
3	£500	£1,500
4	£500	£2,000
5	£500	£2,500

As you can see, the amount of the asset depreciated each year is exactly the same: £500. At the end of the five-year life of the asset, the computer's original cost of £2,500 has been fully depreciated – very straightforward.

Double-declining balance

The *double-declining balance method* of depreciation is what is known as an accelerated method of depreciation because it pushes the majority of the total depreciation amount into the early years of ownership. The double-declining balance is calculated by multiplying the *book value* (the original cost of a fixed asset, less cumulative depreciation) by double its straight-line rate. So, in the example of a computer valued at £2,500, with a straight-line rate of 20 per cent per year, the double-declining balance method allows a rate of 40 per cent per year of the asset's book value.

Table 11-2 shows the results of applying the double-declining balance method to a computer valued at £2,500.

Table 11-2		Double-declining Balance Depreciation	
Year	Book Value	Depreciation Expense	Cumulative Depreciation
1	£2,500	£1,000	£1,000
2	£1,500	£600	£1,600
3	£900	£360	£1,960

Year	Book Value	Depreciation Expense	Cumulative Depreciation
4	£540	£216	£2,176
5	£324	£130	£2,306

The main reason for wanting to accelerate the depreciation of an asset is that this method reflects the real world. Think of how quickly your new car depreciates when you drive it off the forecourt for the first time. Immediately anything is put to use, it loses its resale value; and double-declining balance depreciation reflects this much more accurately than straight-line depreciation. It also underlines the fact that, however you depreciate, eventually you have to pay for the particular piece of equipment in full, and normally write it off altogether.

Sum of the years' digits

The *sum of the years' digits method* of depreciation is another way to accelerate depreciation. In this method, first determine how many years of life an asset will have. Then add the digits together to create the denominator of a fraction, with the year of depreciation as the numerator, in reverse order (lost yet?). The fraction is multiplied by the asset's original cost to determine the depreciated value.

In our example of a computer with an effective life of five years, first find the sum of the digits, $1+2+3+4+5 = 15$. This is your denominator. Table 11-3 shows the calculation involved to determine depreciation of the computer over its useful life.

Table 11-3		Sum of the Years' Digits Depreciation		
Year	Original Cost	Fraction	Depreciation Expense	Cumulative Depreciation
1	£2,500	5/15	£833	£833
2	£2,500	4/15	£667	£1,500
3	£2,500	3/15	£500	£2,000
4	£2,500	2/15	£333	£2,333
5	£2,500	1/15	£167	£2,500

As with the double-declining balance method of depreciation, the sum of the years' digits method pushes depreciation into the early years of an asset's life. Again, this is a much more genuine reflection of the real world than straight-line depreciation.

Using Budgets and Estimates

One of the keys to running a successful business is the ability of owners and managers to predict how a business will perform financially. If you can accurately predict a firm's performance, then you can be certain that resources such as money, people, equipment, manufacturing plants, and the like are deployed appropriately and in the most effective way.

A *budget* is a written estimate of how an organisation – or a particular project, department, or business unit – will perform financially.

The real value in budgets comes when you compare these estimates of expected performance with actual performance. When the figures match, you have a quick way of knowing that your organisation or project is performing just as it should. When the figures between your budgeted performance and actual performance differ markedly, then you know that you need to take a very close look at what's going on. The process of comparing expected financial results with actual financial results is called *variance analysis*, which we discuss in more detail in the 'Variance analysis' section, later in this chapter.

So, with the speed of business increasing all the time, and with raging change all around us, why bother doing budgets at all? Budgets offer the following benefits to organisations:

- ✓ **Budgets are milestones on the road to your goals.** Every organisation has (or at least should have) goals. Budgets are a quick and easy way to see whether your organisation is on track to meet its financial goals. If, for example, you have already spent half of your travel budget but you're only one-quarter of the way through the year, you know that you'll probably have an overspending problem.

- ✓ **Budgets make decisions easier.** When you budget a project, new initiative, or business activity, you'll quickly have a picture of what it will cost. Armed with that information, you can decide whether the costs you'll incur make good business sense or not. Will you make money or lose money as a result? How much money? For how long? The answers to these questions are important elements in the decision-making process, and you can find them in the budgeting process.

- ✓ **Budgets can be fast.** A budget can be as simple as a few figures scribbled onto the back of an envelope. A budget also can be a simple, one-page spreadsheet. Not every budget needs to be complicated. With simple budgets, you can make changes quickly, and print them out or e-mail them immediately.

- ✓ **Budgets can be flexible.** You need to be able to make changes according to circumstances. Perhaps you need to take on extra staff to take care of an unexpected order. Your budget can accommodate the change and create an up-to-date picture of how your organisation is performing. Or you can simply freeze your budget to see the variance between what your budget predicted and what really happened. No matter how fast your markets are moving, you can always keep up, no matter where you are.

✔ **Budgets are positive.** You need to look at budgets from the point of view that they are there to guide you and to predict what you intend to happen. Creating a budget in which the actual results match your expectations is exciting. The only thing that's a bigger thrill is when your results are even *better* than you expected!

Budgets are a financial check on everything that you set out to do, and the forecasting processes that you used to predict the outcomes. So make them as accurate as you possibly can, and ensure that you note especially where the discrepancies arise, and the reasons for these discrepancies.

Different kinds of budgets

You can budget any activity in your organisation that has a financial impact, such as a budget for self-managing work teams, research and development projects, or office refurbishments. Here are some of the most common budgets used in business today.

✔ **Cash budget:** A cash budget is an estimate of a company's cash position for a particular period of time. By using your current cash position as a baseline, you can estimate all cash inflows (sales) and outflows (expenses) during whatever time period you specify – say, a month – to determine a projected cash position at the end of the period.

✔ **Operating budget:** The operating budget shows a business's forecasted revenues along with forecasted expenses, usually for a period of one year or less.

The operating budget is a top-level budget; the following budgets are more detailed items in the operating budget.

✔ **Staff budget:** A staff budget takes every person in an organisation, department, or project and multiplies the number of hours they're expected to work by their wage rates. The result is the total staff cost that will be expended for a set period of time.

✔ **Sales budget:** This is an estimate of the quantity of goods and services that you'll sell during a specific period of time. In the case of products, you determine total revenue by multiplying the total number of units projected to be sold by the price per unit.

✔ **Production budget:** The production budget starts with the sales budget and its estimates of the total number of units projected to be sold. This budget then translates this information into estimates of the cost of staff, material, and other expenses required to produce them.

✔ **Expense budget:** Every business – from a one-person home business to a huge multinational corporation with tens of thousands of employees – incurs a variety of expenses during the course of normal operations. For example, expense budgets are prepared for travel, utilities, office supplies, and telephone use.

✔ **Capital budget:** If you plan to buy fixed assets with a long, useful lifespan (many organisations consider this to mean a year or more), then you budget for them in your capital budget. Items in your capital budget might include buildings, production machinery, computers, copiers, furniture, and anything else that has a long life.

To see what an operating budget looks like, see the sample budget in the sidebar 'A sample operating budget'.

Putting a budget together

The best kind of budget is the one that works. The three key approaches to developing a budget that works are bottom up, top down, and zero-based methods. Each has its advantages and disadvantages, and each approach can work well, although the pendulum is clearly swinging in favour of the bottom up approach.

✔ **Bottom up:** In bottom up budgeting, supervisors and middle managers are asked to prepare the budgets and then forward them up the chain of command for review and approval. These middle managers have the benefit of a close working knowledge of the organisation and its financial performance. As a result, bottom up budgets tend to be pretty accurate. In addition, bottom up budgets can have a positive impact on employee morale because employees assume an active role in providing financial input to the budgeting process.

✔ **Top down:** In this approach, budgets are prepared by top management and imposed on the lower layers of the organisation, generally without any consultation or involvement on the part of those outside of top management. Top down budgets clearly express the performance goals and expectations of top management. These budgets, however, can be unrealistic because they don't incorporate the input of the very people who implement them.

✔ **Zero-based budgeting:** Zero-based budgeting is the process in which you prepare estimates of your proposed expenses for a specific period of time as if for the first time. In other words, each activity starts from a budget base of zero. By starting from scratch at each budget cycle, you take a close look at all your expenses and justify them to top management, thereby minimising waste.

A sample operating budget

A picture is worth a thousand words, so here's what a real monthly operating budget looks like for a typical company with annual revenues of about £1 million.

Sprocket Company

Revenue	Monthly Budget
Product sales	£81,250
Royalties	£1,000
Web site ads	£8,500
Other income	£100
Total revenue	**£90,850**
Expenses	
Rent	£1,403
Wages	£10,000
Taxes	£1,325
Licences and permits	£100
Insurance (public liability)	£1,000
Insurance (other)	£500
Advertising and promotions	£5,000
Dues and subscriptions	£300
Training	£400
Miscellaneous	£100
Office supplies	£2,000
Outside services	£2,000
Postage and delivery	£2,500
Printing	£2,500
Telephone	£1,000
Entertainment	£50
Gifts	£50
Meals	£500
Travel	£5,000
Commission	£2,000
Cost of goods sold	£5,000
Interest	£100
Total expenses	**£42,828**
Profit (Loss)	**£48,022**

Budgets are prepared for small operating units or departments. These budgets roll up into larger budgets – for divisions or groups – which then are combined into an organisation's overall budget. In this way, managers at all levels of an organisation can play a role in an organisation's financial health and well-being.

Budget tricks of the trade

Budgets provide a kind of early warning system that, when compared to actual results, can inform you when something is going wrong that needs your immediate attention.

When your expenditures exceed your budget, you can do several things to get back on track:

- **Review your budget.** Before you do anything else, take a close look at your budget and make sure that the assumptions on which it is based are accurate and make sense in your changing market. If your market is growing quickly, you may need to adjust up your estimates. Sometimes, the budget – not the spending – is out of line.

- **Freeze spending.** One of the quickest and most effective ways to bring spending back in line with a budget is to freeze spending. For example, you can freeze expenses such as pay rises, new staff, and bonuses.

- **Postpone new projects.** New projects, including new product development, acquisition of new facilities, and research and development, can eat up a lot of money. If spending is over budget, a common solution is to postpone new projects until you have enough revenue to support them. However, be sure to carefully balance this desire to bring spending back into line against the need to develop new products and services. If you're too zealous in this area, the result can be disastrous for the future growth and prosperity of the company.

- **Lay-off employees and close facilities.** When you're trying to cut expenses, the last resort is to lay off staff and shut down facilities. Although these actions result in an immediate and lasting decrease in expenses, you'll also face an immediate and lasting decrease in the talent available to your organisation. In addition, the morale of those employees who survive the budget cut can suffer.

Keeping Your Eye on the Figures

You need to review and analyse accounting reports to determine the financial health of your organisation. By regularly reviewing accounting reports and analysing the information they present, you can make better, more informed decisions.

In this section, we look at some ways that people keep their eyes on the figures in an organisation.

Variance analysis

One of the simplest ways to use a budget to keep your eye on the figures is through the use of variance analysis. In simple terms, *variance analysis* is a comparison of the financial estimates that you budgeted for a particular period with your firm's actual financial results. The variance is the difference between budget and actual, and it can be a positive or negative figure, or zero.

In the monthly expenses in Table 11-4, look at the variance between the budget and the actual figures (brackets around a figure mean that it's negative). This method gives you an immediate picture of financial issues that may require a closer look on your part.

Table 11-4	Variance Analysis		
Expenses	*Budget*	*Actual*	*Variance*
Rent	£1,403	£1,403	£0
Wages	£10,000	£12,500	£2,500
Taxes	£1,325	£1,500	£175
Internet access	£60	£0	(£60)
Licences and permits	£50	£50	£0
UPS service charge	£25	£100	£75
Telephone system	£200	£200	£0
Insurance (public liability)	£1,000	£1,500	£500
Insurance (other)	£500	£500	£0
Total expenses	£14,563	£17,753	£3,190

In this example, fixed expenses were originally budgeted at £14,563 for the month. However, when the month ended, the accounting system reflected actual fixed expenses of £17,753. This resulted in a total variance – or over-spending – of £3,190.

After you've determined that you have a budget variance for the period in question, the next step is to decide whether it is significant and, if so, to figure out why it occurred. In Table 11-4, a variance of £3,190, which is 22 per cent of the original budget of £14,563, is definitely significant and warrants a very close look by the responsible manager.

Audits

The accuracy of accounting records and reports is incredibly important, especially to two groups of people. The people within your organisation rely on accounting information to make informed business decisions. And the investors and lenders outside of your organisation rely on accounting information to make informed decisions on the use of their funds.

For these reasons, organisations conduct regular *audits* or checks of their accounting systems to ensure that results are accurate and that the system treats all financial information fairly and honestly.

The two key kinds of audits are:

- **Internal audits:** These audits are conducted by employees of your organisation as an internal check to ensure the integrity of accounting information and the reports that are generated from this information. Many large companies have entire departments devoted to this task, and make this an annual event.

- **External audits:** External audits involve examination of a company's accounting system by an unbiased, outside individual or organisation – either an accountancy practice or chartered accountant. External audits are typically conducted on an annual basis, after the end of a company's financial year. Companies use these audits to ensure the integrity of the numbers that go into annual reports and financial statements, and to guard against fraud.

Accounting provides a kind of scoreboard for an organisation. As such, understanding how accounting works and how to get the most out of accounting reports is an important skill for *any* manager or aspiring MBA. For a much more complete discussion on accounting, have a look at *Understanding Business Accounting For Dummies* by Colin Barrow and John A Tracy (Wiley), which is a clear, comprehensive, and concise guide.

Chapter 12

Making Sense of Financial Statements

*A*s a studious, hard-working MBA candidate – and even if you *aren't* so studious or hard working – you need to know that management has four traditional functions: Planning, organising, leading, and controlling. Each of these management functions has its own characteristics, but *controlling* is the focus of this chapter.

Most experienced businesspeople feel that they can get a fairly accurate, intuitive sense for the success of their operations or of a project or product by simply asking the right people the right questions. But such an approach doesn't provide all the answers. In addition, such personal assessments are inherently risky because they can overlook important information that is critical to an understanding of exactly what is going on in a business. You can gain such insight only by closely reviewing and analysing hard, objective data. In most organisations, this hard, objective data takes the form of accounting reports and financial statements.

In this chapter, we take a close look at the most commonly used financial statements so that you know when and how to use them to better gauge the progress of your business.

Following Financial Statements

Managers often receive a variety of financial and project reports that are tailored to their exact needs. For instance, a software engineer might receive a weekly staff report that shows exactly who worked on each of the team's software projects, how many hours each employee worked, the cost of those hours, and a variance above or below budget. An accounts receivable manager might get a 'blacklist' of receivables that shows who owes money to the company, how much, and for how long. And members of a production team might receive regular reports on the cost of products returned to the company because of quality problems.

However, when it comes to assessing the overall financial health of an organisation, three key financial reports are universally used throughout the wide world of business. These reports – known as *financial statements* – are

- The balance sheet
- The profit and loss account
- The statement of cash flow

Each of these reports offers a unique perspective for looking at a company's financial health. Think of a doctor who, when faced with a patient with some undetermined illness, orders not only a blood test but also an X-ray and a complete physical examination. No single financial report tells the full story. You can understand the complete picture only by reviewing all the financial statements and sometimes by digging even deeper for more information.

A manager or business owner needs to keep close tabs on the organisation's performance. Managers need to make changes in the allocation of company resources to maintain a high level of financial return. If you're part of a self-managing work team, or if you work for an *open-book organisation* – one that shares financial and other performance data with all employees – then you, too, are familiar with financial statements and the information that they provide.

Banks need financial statements to make judgements on whether to extend loans or lines of credit. Accountants need the information to assess the health of the organisation. And investors and financial analysts also need the information provided within financial statements to determine the attractiveness of a particular organisation when compared with a wide range of other investment opportunities.

Financial statements tell their readers the following important information:

- **Liquidity:** The ability to quickly convert assets into cash to pay expenses such as payroll, supplier invoices, creditors, and others.
- **General financial condition:** The long-term balance between debt and *equity* (the assets left after you deduct liabilities).

✔ **Share capital:** The periodic increases and decreases in the company's net worth.

✔ **Profitability:** The ability of the company to earn profits, and to earn them consistently over an extended period of time.

✔ **Performance:** The organisation's performance against the financial plans developed by its management team or employees.

As you review financial statements for *your* organisation, remember there's no such thing as a good figure or a bad figure. If a particular figure isn't what you expect it to be, that's your cue to research *why* the figure is different from what you expect. For example, the fact that profit declined from one period to the next may seem at first glance to be a bad thing. However, the decline may be a result of your finance director's decision to *reapportion profits* (reducing profits and investing them elsewhere in the company, perhaps in equipment or research and development) to minimise the impact of income taxes on the company.

Taking a Snapshot: The Balance Sheet

The *balance sheet* is a snapshot of the financial health of an organisation at a particular point in time. The famous tagline on the heading of any good balance sheet is usually something like 'As of December 31, 2007' or 'At December 31, 2007'. The balance sheet reveals the financial picture not for a period of time, but for that exact date only. The company's financial picture could be vastly different on January 1, 2008 (for example, if a large capital payment is due on that date).

As a reminder, here's the accounting equation again:

Assets = Liabilities + Share Capital

Assets include cash and things that can be converted to cash. *Liabilities* are obligations – debt, loans, mortgages, and the like – owed to other organisations or people. *Share capital* is the net worth of the company after you subtract all liabilities from the organisation's assets. (For a much more in-depth discussion about assets, liabilities, and share capital, see Chapter 11.)

A typical balance sheet looks something like Figure 12-1.

As you can see, the value of PinkPetunias.com's assets is exactly balanced by its liabilities and share capital. Because of the accounting equation, no other option exists. The balance sheet shows that assets are paid for by a company's liabilities and share capital. Conversely, the assets are used to generate cash to pay off the company's liabilities. Any excess cash after liabilities are paid off is added to share capital as profit.

PinkPetunias.com
Consolidated Balance Sheet - As of December 31, 2007
(In millions)

ASSETS
Current Assets

Cash and cash equivalents	£25
Accounts receivable	150
Stocks	50
Total Current Assets	225

Fixed Assets

Equipment	200
Furniture, fixtures, and improvements	150
Allowance for depreciation and write-off	(20)
Total Fixed Assets	330

Total Assets	**£555**

LIABILITIES AND SHARE CAPITAL
LIABILITIES
Current Liabilities

Repayments to bank	10
Accounts payable	50
Wages and Salaries	75
Taxes payable	20
Deferred taxes	10
Current portion of long-term debt	5
Total Current Liabilities	170

Long-Term Debt	100
Deferred Rent Expense	50
Deferred Taxes	50
Total Liabilities	**370**

SHARE CAPITAL

Ordinary shares	100
Additional paid-in capital	60
Retained earnings	25

Total Share Capital	**185**
Total Liabilities and Share Capital	**£555**

Figure 12-1:
The balance sheet for a fictional online company.

In the balance sheet, assets are listed in order from the most liquid (readily convertible to cash) to the least liquid, while liabilities and share capital are listed in the order in which they're scheduled to be paid. And, don't forget – current assets can be converted to cash within a year; current liabilities are scheduled to be paid within a year.

By reviewing changes in a company's balance sheets over time, managers, bankers, investors, and others can pick up on trends that may affect the long-term viability of the firm and that may either positively or negatively impact the value of its shares. In Chapter 13, you find out how to use financial ratios and forecasting tools to make sense of these figures, changes, and trends.

Making Money: The Profit and Loss Account

Businesses can exist to leave a lasting legacy in the world, or to employ thousands of people and pull a region out of an economic slump. But the number one reason that businesses exist is to make money, pure and simple. Because making money is such an incredibly important part of the day-to-day focus of any business, companies need a quick and easily understood way of figuring out how much money a business is making – the profit and loss account.

A profit and loss account is more than a snapshot of a business's financial position on one particular date (like the balance sheet). The profit and loss account tells its readers three key pieces of information:

- ✔ A business's sales volume during the period of the report.
- ✔ The business's expenses during the period of the report.
- ✔ The difference between the business's sales and its expenses (in other words, its profit or loss) during the period of the report.

Figure 12-2 shows what a typical profit and loss account looks like.

Figure 12-2 shows that PinkPetunias.com had £49,000 of net sales revenue and a cost of goods sold of £10,000, leaving the company with a gross profit of £39,000. However, this gross profit was further reduced by the expenses of selling products and running the company (advertising, printing, rent, salaries, bonuses, and so on) and by income taxes. The result is a net income of £9,000. Divided by 250,000 shares of stock in the hands of investors and the company, this works out to an earning per share of £0.036.

PinkPetunias.com
Profit and Loss Account - Twelve Months Ended December 31, 2007
(In thousands)

REVENUES
Gross sales	50
Less: Returns	(1)
Net Sales	49

COST OF GOODS SOLD
Beginning stocks	50
Purchases	10
Less: Purchase discounts	(2)
Net purchases	8
Cost of goods available for sale	58
Less: Ending stocks	48
Cost of Goods Sold	10

GROSS PROFIT   39

OPERATING EXPENSES
Total selling expenses	5
Total general expenses	10
Total operating expenses	15
Operating income	24

Other income and expenses	
Interest expense (income)	5
Total Other Income and Expense	5

Income before taxes	19
Less: Taxes	(10)
Net Income/Profit	9
Average Number of Shares	250,000
Earnings Per Share	£0.036

Figure 12-2:
An example
of a profit
and loss
account.

Keeping More Money Than You Spend: The Cash Flow Statement

For any business, cash truly is king. You need cash to pay employees, to purchase supplies, and to pay bills. Employees have their own obligations to meet – buying groceries, paying mortgages, childcare expenses, and much more – and they need cash to meet them. Paying employees with other assets such as long-term bonds or plant equipment just doesn't work. And you certainly can't pay employees with profit.

The *cash flow statement* (or *statement of cash flow*) is a specialised report that tracks the sources of cash in a company, as well as its inflows (money coming into a business) and outflows (money going out of a business). It is an extremely valuable tool for ensuring that a company has the cash it needs to meet its obligations *when* it needs it.

A number of different kinds of cash flow statements are each suited to a particular business need. Some are used strictly inside a business, and some are used outside a business, for investors, creditors, and other interested parties. Here are a few of the most common types of cash flow statements:

- ✔ **Simple cash flow statement or cash budget:** The simple cash flow statement arranges all items into one or two categories; usually cash inflows and cash outflows.

- ✔ **Operating cash flow statement:** The operating cash flow statement limits analysis of cash flows to items involved in the operations of a business, and not its financing.

- ✔ **Financing cash flow statement:** The financing cash flow statement includes cash raised by issuing new debt or equity capital, as well as the expenses incurred for repaying debt or paying dividends on shares.

- ✔ **Statement of cash flows:** The statement of cash flows is typically an external statement that depicts the period-to-period changes in balance sheet items and the actual money amount for the period in question for profit and loss account items. This statement shows the following categories: (1) operating cash inflows and (2) outflows; (3) priority outflows such as interest expense and current debt payments; (4) discretionary outflows such as equipment charges; and (5) financial flows, which represents money you borrow and have to repay.

Although you can find plenty of different kinds of cash flow statements, don't forget the first rule of cash management: Good business health is a positive cash flow.

Life's an open book in these organisations

In recent years, many organisations have taken a much more open approach with employees in their dealings with the financial aspects of the business. In part, this has been driven by managerial expertise; and it has also been reinforced by UK and EU legislation requiring organisations to open up information to employees, and to consult them on business decisions, as well as matters of employee relations.

Traditionally, the production and analysis of financial statements was always a managerial prerogative. Not only did non-management employees have no need to see these statements (as far as most managers were concerned at least), but it also was generally assumed that employees wouldn't understand the statements anyway.

Fans of open-book management believe that all workers should have access to a company's financial statements. They also believe that employees should be trained in what these statements mean, and in how the work that they do impacts both the company and themselves. Here are the characteristics of an open-book organisation:

- Every employee sees – and learns to understand – the company's finances, along with all the other figures that are critical to tracking a company's performance.

- Employees learn that, whatever else they do, part of their job is to move those figures in the right direction.

- Employees have a direct stake in the company's success.

To make open-book management work, managers must be able to identify the critical figures that make their business work, whether those figures are occupancy rates in the hotel business or number of defects in a manufacturing process. Every business has multiple critical figures for the various functions inside the business that directly affect their profits. These are the figures that employees need to understand. And these are the figures against which employee performance is judged. In a well-executed open-book plan, a portion of every employee's pay is based on reaching agreed-upon targets for these critical figures, and the company pays profit-based bonuses when targets are exceeded. It's a win-win situation for everyone. Knowledgeable employees like the open-book system because, after they understand it, they actually earn more than under more traditional systems.

If anyone is in any doubt over the value of open-book approaches to finances in particular, and management in general, then look at the Japanese manufacturing companies presently operating in the UK. Sharp, Sony, Nissan, Sanyo, and others have all made a practice, right from the start, of opening up all information to their employees. Employees are consulted on, and are expected to contribute to, every aspect of financial performance, business decision-making, and the establishment of production and service delivery schedules and volumes. These companies have been among the most successful in the UK for over 30 years; and despite downturns in some of their markets, they still endure.

Table 12-1 shows a sample cash flow statement – one that's meant for internal rather than external use (remember that numbers in brackets are negative):

Table 12-1	Cash Flow Statement for Internal Use Only		
Cash flows (4th Qtr.)	*October*	*November*	*December*
Cash inflow	£5,000,000	£7,500,000	£6,500,000
Cash outflow	£4,500,000	£8,000,000	£7,000,000
Cash surplus (need) this month	£500,000	(£500,000)	£0
Cash surplus (need) last month	£0	£500,000	£0
Cumulative cash flow	£500,000	£0	(£500,000)

Reviewing financial statements is a great way to get started in the analysis of a company's financial health and its long-term outlook. However, to get the most mileage out of these reports, you need to undertake another, deeper level of analysis. You must apply financial ratios to the figures contained in the balance sheet and profit and loss account, and do financial forecasting. We address these topics and more in Chapter 13.

Chapter 13

Unravelling the Mysteries of Financial Planning and Analysis

*A*lthough cash takes up only one line out of many in a company's balance sheet, it plays an incredibly important role in the day-to-day health of any organisation. Cash pays employee salaries and benefits. It pays suppliers for the vital raw materials, services, and supplies needed to operate a business and to manufacture its products. Cash keeps the lights on and pays for the products that are stockpiled for customers to buy. Without a constant and reliable supply of good old-fashioned money, most businesses would go out of business fast.

Managing, planning, forecasting, and analysing a company's financial situation is always high on the list of priorities for the people who own, manage, and run most organisations. When he was Chairman of the General Electric Company, Arnold Weinstock used to question his senior managers in detail about the financial performance of their particular divisions on a weekly basis. And woe betides any manager, however senior, who could not give precise answers!

Although traditional business practice limited responsibility for knowing the figures to managers and supervisors, business today requires an entirely new perspective on financial management. The pace of business has accelerated in recent years, and hierarchies have flattened, squeezing many managers out of the system. As a result, organisations are increasingly relying on front-line employees to take an active role in financial management. Participative organisations, self-managing work teams, total quality management, and other innovative work practices have blurred the lines between managers and workers in many organisations. For businesses to grow and to thrive today, everyone, not only a company's managers, ought to know the figures in detail, and be able to make sense of them.

With the proper tools, most people can become proficient in managing the finances of their company, division, or department. And, in this chapter, we provide you with the tools to do just that.

Manage Your Finances – Don't Let Them Manage You!

Although every business has many systems and processes that can benefit from proactive management, your company's finances are among the more important areas to manage. Every business – from the smallest start-up to the largest multinational – needs a financial plan. Financial plans serve as blueprints for the financial needs of the company. As such, they allow decision makers to determine when and where funds will be necessary in the organisation, and how much will be allotted. Financial plans also let managers know whether promising new projects or ventures are prudent, or whether they need to terminate old, under-performing ones.

The financial planning process has three parts: Preparing forecasts, developing budgets, and establishing financial controls. Here's a closer look at each part.

Preparing forecasts

If you can count on one thing in business, it's that nothing will stay the same for very long. In business today, change is a constant.

The best managers try to anticipate, forecast, and predict change before it occurs. And, of course, because financial considerations can mean the difference between life and death to a company, financial forecasts and projections are keystones of proactive business management practice. Ask questions like these if you want to prepare accurate financial forecasts:

✔ How many employees will we have on board this year, and will we have the money to pay them when we need to?

✔ Will we have sufficient funds available to invest in new manufacturing equipment that will improve the productivity of our workers while increasing output and lowering rejects?

✔ How much money will we need in order to have enough stocks even for the busiest periods, and will the money be available when we need it?

✔ By what amount can we expect revenues and profit to grow (or, heaven forbid, shrink) over the next year?

✔ What is the timing of payments from our major customers, and how will they affect our cash flow?

These questions are constantly on the minds of all financial directors and managers – and others who are responsible for ensuring that a business can meet all its financial obligations. Managers conduct regular financial planning and forecasting for exactly this reason.

Two key kinds of financial forecasts and projections exist: Short-term and long-term.

Short-term financial forecasts

If a financial forecast is for a period of one year or less, it is considered a *short-term forecast*. Many firms use a variety of short-term financial forecasts and *pro forma* (informal) financial statements to manage day-to-day operations. These types of forecasts and financial statements include:

✔ Cash

✔ Sales or revenue

✔ Profit and loss account (refer to Chapter 12)

✔ Balance sheet (also in Chapter 12)

✔ Receivables or cash receivable (money we're owed by our customers)

Each of these forecasts – and others that an organisation may select – is important to the people in charge of monitoring a company's immediate financial position. But by far the most important forecast for most companies is the cash forecast.

Figure 13-1 is an example of the kind of simplified cash forecast that a typical firm might use on a regular basis. For some companies, 'regular' means daily or weekly. For others, 'regular' means monthly, quarterly, or even longer. The frequency of reporting depends on the needs of the business, and the importance of keeping close tabs on its cash position. The cash forecast in Figure 13-1 is for a business that provides software engineers directly to a large company at a variety of locations across the country. Software engineers are the company's main product, as well as its major expense. In the example, employees are paid weekly, but the company is paid by its client once each month.

Forecasted cash flows	Week 1	Week 2	Week 3	Week 4
Cash inflow (client payment)	£0	£0	£0	£150,000
Cash outflow (payroll)	£20,000	£20,000	£20,000	£20,000
Cash surplus (need) this week	(£20,000)	(£20,000)	(£20,000)	(£130,000)
Cash surplus (need) last week	£0	(£20,000)	(£40,000)	(£60,000)
Cumulative cash flow	(£20,000)	(£40,000)	(£60,000)	£70,000

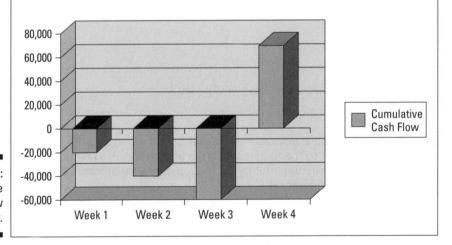

Figure 13-1:
A simple cash flow forecast.

As you can see, in each of the first three weeks of the month, the company incurs a negative cash flow of £20,000. These negative cash flows accumulate, reaching £60,000 by the end of the third week of the month. However, when a £150,000 payment is received from the customer in week four, cash flow goes positive in a big way – to the tune of £70,000.

Using cash forecasts just like this, companies can determine when they'll be taking in more money than they pay out to meet their obligations. They can then use this knowledge to guide decisions on when and how much to pay suppliers, the levels of supplies that they can comfortably keep in stock, the timing of investments in capital equipment, and much more.

Long-term financial forecasts

If you need to plan for a period that extends more than a year into the future, then you need a *long-term financial forecast*. Given how fast the business environment is changing, making plans for more than a year into the future can be tricky. But part of financial planning is planning for change.

Long-range planning has fallen out of favour in many businesses, especially those that realised that months of hard work often led to elaborate, beautifully bound documents that were promptly filed away and forgotten about as soon as they were published. However, as we discuss in Chapter 4, long-range, strategic planning does have a time and a place. Done right, these plans can provide your business with a definite competitive advantage by giving your business focus and direction.

Long-range plans require long-term financial forecasts to support them. Just as in short-term financial forecasts, you can forecast all kinds of financial data with a reasonable degree of accuracy. Here are a few of the most popular kinds of financial data subject to a long-term look:

- ✔ Cash
- ✔ Sales or revenues
- ✔ Profit and loss account
- ✔ Assets, liabilities, and net worth (balance sheet)

The acronym RIRO (rubbish in, rubbish out) definitely applies here. Financial forecasts of any sort are only as good as the data on which they're based. As the horizon for your forecasts extends farther out into the future, the reliability of your forecasts naturally declines, and they become less dependable. Many companies in fast-moving industries are happy to forecast a year into the future with any degree of accuracy. Companies in more stable industries, however, can more safely and accurately forecast for periods of up to five years.

Long-term financial forecasts are built in much the same way as short-term forecasts, but with much longer horizons. These longer horizons require careful attention to long-range trends in markets and technology, and they assume the possibility of greater swings than short-term financial forecasts. Here are some tips for putting together accurate long-term financial forecasts:

- ✔ Look for long-term trends in revenues and expenses. Are revenues and expenses gradually heading up or down over a period of five years or longer? Chart these trends out as graphs and make an educated guess as to where the trends will lead in the future.

- ✔ Are there natural business cycles, and are there natural or predictable cycles that relate directly to our business? If so, are they regular, and what is their frequency? Many businesses and markets go through regular business cycles. By looking at the big picture, you should be able to pick out the cycles and factor them into your long-term financial forecasts.

- ✔ What kinds of random events are most likely to disturb the long-term trends in revenues and expenses? What would happen if your company bought out a key competitor? How would doing so affect revenues and expenses? What if a competitor develops a new process that cuts its cost of production in half? By nature, random events are hard to predict, but the more you can factor them into your long-term financial forecasts, the more accurate your forecast will be.

Long-term financial forecasts are an important part of the long-range planning process. Long term forecasts need to be as accurate and detailed as possible, and especially need to be able to anticipate any problems with cash flow related to possible downturns in markets or matters to do with product and service obsolescence, and/or the bringing of new products, services and ventures to market.

At the very least, the headings required in long-term financial forecasting are as follows:

- ✔ Production and service delivery costs
- ✔ Product and services sales
  - Costs of sales
- ✔ Divestments and acquisitions
  - Management and legal charges
- ✔ Introduction of new products and services
  - Start up costs and exceptional charges

✔ Introduction of new technology

* • Start up costs, implementation costs, training, and development

✔ Overheads, administration, head office costs and charges

✔ Wastage

Additionally, all organisations will have special ventures and new initiatives arising in their own particular set of circumstances. Each figure should be estimated on at least a six-monthly basis (and it is a better and more detailed discipline to produce figures for each quarter) for a five-year period into the future. This needs then to be checked against progress and real costs and charges as the future unfolds.

Developing budgets

The second part of the financial management process is the development and execution of budgets. Budgets are similar to financial forecasts, but much more detailed. For example, while a sales forecast may simply reflect a total revenue estimate of £500,000 for the upcoming financial quarter, a sales budget for the same period is a breakdown of each of the various individual components of the sales forecast. Take a look at Table 13-1, which shows the sales budget for a hypothetical computer components retailer:

Table 13-1	Sales Budget: 3rd Quarter
Item	*Projected Sales*
Monitors	£75,000
Keyboards	£30,000
Hard drives	£100,000
Central processors	£150,000
Software	£25,000
CD-ROM drives	£25,000
Installation	£50,000
Service contracts	£45,000
Total sales budget	**£500,000**

This budget shows how much you're predicting you'll sell of each product during a specific period of time, in this case, a financial quarter. The good thing about budgets is that they not only provide a detailed picture of what the future may bring but also create a baseline against which you can measure actual performance. In the preceding budget, for example, the amount of estimated total sales is £500,000. After the third quarter is over, the accounting system will provide actual results – for each line of the sales budget, as well as an overall total. By comparing budgeted versus actual results, you can quickly grasp exactly where company performance is better or worse than anticipated, and redirect resources accordingly.

If you're still not sure about the whole budgeting process, refer to Chapter 11.

Establishing financial controls

Accounting systems and financial statements and reports are wonderful things, but they aren't worth the silicon they're built from, nor the paper they're printed on, if no one analyses and interprets them. Figures by themselves mean nothing. Figures with context and understanding mean everything.

The whole point of preparing financial forecasts and budgets is to attempt to predict future performance while creating baselines by which you can compare actual results. If results are as predicted, terrific – you're right on track towards your goals. If actual results are significantly less, or significantly more, than predicted then managers know where to begin to look for sources of these variances.

Here are some ways that you can analyse a company's performance:

- **Variance analysis:** By comparing an organisation's actual results versus its budgeted results (for example, its actual revenues versus its budgeted revenues), you get a quick picture of whether a company is on or off track, and by how much. (We discuss variance analysis in detail in Chapter 11.)

- **Ratio analysis:** By comparing certain financial results within a company's financial statements (particularly the profit and loss account and balance sheet, discussed in Chapter 12), you can quickly determine whether the company is operating within the normal limits for its industry. For example, dividing a company's current assets by its current liabilities results in a ratio (called the 'quick ratio') that tells you whether the company is solvent and can meet its financial obligations to its lenders.

✔ **Cost/volume/profit analysis:** By determining which products are the most – and the least – profitable for a company, you can make decisions about where to invest your company's time and resources. Here are a couple of key approaches to cost/volume/profit analysis:

- **Break-even analysis:** A break-even analysis allows you to determine at what sales volume your profitability will break even with the cost to produce your products or services. Using electronic spreadsheets, you can run all sorts of what-if scenarios with a variety of different cost and price assumptions.

- **Contribution margin analysis:** The contribution margin analysis compares the profitability of each of a company's products or services, as well as its relative contribution to the company's bottom line. This analysis quickly points out under-performing products and services that your company needs to either restructure or terminate.

If your company is under-performing, then you can redirect resources to boost performance, or you can change plans to bring expectations in line with reality. If the company is performing better than planned, you can identify the reasons why, and do more of the same. At the same time, you can modify budgets upward to accommodate the improved performance.

You can use many tricks of the trade to determine how a business is performing, based on all sorts of financial data. In the next section, we explore some of the most common.

Financial Tricks of the Trade

In this section we share with you some shortcuts that put complicated processes or data into simple, easily understood terms.

As you read through these financial rules, keep in mind that they can vary considerably for companies in different industries. Manufacturing companies as a group have different ratios than consulting firms or utilities. Be sure that, when you compare one company's figures with the figures for another, you are comparing apples with apples, and oranges with oranges. However, some ratios are common to all businesses, many of which we explain here.

Liquidity ratios

Liquidity ratios are a group of ratios that measure the *solvency* of a business – its ability to generate the cash necessary to pay its bills and other short-term financial obligations. We talk about two of them – the current ratio and the quick ratio.

Current ratio

The current ratio is the ability of a business to pay its current liabilities out of its current assets. In the following example, the 2.5 ratio says that the company has £2.5 in assets for every £1 in liabilities. In general, a ratio of 2 or better is judged to be good, and in fact, many banks require that their borrowers maintain a current ratio of 2 or higher as a condition of their loans. Here's an example of how the current ratio works:

Current ratio = Current assets ÷ Current liabilities

= £250 million ÷ £100 million

= 2.5

Quick ratio (acid test)

The quick ratio – also known as the acid test – is also a measure of a business's ability to pay its current liabilities out of its current assets. However, the quick ratio subtracts stock from current assets, providing an even more rigorous test of a firm's ability to pay its current liabilities quickly. Stock is often difficult to convert to cash because it may be obsolete, or simply not easily or quickly sold on. A ratio of 1.1 or higher is considered to be acceptable.

Quick ratio = (Current assets – stock) ÷ Current liabilities

= (£250 million – £20 million) ÷ £100 million

= 2.3

Activity ratios

Activity ratios are an indication of how efficient your company is at using its resources to generate income. The faster and more efficiently your firm can generate cash, the stronger it is financially, and the more attractive it is to investors and lenders.

Receivables turnover ratio

The receivables turnover ratio tells the average amount of time that your company takes to convert its receivables into cash. The ratio is a function of how quickly your company's customers and clients pay their bills and points out problems that your company may be having in the collections process. The higher the ratio, the better. Here's an example:

Receivables turnover ratio = Net sales ÷ Accounts receivable

= £100 million ÷ £15 million

= 6.67

Average collection period

You can get another very interesting piece of information by using your receivables turnover ratio. By dividing 365 days by the receivables turnover ratio, you find out the average number of days that your company takes to turn over its accounts receivable. This result is also known as the average collection period. In this case, the lower the number, the better, because that indicates that customers are paying their bills quickly.

Average collection period = 365 days ÷ Receivables turnover ratio

= 365 days ÷ 6.67

= 54.7 days

Stock turnover ratio

The stock turnover ratio provides an idea of how quickly stock is *turned over* (sold off and replaced with new stock) during a specific period of time. This information represents the ability of your firm to convert its stock into cash. The higher the number, the more often stock is turned over – a good thing. Figure 13-2 shows an example.

$$\text{Stock turnover ratio} = \frac{\text{Cost of goods sold}}{(\text{Beginning stock} + \text{Ending stock}) \div 2}$$

$$= \frac{£200 \text{ million}}{(£20 \text{ million} + £25 \text{ million}) \div 2}$$

$$= \frac{£200 \text{ million}}{£22.5 \text{ million}}$$

$$= 8.89$$

Figure 13-2:
A sample stock turnover ratio.

Debt ratios

For most organisations, going into debt is a normal part of doing business. Debt can plug the holes when cash flows can't cover all necessary operating expenses for short periods of time. Debt also allows companies that are growing quickly to finance their expansion. However, too much debt becomes a financial burden on any organisation. Debt ratios are a measure of how much debt a company is carrying and who is financing the debt.

Debt-to-equity ratio

The debt-to-equity ratio measures the extent to which a company is financed by outside creditors versus shareholders and owners. A high ratio (anything over 1) is considered bad because it indicates that a company may have difficulty paying back its creditors.

Debt-to-equity ratio = Total liabilities ÷ Share capital

= £100 million ÷ £150 million

= 0.66

Debt-to-assets ratio

The debt-to-assets ratio measures the percentage of a company's assets financed by outside creditors versus the percentage that is covered by the owners. Ratios of up to 0.5 are considered acceptable; anything more may be a sign of trouble. (Note, however, that most manufacturing firms have debt-to-asset ratios between 0.30 and 0.70.)

Debt-to-assets ratio = Long-term liabilities ÷ Total assets

= £50 million ÷ £500 million

= 0.1

Profitability ratios

Profitability ratios indicate the effectiveness of management in controlling expenses and earning a reasonable return for shareholders and owners.

Profit ratio

The profit ratio is a measure of how much profit your company generates for each pound of revenue after all costs of normal operations are accounted for. The reverse of this percentage represents the expenses incurred in generating this profit. For example, if there's a profit ratio of 15 per cent, then there's a cost of generating this profit of 85 per cent. In general, clearly the higher the profit ratio, the better. However, the expected ratio can vary considerably from industry to industry. For example, although greengrocers – who make money by turning over high volumes of stocks quickly – are generally satisfied with profit ratios of just a couple per cent, many software developers have profit ratios of 30 to 40 per cent or more. Here's how to calculate a company's profit ratio:

$$\text{Profit ratio} = \text{Net income} \div \text{Net Sales}$$

$$= \text{£}50 \text{ million} \div \text{£}100 \text{ million}$$

$$= 0.5$$

Gross margin

The gross margin is an indication of the profitability of a firm. To determine gross margin, you use your gross profit, which is what is left over after you subtract *cost of goods sold* (*COGS* is the direct costs of making a product) from revenues. Gross profit tells you how much you have left to pay overhead and make a net profit. In this example, the company's COGS is £25 million, which leaves £75 million (which is extraordinarily high) to pay overheads.

$$\text{Gross margin ratio} = \text{Gross profit} \div \text{Sales revenues}$$

$$= \text{£}75 \text{ million} \div \text{£}100 \text{ million}$$

$$= 0.75$$

Return on investment ratio

Return on investment – better known as ROI – is one of the keys of the world of financial tools. Return on investment measures the ability of a company to create profits for its owners. The ROI gives the percentage that represents the amount of pounds of net income earned per pound of invested capital. As such, this ratio is of great interest to investors, shareholders, and others with a financial stake in the company. Quite simply, people investing in your company want to know how much money they're making, whether or not this is satisfactory, and why.

$$\text{Return on investment ratio} = \text{Net income} \div \text{Share capital}$$

$$= \text{£}50 \text{ million} \div \text{£}150 \text{ million}$$

$$= 0.33$$

Return on assets ratio

The return on assets ratio – also known as ROA – measures earnings (before interest and tax) that a company earns from the total capital employed. In this sense, return on assets indicates the effectiveness of a company's utilisation of capital. A low ROA should cause managers to investigate whether a company is using its assets as effectively as possible; while a high ROA may mean that activities are fully effective, or it may mean that assets could be used to work harder elsewhere. Here's the way to calculate return on assets:

Return on assets ratio = Earnings before interest and tax ÷ Net operating assets

= £75 million ÷ £300 million

= 0.25

Reading an Annual Report

Without a doubt, annual reports are at the pinnacle of corporate communication. With their glowing, future-looking words, their evocative photographs, and their lovely, full-colour graphs, they can be very compelling reading. The point of the annual report is to provide a summary of exactly how a company has performed in the preceding year, and to provide a glimpse of the future. Building a compelling annual report is a real art and science, and more than a few consulting firms are doing very well, thank you, by hiring themselves out to create reports for all kinds of companies.

Annual reports are generally written for shareholders and other investors, although they're also required reading for lenders, banks, potential employees, and MBA students working their way through gruelling accounting and finance classes. Annual reports are produced and published by all public limited companies, and by public service authorities that are accountable to taxpayers. Many privately owned companies also publish their accounts, at least to their own staff and immediate or major backers. For most of the public, the annual report contains the only financial documents they're likely to see. The report, therefore, is the best source of information for most people to determine the financial health of a company and to learn of any potential problems or opportunities.

Reading an annual report can be a daunting prospect if you don't know exactly what you're looking for and where to find it. The final format of the annual report depends on the needs of a company, its industry, and any legal disclosure requirements. The good news, however, is that most reports are now standardised around a common model of nine key parts, making it easy to review any company's annual report when you get the hang of it.

An annual report contains a selection of the following nine parts:

✔ **Statement from the chair or chairperson:** The statement from the chairperson of the board is the traditional place for a company's top management team to tell you what a great job it did during the preceding year and to lay out the company's goals and strategies for the future. It's also a great place to find apologies for problems that occurred during the year, which may or may not have been solved.

- ✔ **Sales and marketing:** This section contains complete information about a company's products and services, as well as descriptions of its major divisions and groups and what they do. By reading this section, you can work out which products are most important to a company, and which divisions or groups are most critical to a company's success.

- ✔ **Ten-year summary of financial results:** Assuming that a company is at least ten years old, many annual reports contain a presentation of financial results over that period of time. This is a terrific place to look for trends in growth (or non-growth) of revenue and profit and other leading indicators of a company's financial success.

- ✔ **Management discussion and analysis:** This is the place where a company's management has the opportunity to present a candid discussion of significant financial trends within the company over the past couple of years.

- ✔ **Financial statements:** Financial statements are the bread and butter of the annual report. This is where a company presents its financial performance data for all to see. At the least, expect to see a profit and loss account, a balance sheet, and a cash flow statement. Be sure to watch for footnotes to the financial statements and read them carefully. You can often find valuable information about an organisation's structure and financial status that has not been publicised elsewhere in the report. For example, you may notice information on a management reorganisation or details on a bad debt that was written off by the company. Also look at the 'Notes to the accounts', which tells you how the accounts have been added up and calculated, and which elements have been placed where.

- ✔ **Subsidiaries, brands, and addresses:** Here you find listings of company locations – domestic and foreign – and contact information, as well as the company's brand names and product lines.

- ✔ **List of directors and officers:** Public companies are required to list the names of their directors and officers, and the nature and level of remuneration (such as salary and share options) that they've received.

- ✔ **Share price history:** This section gives a brief overview of recent share prices, dividends paid, shares and rights issues, and other matters to do with share management. This section also states the names of the stock exchanges on which the company's shares are listed.

- ✔ **Auditors' signatures:** To be considered reliable, true, and fair, a company's financial statements have to be signed off by the company auditors. Look especially at any caveats or qualifiers that the auditors have added to their statement.

Annual reports are the best tool that the public has to review the performance of companies. And most annual reports contain lots of useful information – information that you can analyse to get a sense of the near- and long-term health of the firm. The more often you read annual reports, the better you'll get at it.

So now that you have all this wealth of information, what should you do with it? Here are some definite must dos when reading an annual report:

✔ Review the company's financial statements and look for trends in profitability, growth, stability, and dividends. (Refer to the section 'Financial Tricks of the Trade' earlier in this chapter to check out the most common financial ratios.)

✔ Read the report thoroughly to pick out hints that the company is poised for explosive growth – or on the brink of disaster. Places to look closely for such hints include the statement from the chair, and the sales and marketing section of the annual report. Of course, keeping an eye on the company through the business press or analyst reports also pays off.

✔ Carefully read the auditors' statement to be sure that the firm agrees that the financial statements are an accurate portrayal of the company's financial position.

✔ Carefully read any footnotes to the financial statements. These footnotes often contain information about company assumptions that can be critical to a full understanding of the financial statements.

The seven deadly warning signs in an annual report

To the unwary, annual reports are concocted of marketing glitz, feel-good platitudes, and financial data presented to the best possible advantage.

You need to get past all the hype, and get to the meat of what's really being stated. As you read the report, stay on the look-out for the following warning signs:

1. **Turnover stagnant or falling:** Falling turnover can occur for a variety of reasons – changes in customer and client behaviour, entry of new competitors into the market, and so on. What you really want to know is what the company is going to do to address the problem. Look for precise proposals, and if you can't find any, the chances are that the company still does not see that they have a problem.

2. **Blaming external conditions:** All companies have to operate within the opportunities and constraints of their environment. It is also true that external trading conditions do become difficult in all sectors from time to time, and companies are perfectly within their rights to draw your attention to this. However, if the company has no direct and precise proposal to tackle the difficult trading conditions head-on, they have a serious problem. Companies that put the blame for poor performance on the external environment, with no suggestions for coping with the situation, normally continue their decline.

3. **Large bonus payments to directors and top managers in times of difficulty:** This detail is an almost sure-fire indicator that the company is in difficulty, and that directors

and top managers are insulating themselves against future losses. Anyone who has an interest in the future of the company needs to question the reasons for these bonus payments as closely as possible.

4. **Employee relations difficulties:** In the UK at present, the level of strikes and collective disputes is at an all-time low. With very few exceptions, it takes great ineptitude on the part of management, employees, and their representatives to become engaged in lengthy and protracted disputes. So examine closely the reasons for these disputes where they do occur, and again pay attention to the effectiveness of any actions that management are taking in order to resolve the issues.

5. **Declining profit margins:** Declining profit margins may be for understandable reasons – rising energy costs especially are a matter of present and enduring concern. It may be that the industry has had to restructure simply in order to retain existing levels of customers and clients. Again, examine the figures as closely as you can to see if any of these factors are true; or whether other expenses are rising.

6. **The precision of future plans:** The more precisely that the chair and other top managers lay out plans for the future, the greater the confidence you can have in the company. Additionally, the greater the clarity of these plans, the greater the capability to see in future whether or not they were fulfilled. If, on the other hand, the company is simply making bland statements about its future prospects, then be sure to question closely what it actually intends to do.

7. **Lack of correlation between the chair's statement, other statements, and the figures:** Overwhelmingly, this arises when the chair makes generally positive statements about the future, while the figures show all sorts of crises and difficulties! Of course, the chair and top management may know exactly what to do, but need to keep their plans a secret for commercial confidentiality! Otherwise, if in any doubt, concentrate on what the figures deliver, rather than on the written words.

Chapter 14

It Takes Money to Make Money

....

In This Chapter

▶ Finding out your company's financial needs

▶ Defining first-stage or start-up capital

▶ Discovering second-stage or expansion capital

....

*I*f you had to describe the financial and capital markets of the world in one word, that word would be 'chaotic'. Current and recent upheavals, driven by political turbulence and uncertainty, energy price fluctuations, and economic crises, have left everything in a constant state of flux. So the best way to approach any issue concerning business finance and the acquisition of resources is through a combination of the following opposites:

✔ Meticulous planning in terms of what you want and need the money for and where the returns on investment lie.

✔ Total irrationality and uncertainty, in that however sound your planning is, the resources may be turned down for any reason, including uncertainties and anxieties on the part of the proposed financier or backer.

If you're an entrepreneur, venturer, or the manager of an established organisation that may be thinking of expanding, bear the following points in mind:

✔ Just because something is a good idea, well thought out and meticulously planned, doesn't mean that it will attract the necessary funds and backing.

✔ Those who pull the financial strings and control capital resources are now much more determined to influence the terms and conditions under which finance is made available.

✔ Financial institutions and key backers are now much more strident in their insistence on a large volume of equity in start-ups, and preferential treatment in funding the expansion of existing businesses and organisations.

In this chapter, we look at the best ways in which to know, understand, and be effective in the management of finance and capital resources, whatever the state of the financial world at large.

Considering Financial Needs and Wants

In order to consider financial needs and wants in detail, you have to know the ways in which finances affect your organisation and its products, services, and markets. You have to be able to recognise and accept the constraints under which you have to deliver.

This section is principally to do with entrepreneurial finance, but managers everywhere can benefit from using the professional financial rigour required of all pioneers. There are several stages of financial need, as illustrated in Figure 14-1.

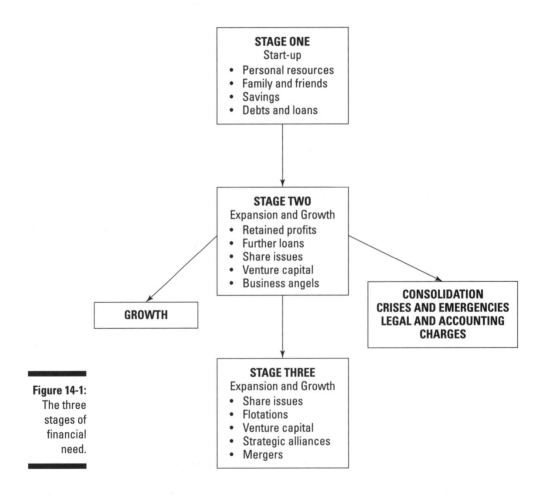

STAGE ONE
Start-up
- Personal resources
- Family and friends
- Savings
- Debts and loans

STAGE TWO
Expansion and Growth
- Retained profits
- Further loans
- Share issues
- Venture capital
- Business angels

GROWTH

**CONSOLIDATION
CRISES AND EMERGENCIES
LEGAL AND ACCOUNTING
CHARGES**

STAGE THREE
Expansion and Growth
- Share issues
- Flotations
- Venture capital
- Strategic alliances
- Mergers

Figure 14-1:
The three stages of financial need.

To begin to address any accurate and professional assessment of financial needs and wants, you have to be able to answer the following series of questions:

- ✔ How much money do you need? What for?
- ✔ Have you the calculations and forecasts to back up your demands for money?
- ✔ Do you need the money all at once, or do injections of cash need to be staggered?
- ✔ What is the benefit to the organisation of this investment?

After answering those questions, you now need to provide the following extra details:

- ✔ How much money do you *need* to make to cover the costs and charges incurred as the result of the investment?
- ✔ How much money do you *want* to make (and the answer: 'Well, obviously, as much as possible' won't do under any circumstances)?
- ✔ How much money do you think your company will make, by when, and how?
- ✔ What can possibly go wrong? (Make sure you fully debate what can go wrong – where things do go wrong, it usually hasn't been debated!)

Now you can present projections of best, medium, and worst outcomes for any venture. Make sure that you do each in full detail, so that everyone knows at the outset what they're letting themselves in for.

Taking financial restraints into account

You may be constrained from doing things your way as an expert manager and MBA by forces outside your control. Your superiors or backers may demand that you follow a particular course of action, whether or not you yourself would have chosen it. They may demand that you sell assets in order to strengthen the balance sheet. Or they may have their own priorities, in which case you may get fewer resources but still have to make your own venture work. Or you may have to take actions that will find favour with the stock market in order to increase the share price and company value.

Whatever the pressures, you have to be able to operate within them. And you need to know at the outset whether any resource constraints or pressures from elsewhere may have the following consequences:

- ✔ If you try to tackle everything, will this lead to everything being done, but not satisfactorily?

- ✔ If you try to tackle only those things that can be done properly, will there be consequences as the result of those things that you don't tackle at all?

Managing corporate capital resources

Managing corporate resources is simple isn't it – you simply do as you're told! We're afraid not. In today's business world, MBAs and managers are responsible for seeing that scarce resources are used wisely and well, and to greatest effect. The days of throwing money at problems haven't actually gone, but with capital project and investment failures and scandals in so many diverse activities and areas, the corporate and managerial world is taking a much more active responsibility in this area.

The following are examples of how things can go wrong if resources are poorly managed:

- ✔ Lack of financial controls on the Channel Tunnel led to sloppy attention to scheduling of work, and resulted in the large debt that the operating company now faces.

- ✔ Problems with the software costs and charges at the (now defunct) Child Support Agency weren't identified and tackled in a timely manner, leaving a £450 million bill for a system which never did the job for which it was intended.

And while these are well-known examples, their equivalent exists in many companies and organisations in all sectors. So you need to grasp financial discipline and apply it as a key part of managerial and MBA expertise. After all, you don't want to be the next high-profile company resignation, or the next senior civil servant hauled up to explain yourself before the public accounts committee, do you?

Stage One: Start-Up Finance

When it comes to finding money for a start-up venture, you're essentially relying entirely on what you can raise from family and friends, any savings that you may have, and any re-mortgage finance that you may be able to raise against the value of your home. You may also decide that you need a loan (which we cover in the next section).

Before you consider acquiring start-up money, you need the following:

- ✔ A detailed description of your idea, product, or service, with prototypes or mock-ups if at all possible showing that it can be commercialised.

- ✔ Sales forecasts based on detailed market research.

- ✔ A precise definition of the market or markets to be served (and 'anyone and everyone' won't do!).

- ✔ Financial forecasts including a cash flow forecast, as well as profit and turnover projections.

You then need to structure all this into a short but comprehensive and precise presentation to deliver to potential backers.

An added benefit of creating a strong presentation is to make sure that you've thought the idea through fully, and that it really does stand up to detailed scrutiny. It doesn't matter if you're trying to convince family and friends (who know and love you), or bank managers, financial advisors, and financiers (who probably don't know and love you) to back you. Ultimately they all want to know the same things – how safe is my money; how are you going to use my money; and when can I have it back?

Given the present state of the financial and capital markets, and the attitudes of those who control and allocate resources, you *have* to be able to prove your case in advance of seeking any short-, medium-, or long-term backing. This is because:

- ✔ New ventures don't have a track record, so that everything that investors and lenders see in the figures is pure speculation.

- ✔ New ventures often fail; indeed, in the UK, 90 per cent of all new ventures fail within two years of start-up.

Dragon's Den (1)

If you want inspiration in how to – and especially how not to – present a clear and concise business plan, watch the television programme *Dragon's Den* (BBC2).

The series (which allows budding entrepreneurs to pitch their business ideas to successful business people for backing) has been running for several years. Yet, the fundamental issues remain the same – all that the *dragons* (the potential backers) want to know is:

- ✔ The idea

- ✔ The size and scale of the markets

- ✔ Projected turnover volumes and potential profit margins

It is quite legitimate that the dragons ask in full detail what they're letting themselves in for – and if you don't have the detail to hand, you simply demonstrate that you yourself don't know. And if you don't know, you can't expect backing!

✔ Most new ventures have no specific selling points such as real invention, intellectual property rights, or other specifics that would give them a head-start in the marketplace.

✔ Many entrepreneurs and pioneers often don't have a track record of successful ventures in the past.

Debts, loans, and overdrafts

If you're serious about your venture, you're going to need the support of your bank manager or financial advisor. Shop around for a good one and stick to them like a limpet. In your meetings with bank managers and financial advisors, be open and honest with them. State what you want from them, and why. Give them figures in full detail; give them timescales and projections for when they can expect to see the loan or overdraft paid off. And make sure that you establish where their concerns lie – you are, after all, using their resources for your purposes, and they're entitled to know when you're going to start producing results.

You can go to a specialist loan company, or even load up on your credit card to get funds for a start-up venture. This form of debt is very easy to acquire but it's also very expensive in terms of repayments, fees, and interest charges. If you decide to go down this route, know exactly what you're letting yourself in for. And if you have any choice in the matter – avoid it!

It really does take money to make money

The main costs associated with raising capital at Stage Two are:

✔ The interest rate, including any in-built variations

✔ Returns on investment demanded by investors

✔ Costs of seeking capital

✔ Other fees and charges, especially accountants' and legal fees

The balance of these costs varies between ventures. However, you have to be prepared to face them all; and even if you're willing to do much of the hard work associated with raising money, those whom you approach may expect things to be done through legal or accountancy channels.

The total cost of raising capital at this stage can reach as much as 25 per cent of the total amount of money you seek. We suggest that you in-build this figure into any future projections for investment, turnover, growth, and revenues. Some companies even deliberately add a proportion that they quite openly and legitimately set aside for this purpose. Facing such a bill before any investment is made can be off-putting to potential investors. However – it all has to be paid for! Whatever your approach, make sure that you have include the 25 per cent figure in your calculations.

Stage Two: Financing Growth and Expansion

Financing growth or expansion is generally used to take the business into new markets, products, or services. To grow effectively at this stage, most businesses have to seek some form of expansion capital. In this section, we look at different ways to raise that capital.

Retained profits

Consider retained profits as one of your major sources of investment finance. It is both legitimate and tempting to pay yourself now for the fruits of your (hopefully!) highly successful and effective labours. However, if and when you do need finance for expansion and development, your ability to prove that you've been wise enough to plough back a proportion of what you've earned independently, always goes down well with potential backers.

Share capital

If you sell shares in your company, you're asking people to invest in the company in exchange for a part ownership. You sell shares when you're willing to give up part of the ownership and control in return for the resources that give you the opportunity to develop and implement your ideas, products, and services. You have to strike your own balance as follows:

✔ How much ownership are you willing to give up?

✔ What is the share capital going to deliver that your own resources can't deliver?

✔ How much of a stake in the company are you going to offer shareholders in return for their investment?

✔ What are you going to pay out in dividends; when; and under what circumstances?

Weighing up loans and shares

To raise money to grow and expand, you can seek share capital or use debt financing. Neither one is best – it varies in all cases. Before making a decision, bear in mind your obligations – how easy it will be to meet your obligations to shareholders; or how easy it will be to make repayments to the bank.

Dragon's Den (2)

The *dragons* – the potential backers – in the television series have often been interested in ideas, but have baulked at the relatively small percentage of ownership on offer, in return for relatively high levels of investment.

You need to be realistic about the amount of control that shareholders are going to want if they're to invest in your business. Look at the situation from their point of view by placing yourself in their shoes – if you were going to be asked to invest a certain amount in your own business, how much control would you expect? The most common lesson from the *Dragon's Den* seems to be that entrepreneurs and pioneers over-value their company's ideas, products, and services by a factor of about 2. So if you're offering a 10 per cent stake in the company in return for a particular investment, you need to be thinking of eventually agreeing to a 20 per cent stake.

You also need to bear in mind the risk to yourself. If you go for debt finance, are you willing to risk your home in return for the ability to pursue your own ideas as you see fit, unhindered by shareholders' demands? The answer will quite legitimately be 'yes' in some cases, and 'no' in others.

Your own preferences

You have to make the choice based on a combination of your own personal preferences, combined with a cold evaluation of what's right for the business. You can also use the sale of shares as the opportunity to acquire and use the shareholder's own expertise; and while this means that the venture is no longer your own 'baby', your action may greatly benefit the business as a whole.

Your shareholders' preferences

In practice, nobody is going to buy share capital in your company at the outset unless they like your ideas, products, and services – and unless they like, trust, and respect you, and have confidence in you as the driver of the venture. In most cases, they seek to bring their own expertise to bear whenever it is of value to the business. Otherwise, shareholders are entitled to expect dividend payments, influence (if not control) over the future direction of the business – and they expect the shares themselves to rise in value in future!

Selling shares to the public

You can sell shares in your company to the public privately or through stockbrokers on a stock exchange. Shares are given a face value (usually low, either 1p, 10p, 50p, or – at most – £1). However, you then sell them for what you can get for them; and with attractive and high-profile stock market flotations, what you actually get for your shares can be very high indeed.

Opting for venture capital

Venture capitalists exist to provide finance and capital resources for start-ups, business expansion, mergers, take-overs, and acquisitions. Their job is to evaluate business plans and proposals. With the business plans that they like and have confidence in, venture capitalists put in the finance and may introduce a measure of control and influence over the future direction of the company and its activities. Venture capitalists often insist on bringing their own people into key management positions. Some venture capitalists can, and do, insist on appointing their own CEO – which can mean that you're out of a job, or at least out of your present job!

What do venture capitalists look for?

The venture capitalist's concern and priority is to move the business along as fast as possible. The venture capitalist has bought into the business because they can see the potential in the products and services on offer, and now wants to maximise and optimise their return on investment as quickly as the business, products, services, and markets served will allow. In particular, the venture capitalist looks very hard at the growth and development aspects of the business, because this is where their value is created. Venture capitalists won't normally take any interest in a steady business or one that has grown already to its full potential. Venture capitalists may also seek to cut costs. Most venture capitalists have their own cost and overhead regime that they'll probably introduce when they assume influence and/or control.

Flotation

Flotation, or selling shares, whether on the stock market or privately, is a serious business. You need to prepare a *prospectus*, which is a legal document setting out the value of the company, the number of shares to be sold, and what is to happen to the money once it has been raised.

You have to prepare all this information several months in advance of the actual flotation or sale of shares. You incur legal fees and accountants' and auditors' costs, and these have to be paid in advance.

Also – most important of all – you have to be aware that market conditions can, and do, change very rapidly. A flotation that was mooted during advantageous trading conditions may have difficulties when the great day for flotation finally arrives, because other events have occurred since – interest rate rises, stock market downturns, corporate scandals, or political upheaval.

Be realistic about what you're going to achieve. Have best, medium, and worst outcome projections when you're considering shares, issues, and stock market flotations. Take a fully informed view of the worst possible outcome, and what this will mean for the present and future of your business.

What happens when you find a venture capitalist?

If you do go down the venture capital route to expansion, assume the following:

- ✔ You've considered all the alternatives and have chosen this one above all the other choices.
- ✔ You know what you're letting yourself in for, and so won't be shocked by any demands that a venture capitalist may make in terms of influence and control.
- ✔ You have a fully detailed and costed business plan.

 As well as your short presentation about your business (see the section 'Stage One: Start-Up Finance'), now fully updated as the result of your present successes, have a one-page synopsis available. That way, a venture capitalist can see what your business is and why you're now asking for money – at that point, the venture capitalist is either interested or not. If they're interested, then give the rest of your presentation. If the venture capitalist is interested, bear in mind that they will want everything set out in a contractual form – and this means engaging lawyers and accountants for the purpose, so make sure that you have included this fee in your projections.

Flying with business angels

Business angels are private investors who put money into new ventures, growing firms, and new products and services. The difference between business angels and venture capitalists is that the business angel normally treats each case presented to them on its own merits, rather than seeking to apply the standard venture capitalist formula of control, direction, and growth. People who work with business angels normally (but not always) retain overall control of the business, though the business angel will certainly want some influence. But in treating each case on its own merits, an angel is more likely to support an optimum and longer-term growth rate that is appropriate to the business itself, rather than operating to fixed minimum assured percentages.

 If you do go down the business angel route, you're effectively seeking private investors who are going to take an active interest in you and your company. You need to have the confidence that you can work with your angel, talk over problems and opportunities as they become apparent, and ask them for advice and support whenever necessary. As well as the money, you're seeking support and involvement on an individual and personal level, as well as in the interests of the business.

Stage Three: Locating Other Ways to Raise Capital

You can use ways other than debt and equity to raise capital or find the resources necessary to grow the business. Stage Three of financial need is yet more growth and expansion, and may additionally involve some consolidation. So share issues and flotations also come into Stage Three.

At this stage, you also need to consider the possibilities of mergers and strategic alliances, which we cover in this section.

Mergers: Can we all just get along?

One way that entrepreneurs manage to grow their companies is by merging with a larger company or one that has compatible products or services. A merger is similar to a sale, but it's also very much like a partnership. You really need to know the other company well, because, like a marriage, you're hoping that it will last a long time. Here are some other factors to consider before joining forces permanently with another company:

✔ Make sure that the culture of the other company is compatible with yours; otherwise, everyone will have trouble working together. Here's an example. Suppose that you've encouraged a very casual culture in your organisation, where people don't clock in at a certain time but, instead, are responsible for certain tasks and projects. Now suppose that the company with which you're merging has a very traditional culture based on a hierarchical style of management and everyone arrives at 8 a.m. and leaves at 5 p.m. Merging the two cultures is going to be very difficult.

✔ The two companies need to be complementary in what they do, so that joining them produces *synergy* (that is, that the whole is greater than the sum of the parts).

✔ The two companies benefit from being geographically close. If not, the two companies need to be able to make immediate contact whenever required. And however close or distant your geographical proximity, you need to have the mechanisms for meeting whenever crises and emergencies occur.

✔ Make sure that the company you want to merge with is successful and growing in its industry.

✔ Check the company's financial statements to make sure that it's in a healthy position. Ask whether the company has audited tax returns and a business plan. Check to see what the company's bankers think of the business.

✔ Interview the company's customers and suppliers.

A merger is forever (technically), so be sure that the acquisition will give you the strength and resources you need to grow your company.

Strategic alliances

Very simply put, a strategic alliance is a partnership between two or more businesses. A strategic alliance is an excellent way to share core competencies and reduce the costs of research and development, marketing, and raw materials. Strategic partners invest time, money, and expertise in your company – they're really stakeholders. Strategic alliances have helped many a company to grow without having to raise costly outside capital and without giving up any equity in the company.

To be successful, a strategic alliance should be a win-win situation for both companies. To make sure that you create an effective alliance, heed the following advice and find a partner that:

✔ Is financially healthy with, or without, your company.

✔ Deals with other companies to find strength in diversification.

✔ Has experience doing strategic alliances. Just like a sophisticated investor, such a partner understands the risks and knows better how to make the partnership work.

✔ If possible, find a company that has excess capacity, so that you don't have to expend extra capital in plant and equipment.

Joint ventures

Another way to raise finance and resources, or at least to spread the load, is to engage in joint ventures with particular partners. Successful joint ventures are founded on the same principles as mergers and strategic alliances. Again, the key priorities are to make sure that your culture is compatible with that of the partner; you have mutual personal, professional, and occupational respect and understanding; and the finances of both your company and your joint venture partners are strong enough to sustain the venture through to fruition.

The additional benefit is that engaging in a joint venture gives you entry into new markets, areas, locations, and activities without bearing the full risk. While you're working on the joint venture, evaluate the particular activities or locations for future possibilities. Whether or not the joint venture is going to lead to other activities in the particular location, then you've been able to take advantage of finding out about these without incurring full research costs.

Chapter 15

Understanding Stocks and Shares

. . . .

In This Chapter

▶ Understanding the context in which stocks and shares are traded

▶ Setting objectives for buying and selling stocks and shares

▶ Watching share prices rise and fall

. . . .

*S*tocks and shares are portions of companies purchased by people invest-ing in them. Buying and selling stocks and shares is the usual way of rais-ing the substantial sums of capital finance needed for business expansion, and the acquisition of new assets and equipment.

Entrepreneurs, business managers, and MBAs need to know enough about stocks and shares, and how stock markets work, because:

✔ If you're an entrepreneur, you need to know and understand how stock markets work and how potential investors will approach your shares with a view to buying.

✔ If you're a corporate or business manager, you need to know and under-stand the opportunities and consequences of selling shares in your company.

In this chapter, we cover the environmental issues and constraints that affect the ways in which stocks and shares are traded, the reasons why people invest, and why they withdraw their investments and move their funds around. We start by looking at those things that can, and do, affect the stock markets themselves, and the attitudes of those who work in them.

Being Careful

As is the case with all aspects of business and management, before making any important decisions, always ask yourself the key question: What can pos-sibly go wrong? The stock market begins to rise, people – small private investors, as well as professionals and corporations – put their cash into shares and they watch the market and their investment rise and rise. The value of their shares grows to 3, 4, 6 or even 10 times the initial investment. And then there's a crash. The professional and corporate investors take a hit, and the private investor loses the lot.

The Financial Services' Authority (FSA) requires that all firms operating under its remit notify their customers that: 'The value of investments can go down as well as up. You may not get back the full value of your payments in.' In other words: 'Don't bet what you cannot afford to lose.' This advice applies equally to all stocks and shares.

Stock market *crashes* (when there's a collective loss of confidence on the part of all those who work on a particular stock market, causing mass selling of stocks and shares at sharply falling prices) can be caused by anything. One crash on the Tokyo stock exchange was caused by a broker accidentally hitting the 'sell' rather than the 'buy' key on his computer. At present, be aware that fluctuating interest and currency exchange rates; the price of essential commodities such as oil; and political and economic volatility all affect investor confidence. Investor confidence (or lack of it) is what causes investors to place investments in shares (or not) in the first place.

If you do have a large portion of your own resources tied up in the markets, or else are seeking resources in the markets, know and understand what can possibly go wrong as the result of stock market crashes, and the consequences and effects on your business or organisation.

Understanding Shares

If you sell shares in your company, you forego a part of the ownership and control of the business, and you also give up your right to the profits and *dividends* (the cash return per share to which shareholders are entitled) for that proportion of the company which you have sold off. This share of the company now becomes the right of the shareholders as their reward for the risks that they've taken in investing in you.

Normally, the liability of shareholders – what they must pay up in the event of business collapse – is limited to the face value of the shares. However, if the shareholder bought the shares at above face value, they'll normally lose the whole of their original investment.

Types of shares

Essentially the three types of shares are ordinary shares; preference shares; and debentures.

Ordinary shares

Ordinary shares are exactly that – ordinary! Each share represents the proportion of ownership held by the shareholder in the business, relative to its full capital value. Dividends are paid out in the form of dividends per share. Shareholders therefore receive a return on their investment in direct proportion to the amount of money that they've put into the business.

Preference shares

Preference shares are also exactly what they say! Preference shares are sold on the basis that they attract preferential rights. In particular, preference shares may give a guaranteed dividend, either as a percentage, or as an absolute figure per share held. In return for this preferential treatment, however, preference shareholders don't normally exert influence or have any control over the business.

Debentures

Debentures are fixed-term, fixed-value loans issued in the form of share certificates. Debentures normally carry a fixed rate of return. Again, because a guarantee is attached to them, debenture holders don't normally exert control or influence over the business. Shareholders may be individuals, groups, or business entities. Companies, corporations, and (especially) pension funds hold large blocks of debentures in organisations as part of their overall investment strategies and policies.

Rights' issues

Shareholders and their representatives may be asked to approve rights' issues. *Rights' issues* are the sale of new shares to existing shareholders – asking for them to put more money into the company or organisation in which they're already investing. You may seek rights' issues because your company is in good shape and now needs a cash injection for further expansion, or because your company is in trouble and needs a cash injection to stave off a crisis. Shares issued under rights' issue conditions often carry preferential conditions, including guaranteed rates of return.

Investing in Shares

If you or your company is selling shares to the public, the public need to understand what they're getting in return. You therefore have to be clear in your own mind about the precise purpose of the investment for which you're asking, and may even have to do a bit of research.

When The Body Shop first floated on the stock exchange, the stockbroking industry was initially alarmed that much of the capital raised was to be used on environmental projects, and on securing supplies from the developing world at Western prices. So Gordon and Anita Roddick, the company's founders, had to spend a great deal of time and effort explaining their different approach, relating these differences to organisational sustainability, and gaining support for a very different attitude to organisation growth, sustainability, and profitability.

Make sure that you can complete the following statement clearly and accurately:

> 'The purpose of investing in this company is . . .'

By completing the statement, everyone then knows and understands where they stand. You become immediately attractive to investors whose objectives match your own; and you don't waste the time of people whose objectives don't match your own.

In general, investors with funds to place are looking for one of the following:

- ✔ Bargains
- ✔ Growth
- ✔ Dividends
- ✔ Companies they like

Bargains

Especially at *flotation* (that is, when you first offer shares in the company for sale on a regulated stock market), some organisations have their shares under-priced to ensure that all the shares sell, and to provide an instant return to investors in the form of immediate sell-on capability. Otherwise, you can find bargains in steadily performing, sound, and unspectacular organisations. If you're a steady and sound organisation, emphasise these aspects when asking your brokers to secure additional sales, and when asking your present shareholders for additional funds through rights' issues.

GEC Marconi

When Arnold Weinstock left technology giant GEC Marconi, he'd been CEO for over 20 years. During that period, he kept everything concentrated on the sale of products and services, and when he departed, he left a cash reserve of £2.5 billion. The share value was £3.

Weinstock was replaced by a new chairman, George Simpson, and a new management team was installed. The new management team stated that the shares were grossly under-valued, and that they should be up to £15 per share.

The new management team began a programme of expansion through acquisition. The stock market became very excited and enthusiastic. Staff were encouraged to buy shares in their own company. The share value rose from £3 to £12 over the next 18 months.

At the end of this burst of acquisitions, the stock market then looked for consolidation – and for business performance in terms of turnover, sales volumes, and profits.

However, it became clear that the company had heavily overpaid for many of its acquisitions, and that the business volumes were not going to be delivered. The share price started to fall and stockbrokers and financial analysts looked harder at the business potential of all of the acquisitions. They found little or no business potential. The company collapsed. Shares that had traded weeks earlier at £11 or £12 now fell to 10 pence. The cash reserve left behind by Arnold Weinstock was gone. Additionally, by pursuing the programme of acquisitions, the company had neglected its core business – high technology radar and defence systems and equipment.

Remember: Firstly, if you concentrate on the share price to the exclusion of everything else, the business invariably suffers. Secondly, if you concentrate only on growth and acquisition, the core business will suffer. Thirdly, if you grow share values by large amounts, then you have to be able to sustain them through business consolidation and output. Fourthly – and probably most important of all – remember that anything that can go up, can also come back down again.

Going for growth

If you're offering shares on the basis of the growth potential available to investors, make sure that you can deliver, and make sure that you can sustain, that growth. Of course, blips will occur in share values, some caused by movements in the stock markets in general. However, if you offer shares on the basis of growth, this growth is ultimately sustained by the soundness and strength of your business overall, and the volume of products and services you produce and sell.

Dividends

Dividends are the legitimate and expected returns on investment in which a proportion of the company's profits are returned to shareholders in the form of an income per share held.

As long as the company delivers levels of profits that allow for attractive dividends to be paid, all is well. However, if the fundamental attractiveness of your share is the dividend paid, then you have to be able to sustain this during adverse trading conditions. If adverse trading conditions happen you have the following choices:

- ✔ Don't pay a dividend this time, and explain in detail why you're not doing so to all of your shareholders.
- ✔ Pay the dividend in full this time, and explain why this may not be possible next time.
- ✔ Pay the dividend in stages, for example half now and half in six months' time.

In exceptionally poor trading conditions, some organisations (especially large organisations) continue to pay dividends out of capital resources. The purpose of doing so is to continue to deliver what the shareholders expect, and also to try to secure their loyalty over the difficult times. But you have to have clear proposals about how you're going to survive the bad conditions – otherwise the shareholders will take the dividend and run.

Companies you like

People often invest in companies they like, as well as seeking returns on investment. People invest in football clubs because they support them; in travel companies because shareholders get cheap tickets; civil engineering because they want to be associated with 'building the world'. If people invest in you because they like you, make sure that you manage their perceptions and that they continue to like you! Keep the confidence of your shareholders, reward them when you can in the ways that they expect, and keep them notified about any changes in the company or the sector that may happen.

People invest for a variety of reasons, and have to accept the consequences as well as the opportunities of putting their money into particular ventures. So if people are investing in you because they like you, they're taking the returns that are on offer from you. If investors wish to invest in civil engineering, it means that they're prepared to take the returns on offer from civil engineering. If people want a 35 per cent return on investment per annum, they have to invest in sectors where a 35 per cent return on investment per annum is on offer.

When Share Prices Rise . . .

Everyone likes to see share prices rise. This situation means that everyone's happy. Investors are seeing a return on investment. Financial analysts have confidence in companies. Share volumes traded on stock markets are steady and assured. Share prices rise for many reasons, including:

✔ Companies have excellent trading volumes.

✔ Turnover and profits are growing in line with forecasts, or exceeding forecasts.

✔ Top and senior management have proposed and implemented a clear strategy, which is bringing all the anticipated benefits.

All good and sound so far. However, the following reasons also very often produce at least an initial share price rise:

✔ **Cost-cutting measures including sales of assets, and withdrawals of some of the less profitable product and service lines.** From a managerial point of view, these measures often bring about a conflict – that in return for the rise in the share price, the organisation goes through a period of internal turbulence and upheaval that may, or may not, produce the desired efficiencies over the longer term.

✔ **Reducing payroll as a percentage of capital employed.** This action is certain to mean either redundancies and lay-offs, or the outsourcing and subcontracting of particular activities and functions to other organisations. Again, a potential conflict exists between managing the share price and managing the business.

✔ **Employing top brand consultants to restructure the business.** Stock markets and financial analysts like to see top brand consultants (such as the prestigious management consulting firm McKinsey) employed by companies and organisations, because they perceive that restructuring will result in job losses, cost cutting, and greater efficiency.

✔ **Going into new markets, activities, operations, and locations.** Often described as 'exciting new ventures', the paradox is often that share prices rise because the company is going into something new, rather than sticking to what it is good at.

✔ **Being involved in merger, acquisition, and take-over activities.** Doing so results in rises in the share prices of under-performing or failing companies, especially if their products and services are sound but are simply being badly led and managed at present. More generally, in merger and acquisition activity, shareholders assume that the merged companies will achieve economies of scale and sales of duplicated assets, leading to windfall profits and returns.

- ✔ **Following fashion and fad.** If you can secure a fashionable or high-profile angle for a share flotation, you may gain additional interest. However, investors are more wary of becoming involved in high-profile companies and share flotations because of their experiences during the dot.com boom of the 1990s – in which most people lost everything.

- ✔ **Appointing a high-profile chairperson or CEO.** Shares rise when such a person arrives with the full confidence of the stock market, or when they bring with them an impressive track record from their previous job.

Share prices tend to rise on *rumours* of the preceding list of events, as well as the reality. If you start a rumour, you may have to sustain it in reality because of the commentary and speculation that you may receive as the result – so watch it!

Much of share price rising and falling is irrational and behavioural – and above all, subjective. What stock markets and financial analysts like to see has to be made to work in practice; and this is entirely dependent upon the quality, expertise, and commitment of the leadership and management of the particular company or organisation.

. . . And Fall

Just as share prices rise for a variety of reasons, share prices fall for different reasons, too. The main reason for share prices to fall is because of the declining performance of a company (at least until it becomes a take-over target). The other main reasons for share price falls are:

- ✔ **Loss of confidence in top management.** This happens when, for whatever reason, the stock market and financial analysts lose confidence in the ability of company top management to continue to deliver results and performance. This may be caused by something as simple as personal dislike, right the way through to being uncertain about future plans and proposals for the company, and its products, services, and performance.

- ✔ **Lack of certainty over succession.** This occurs when a powerful, dominant, or expert chairperson or CEO has been in the post for many years. Uncertainty is sure to be a key concern when, for example, Michael O'Leary leaves Ryanair, and Richard Branson leaves Virgin.

- ✔ **A quick succession of CEOs.** This often happens after a powerful or expert CEO has left. The company shareholders and their representatives appoint a new person, who then does not quite deliver what was expected, and so is replaced, and the same thing happens again. The continued uncertainty that this scenario brings accelerates the wider loss of confidence further still.

✔ **Change of direction.** Share prices can fall when the realities of 'exciting new ventures' kick in. The excitement must be paid for through the delivery of products and services in the reality of the new markets and locations – or overall performance will decline.

✔ **Lengthy employee relations disputes.** In the UK at present, lengthy strikes and disputes are rare. When a strike does occur, shareholders' representatives want to know immediately what top management is going to do to resolve it.

✔ **Restructuring costs.** Restructuring and cost-cutting initiatives are one reason why share prices rise! But then the reality kicks in. The company doesn't quite achieve the projected cost cuts, or doesn't achieve them as quickly as expected, or perhaps has to make additional charges for the turbulence and upheaval caused. The stock market gets wind of this, and having supported the cost-cutting initiative, it now withdraws its support when the company does exactly what it said it was going to do!

Many of the reasons for share prices to fall are based on business performance, and the continued confidence in top management. Shareholders need to have concerns like the ones in the preceding list addressed. And if you can't (or won't) address these concerns, then performance declines and loss of confidence will accelerate faster still because shareholders will conclude that you're complacent, negligent, or incompetent in relation to managing your organisation in difficult times and conditions.

Strong and steady: Tesco

In recent years, Tesco, the supermarket giant, has accrued regular profits, turnover, and market share every quarter. At present, the company commands something over 30 per cent of the supermarket sector, and behind the French company Carrefour, it is the largest company in the supermarket sector in the European Union. Tesco is undertaking planned expansion in Poland, Hungary, and elsewhere in Eastern Europe, and the Far East; and it has plans to begin operations in the US.

The share price, however, remains relatively stable. Dividend levels are more or less assured and this, together with the fact that the shares hold their value, is attractive to investors.

The stock market at large, appears to be unimpressed with the fact that, each time Tesco announces record profits and expansion plans, it also announces the creation of several thousand new jobs. This is because Tesco has set its priority on managing the business and delivering excellent customer service (which requires intensive staffing), rather than managing the share price (which requires staff cuts).

Getting expert help

You incur corporate costs as the result of offering shares for sale simply by being in business and structuring the organisation in that particular way. Your company needs its own brokers, auditors, and corporate lawyers to call when required. Companies also need to manage their own *shareholders' register* (which does exactly what it says on the tin) to ensure that it is accurate at all times, either by internal experts or by specialist providers if you don't want the expense of a shareholder services department or function in-house.

Expert help of this kind should provide you with up-to-the-minute reports on any material fluctuations in your share price (and the real or apparent reasons for the fluctuation), and any potential take-over bids that you may face.

If managed properly, outside expert help can provide excellent advice on the appointment of directors and top managers, potential acquisition targets for yourself, managing shareholder loyalty, and the balance required by shareholders in terms of re-investing retained profits in the business, and paying out dividends.

Considering Other Aspects of Corporate Finance

Corporate finance and the sale, purchase, and management of stocks and shares takes place in the same world as stocks and shares and is subject to exactly the same pressures. You need to know the effects of such things as the retail prices index, interest rates, and exchange rates on the fundamental financial strength of your organisation as a whole, and its capability to raise funds when required. We cover those topics in the following sections.

Retail prices index

The *retail prices index* (RPI) is a reflection of both the movement of retail prices, and of an economy's inflation rate. You find the RPI in any of the business pages or Web sites of the *Financial Times*, *The Times*, *The Daily Telegraph*, or *The Economist*. You need to keep an eye on the RPI because it affects decisions concerning interest rates and currency exchange rates, as well as the buying habits of customers and clients. Interest rates and consumer buying habits in turn affect the wider confidence of the financial markets, and the willingness, as well as the ability, to make funds available for investment.

Of particular importance are those prices that affect the ability of companies and organisations to do business using their existing cost base, such as changes in prices of fuel, oil, gas, electricity, water, transport, and distribution. These prices affect everyone, so they're certain to put pressures on your suppliers and distributors too. All the time that you pay money out on these essential commodities, it affects both the ability of investors to invest, and wider confidence.

Interest rates

Interest rates are the rates established at which banks and other finance houses lend money to those who need or want it. In the UK, interest rates are set by the Bank of England, and these are reflected in the interest and other charges made by retail and merchant banks and other financial institutions. Interest rate changes can, and do, affect your ability to raise finance because rises in interest rates:

✔ Reduce the amount of money available for investment elsewhere.

✔ May mean that you incur additional charges several months or years into the future if those who lend you money insist on long-term contracts with you, or if you accept a lower rate of interest for the early period of the loan, and then have to make good the repayments on the rest of the loan at higher rates.

✔ May affect your customers' ability to buy from you, or the prices that suppliers may have to charge you.

Currency exchange rates

Currency exchange rates are very important if any part of your operation is dependent on something from overseas. Currency exchange rates additionally affect key commodities such as oil (priced in US dollars), gas (priced whole-sale in euros, Swiss francs, and US dollars), and electricity (priced wholesale in euros).

Hedging

Hedging means buying key commodities at assured prices, agreed with suppliers, for periods many months or years in advance. You can hedge against the price of oil, gas, electricity, telecommunications, and currency.

Hedging is attractive because it gives you the opportunity to buy at fixed and assured prices when these are otherwise rising. On the other hand, hedging normally means tying up large volumes of capital immediately, and of course, you'll lose if the prices of the particular commodities come down. Also, remember that all the time that money is tied up in paying up front for commodities (however essential these may be), you lose the use of that money for the period of time. So you really do have a complex decision to make.

Part IV
Marketing in the New World

In this part . . .

In this part, we help you find out how to understand your customers' needs, and we show you how to provide world-class customer service. We discuss the best approaches to developing a marketing plan, and we take an in-depth look at advertising and promotion. To conclude, we present various sales methods and techniques.

Chapter 16

You're Nothing Without a Customer

In This Chapter

▶ Understanding your customers' needs

▶ Getting acquainted with your customers

▶ How to keep your best customers

▶ Taking care of dissatisfied customers

*W*e're amazed at how often owners get so wrapped up in the day-to-day operations of their businesses that they stray far afield from the one thing that will ensure their success – the customer. Businesspeople often become so focused on trying to find the best products, setting up employee incentive programmes, paying bills, and finding new ways to market their business that they forget about the customer. But without customers, you have no business. The customer is the beginning, middle, and end of a business. Yet, too many CEOs and MDs assume they know what the customer wants, so they never bother to ask. They think that they're providing customer service, but what is customer service if you don't know what the customer wants?

Here's a quiz to start this chapter. Answer the following questions as honestly as you can without spending any time on them.

✔ Who is the most important person in your business?

✔ Who pays your employees?

✔ Who designs your products and services?

✔ Who determines when it's time to grow the company to the next level?

If you haven't guessed by now, the answer to each of these questions is *the customer*. In this chapter, you find out why the customer is all important. You also discover some ways to build long-term customer relationships that will greatly increase your business's potential for long-term success.

Understanding Your Customers' Needs

In order to understand your customers' needs, you first have to understand the types of customers that you're serving. You can break customers down into types as follows:

- **Loyalists:** Loyalists are your best customers. They're pleased to do business with you because you provide the products and services that they want, and the benefits and satisfaction that they seek. A large loyalist customer base is essential for long-term survival.

- **Mercenaries:** Mercenaries choose purely on price. Your products and services have a fundamental utility to mercenaries, but if your prices rise, mercenaries will shop around.

- **Hostages:** Hostages have to buy products and services from particular sources, possibly because only one outlet is in their particular location – such as one restaurant, chip shop, or supermarket.

- **Apostles:** Apostles are extreme loyalists. Apostles identify very closely with companies that provide their products and services. They expect to be delighted at every visit and with every purchase. As long as everything is going well, apostles will sing your praises to the roof. However, if anything goes wrong, apostles normally turn very quickly into terrorists!

- **Terrorists:** Terrorists are dissatisfied customers who want their revenge on you! Terrorists complain to trading standards authorities, the Advertising Standards Authority and anyone else who'll listen. Terrorists go to great lengths to get their problems, issues, and complaints aired on consumer affairs television programmes such as *Watchdog* – anything to make sure that you now suffer as the result of letting them down.

After you understand your customer types, you discover the secret to understanding your customers' needs. All you have to do is ask. What a concept! Yet many businesses still don't see customer needs as important, and so they don't interact with them. The two fundamental reasons for interacting badly with customers are that managers or business owners:

- Assume that because they started the business, they must know what their customers want. Wrong!

- Assume that if they're getting their products or services out on time and with good quality, they've done all they need to do to satisfy the customer. Wrong again!

Today, just keeping your customers satisfied isn't enough. You have to build long-term relationships with them. Customers are jaded because they're bombarded with an endless variety of products and services, so many, that they end up frustrated and ultimately choose based on price, convenience, familiarity, or habit.

This situation is one that most businesses can't survive. Especially, competing on price alone is a no-win situation for everyone. You have to show your customers that dealing with your company offers intangible benefits that make it a better choice than the competitors.

Here's a look at how to better understand the customer.

The customer is the person who pays you

If you agree that the customer is the person (or business) who pays you, the one who controls the purchasing decision, defining who your customer is will be easier. Suppose that you own a restaurant. Your customers are naturally the people who come to your restaurant because you're delivering your food products directly to them. Now consider a more complicated example: You manufacture bicycles that are geared toward racers and are sold through retail outlets. Who is your customer? Your first guess may be that the customer is the retail outlet, because it buys the bicycles from you to sell to its customers, the racers. And in some instances, you'd be right if you, the manufacturer, sold direct to the retailer. The more likely scenario, however, is that you sell to a distributor who then locates retail outlets for the bicycles. In that case, your customer is the distributor because the distributor pays you, and the retailer pays the distributor.

Think about the difference between the customer and the end-user. In the case of the restaurant, the customer and the end-user are the same. Where they are not the same, however, you have to satisfy both. In the bicycles example, you have to provide products that the retailer is happy to sell on; and the cycles have to appeal to the retailer's customers also – the end user. And so you have to appeal to the needs and wants of both.

Consider the following:

- ✔ Manufacturing staff at Dutton Engineering Ltd. know that the customer pays their wages to such an extent that they're fully empowered to take any action necessary to ensure that the products go out on time.

- ✔ The barrister, Anne Mallalieu, places a high value on her personal reliability and integrity, as well as her legal expertise. This, she says, is what those using her services expect. She stated (perhaps a little fancifully): 'If I don't maintain my reliability and integrity, I don't eat.'

- ✔ Nissan UK made its immediate mark in the UK car market by promising same-day delivery on all models to customers at a time when the industry standard was a delivery period of between two and three weeks.

Customers want benefits, not products

We're amazed at how many companies take the 'Field of Dreams' approach to product or service development – that is, they think that if they build it, the customers will come. Nothing could be further from the truth. Customers are normally very knowledgeable. They know exactly what they want, when they want it, and how they want it. As a business trying to get customers to buy your products and services, you must give them exactly what they want.

Ryanair know that their customers want low fares. So, their advertising, marketing, and Web site project their low fares. However, during their early period of success, Ryanair concentrated too heavily on low fares – and not enough on service reliability. To amend the situation, throughout its period of expansion over the past five years, the company has concentrated on the combination of low fares and service reliability – both of which really benefit the customer. The company now regularly publishes its reliability figures, which compare very favourably with other operators in the market.

Assuming that customers buy based on the features of your product or service – the bells and whistles – is a mistake. Customers are more interested in what the product or service can do for them – they want to know 'what's in it for me?'. Take this example. Suppose that you have an Internet-based travel company that offers adventure tours to exotic places. Some of the many features of your product or service might include the following:

- ✔ Your company puts the whole trip together so that all the customer has to do is show up.
- ✔ Your company provides a wealth of information about the exotic location.
- ✔ Your company supplies an on-location guide.

These services are all well and good, but they don't address the needs of the customer in the form of benefits that let them know why they should do business with you. Try taking each of the features in the preceding list and turning them into benefits for your customers.

- ✔ Customers save time and money by going to one place for all of their travel needs.
- ✔ Customers save time when looking up location information and have a means of discovering more about their destination.
- ✔ Customers have the security of knowing that a representative of your company will be on site to take care of any last-minute needs.

Now you're looking at the features from the customer's perspective. The customer needs to be aware of these benefits before making a purchasing decision. Think like a customer; think in terms of benefits, not products or features.

Talking to Your Customers Is a Must

How do you know what customers want and expect from your business if you don't ask? Think about how much easier it would be to sell a product or service if you knew that you had a ready and willing customer. 'Impossible,' you say. 'You won't know if customers want your product or service until you get it out in the market and see if they buy it.' But that approach is just guessing. Most businesses can't afford to play that game. If you start talking to customers when you're in the concept stage of your product or service, you can be sure that you're giving them what they want when the product or service finally hits the market.

Building relationships

Today, building customer relationships and loyalty is critical to success. In marketing terms, this approach is called *relationship marketing*, and it has to do with building trust and satisfying customers in a way that results in shared customer and company goals. In short, you make your customers part of the team. Relationship marketing is very different from the transaction focus that has pervaded marketing for decades. In transaction marketing, the focus is on the sale. In relationship marketing, the focus is on the customer. Take a look at Table 16-1 to see how different the two approaches are.

Table 16-1	Transaction Focus versus Relationship Focus
Transaction Focus	*Relationship Focus*
Concern yourself with getting the sale	Build a long-term relationship with the customer
Sell the features of the product/service	Sell the benefits of the product/ service
Think about customer service after the sale	Provide fanatical customer service
Limit your commitment to the customer	Be totally committed to the customer
Minimise customer contact	Talk to the customer continuously

Relationship building is a real strategy with real benefits. It requires that you change the way you do business, but those changes will actually improve your business in many ways. If you're in better touch with the changing needs of your customers, you'll make fewer mistakes. Customers will buy more from you because they feel that they have a vested interest in your company because you listen to them and give them what they want.

Another benefit of great customer relationships is that when problems occur (and they always do!), your customers will talk to you about them instead of immediately changing their allegiance to your competitor. Because you have spent time with them, they feel that they owe you their loyalty. This loyalty is a huge benefit to you because working to keep your current customers is far less costly than trying to find new ones. The goal today is to maintain your customers for life.

Yet another benefit of customer relations, and perhaps the most important one from a business survival standpoint, is that over the life of your relationship with your customers, you'll realise the full value of those customers. They will give your company far more than the mere sum of their transactions with your business. Your company will improve in direct correlation with what you find out from your customers, and as a result, your competitors will find it much more difficult to negatively affect your business.

Tracking your customers

To begin to build relationships with your customers, collect some information on them. Relationship marketing is more than simply creating a database of customer information. This approach involves interacting with your customers and running experiments to find out what works. So the information-gathering process isn't one-way – it's two-way. Information is going back and forth between you and your customers continuously. Remember, the goal is to attract customers who'll be with you for life. We'll even go so far as to say that your focus shouldn't be on selling products, but on managing customer relationships and providing customers with solutions to their problems. In essence, your business becomes a broker to your customers for all their needs relevant to your industry. Remember that information is the key to success. You want your customers to see your business as their information source.

Doing some experiments

Simply collecting a lot of information isn't enough. You have to do something with it. The customer information needs to answer your questions. So you set up some experiments to test what you believe is reality. Consider this simple example. Suppose that you own a restaurant and you want to introduce a new category of foods that your customers are not used to eating. What kind of information do you need to gather to make your decision? You may want to find out the following types of information:

- ✔ Who responds most favourably to these new flavours? Are you drawing in new customers as a result? Are your current customers enjoying the new foods?

✔ Have you priced the meals correctly? Is price affecting the customer's choice?

✔ How is the food being presented? How does appearance affect the customer's desire to try the food?

You can probably come up with many other ideas to test. By testing the questions you want answered, you can try several versions and discover which one will give you the result you want.

Even very large companies like American Express learn from testing ideas. American Express's merchandise services division was suffering enormous losses. From experimentation, it found out that it was too product-focused – sell, sell, sell! When it shifted to a customer focus and started managing customer relationships, the company succeeded. American Express also began rewarding its salespeople for customer longevity and repeat sales rather than just one-time sales.

Starting a conversation

Customers believe that product/service companies contact them for one reason and one reason only – to sell them something. But relationship marketing is much more than just selling – it's a dialogue with the customer.

Now, be honest, you think that the first time you try to have a dialogue with your customers without trying to sell them something, they'll probably be suspicious because they're not used to being treated in that way. They'll be waiting for what they expect to be the inevitable punch-line – the moment when you tell them about a new product or service that you want them to buy. Won't they be pleasantly surprised when you don't? This moment could be the start of a beautiful relationship!

Don Peppers and Martha Rogers, the relationship marketing gurus, suggest three approaches to starting a relationship with your customers in their book *The One to One Future: Building Relationships One Customer at a Time* (Currency/Doubleday):

✔ For the first few times you contact the customer, don't try to sell something. Start with getting-to-know-you conversations in which the customer finds out about your company and you discover something about the customer's needs.

✔ Set up a voice mail system so that you can get feedback from your customers at any time, but be sure to respond within 24 hours.

✔ A Web site is a good place for customers to voice their complaints or praise your company. A Web site's also a great way to deliver information to the customer and even provide incentives for responding to company questionnaires.

Keeping a customer information file

To really get to know your customers, begin to systematically organise all the information you collect from a variety of sources into one central file – the *customer information file*. The contents of the file depend on the type of business you have and the kinds of customers you deal with. But in general, certain information is pretty common to all businesses. As well as keeping track of your customers' contact details, a record of upgrades, and complaints received, also look for answers to the following questions:

- ✔ When was your customer's last purchase and what did he or she buy?

- ✔ How often does your customer make a purchase?

- ✔ How much does your customer spend on average per purchase?

- ✔ How much has your customer spent over the past year?

With all this information in hand, you can now begin to look at patterns of behaviour and make decisions about how best to satisfy your customers.

Keeping Your Best Customers

Companies make two major mistakes that keep them from increasing their sales and improving their profits (something that doesn't always occur simultaneously, by the way). They get themselves trapped in a continual cycle of scrambling to find new customers, and they spend enormous amounts of time and money trying to keep all of their customers. Both strategies tend to backfire.

In the first place, most companies lose about 25 per cent of their customers every year. Because acquiring a new customer costs about five times as much as it does to maintain an existing one, it stands to reason that you'll save a lot of time and money by focusing on the 75 per cent of those customers who stay with you. Almost 65 per cent of the average company's business comes from current, satisfied customers. Now take a look at these three eye-opening statistics:

- ✔ If each day for one year, your company loses one customer who spends about £50 a week, the next year your company will suffer a decline in sales of £1 million!

- ✔ Approximately 91 per cent of your dissatisfied customers will never buy from you again. And they'll tell at least another nine people why they won't buy from you.

- ✔ About 90 per cent of your dissatisfied customers won't even bother to tell you that they're unhappy. They'll just stop buying.

If these statistics don't make it very clear that the most important customers are the ones you already have, we don't know what will. These figures also tell you that you're wasting your time and money on your worst customers. The next section discusses how you can decide who your best and worst customers are.

Identifying your best customers

Building relationships with all your customers probably seems like a daunting task, especially if you have thousands of customers. That doesn't seem like a very manageable number, even with technology to help. But it can be done. If you've got rid of your worst customers – those that don't pay, never buy, return everything (you get the picture) – then you need to analyse your database for your best customers. Who are your best customers? Very simply, they're the customers who account for the greatest percentage of your sales. About 25 per cent of your customers account for 95 per cent of your revenues. These are the loyal, repeat customers who cost you the least to maintain and send more money to the bottom line.

If you've created a customer information file, finding the best customers – and the worst ones – is easy! Encouraging you to get rid of your worst customers may sound harsh, but the reality is that they're the ones who have a bad history with your company. They buy infrequently and in so little volume that if you ran through the figures, you'd find that keeping them is actually costing you money! The most valuable customers, on the other hand, make you money.

You can use statistical measures to determine who's a valuable customer; or you can look at the total revenue generated by each customer and the frequency of purchases. Compare that data against other customers. Or you can take the top 25 per cent of your customers and see what they contribute to your total revenues.

For a moment, look at each customer as a series of transactions over time. Calculate the present value of future purchases based on the customer's buying patterns to date. To that figure, add what you think is the value of referrals from that customer and then subtract the cost of maintaining the customer (advertising, promotions, and so on). That final figure is your customer's lifetime value to your company. (Chapter 10 covers present value in more detail.)

Identifying your best customers is the first step. You need to find ways to encourage them to *remain* your best customers.

How do I love thee? Let me count the ways

You have lots of ways to let your customers know that you really want their feedback and you care about them. For starters, you can try:

- ✔ Free-phone customer service hotlines

- ✔ Mystery shoppers who evaluate how customers are treated

- ✔ Personal visits to customers

- ✔ Tours of your facilities for customers

- ✔ Telephone or postal surveys

- ✔ Customer exit interviews (for when you lose a customer)

- ✔ In-person interviews

- ✔ A Web site to provide answers to problems quickly

- ✔ Focus groups

- ✔ Meeting customers at trade shows

- ✔ Special events for customers

- ✔ A customer advisory board to the company

- ✔ Observation of customer behaviour

Rewarding your best customers

Rewarding your best customers doesn't have to be an enormous and costly undertaking. Often the simplest things make customers want to come back. For example, memorising your customers' names and using them when you see them is a very powerful reward. Customers love to feel that they're important to the company and that you respect what they're contributing to its success. Remembering important customer dates like birthdays and anniversaries (this goes for businesses as well as people) shows that you're interested in the customer. This gesture also gives you a chance to suggest something that your company can do to help them make that day special.

The next sections discuss a few more strategies for making sure that you keep your best customers.

Frequency awards

Airline frequent flier programmes have spawned many clones for other industries. The basic principle of the frequency programmes is that the more your customer buys from you, the more benefits they get and those benefits increase with use. The purpose is to encourage customers to look to your company first for all their needs.

Frequency programmes are very beneficial to companies because they help to build up a strong bond of loyalty and identity with the customer. Loyalty cards also enable companies to track every consumer purchase so that specific marketing initiatives can target individuals.

Loyalty cards

Today, most supermarkets and department stores have loyalty cards. These enable customers to build up point collections, which they can then exchange either for goods and services at a later date, or for price discounts.

Coupons

Coupons are also issued by supermarkets and department stores. The most familiar coupons are those that allow for, say, a 10 per cent discount on the next visit to the shop, provided that you spend a minimum of £50.

Building a win-win strategy for great customer relationships

After you find out how to identify your best customers and reward them, consider how to keep them happy for life. Our win-win strategy is based on four principles of the current marketplace, which we describe in the following sections.

Owning your market

If you want to be successful today, you have to create your own niche in the market. You need to develop aims and objectives to help you achieve market leadership in some aspect of your business. When you're the leader, people look at you differently. You have an automatic edge over your potential competitors. You also set the standards in the market and can encourage others to develop products and services that are complementary to yours.

So how do you create a niche, and what does this have to do with customer relationships? If you find customer needs that aren't being met by others in your industry, you have found a niche that your business can serve. For example, Innocent Smoothies, the whole fruit branded soft drinks company, found and developed a niche in the market for people who are concerned about having their 'five a day' fruit and vegetable intake, but who are often too busy to prepare fresh food for themselves.

Niches are defined by customer needs, so talk to your customers.

Positioning your company

Positioning is simply attempting to control the way people perceive your company and its products. Products come and go, but if you position it right, your company will last for a long time. Therefore, you need to spend as much or even more time positioning your company in the market with customers than you do positioning your products and services. Taking a proactive approach to positioning your company is important, because if *you* don't position it, your customers, distributors, suppliers, and competitors certainly will. And they may not position the company the way you want.

With positioning, perception is reality. This situation means that whether what is perceived is true or not, the customers decide based on their perception. So the perception of your company and its products must be a positive one. Two identical products can be perceived differently depending on how they're marketed. For example, a brand name product may have exactly the same ingredients as a generic brand next to it on the shelf. Many consumers purchase the name brand for more money just because they perceive a difference, even though there isn't one.

Because an important ingredient in brand loyalty is integrity and reputation, you need to position your company as one that is focused on the customer.

Mass customisation

One great side benefit of technology is that it allows businesses to customise their products and services to the specific needs of each customer. Mass customisation is giving your customers what they want, when they want it, and in the specific way they want it. Anything that can be digitised can be customised, so manufacturers who use computer-aided manufacturing techniques can program in customer changes as easily as pushing a few buttons. Companies that produce written documents can easily customise wording to speak directly to a specific customer. Mass customisation can be employed in many other areas, for example:

- Clothing, in which shirts and trousers are produced precisely to fit the individual customer, and which may include additional pockets, special buttons, and other features.
- Cars, in which customers are given specific audio packages and computer systems.

Of course, the fundamental requirement for mass customisation is a good relationship with your customers, so they can guide you in your efforts to give them exactly what they want. And if you really want to know what they want – ask them!

Focusing on things you can't touch or see

Businesses often become so product-focused that they can't see what's really significant. The most important things about your company and its products and services are the intangibles that you can't see or touch such as quality, customer focus, and reliability. In a market where products and services rapidly become commodities, these intangibles become the differentiating factor in putting your business in front of your competitors. When your competitors start competing based on price alone, the only way you'll gain an advantage is by adding value with intangibles. Customers tend to buy from a business with which they have an ongoing relationship and where they perceive value because they've invested time and effort with you and vice versa.

Dealing with Unhappy Customers

No one's perfect, and that includes good companies. Even good companies sometimes have temporarily unhappy customers.

You need to work out how to deal with complaints positively. Remember that complaints are merely a way to find out how to improve your company. Continuous improvement is one of the core principles of successful businesses today.

Letting your customers complain

Give your customers some reasonable methods for complaining. Some customers are incensed when you give them a free-phone number for customer service and they have to leave a voice mail message for some unknown person who may never respond. Pizza Hut has a better approach. It provides a free-phone number but human beings answer the phone. Talking to a person makes customers feel the company really is interested in hearing what they have to say. After the conversation is over, the customer's comments are sent to the manager of the particular restaurant in question. That manager must call the customer within 48 hours and resolve the problem.

Some of your customers may not require that human touch to handle their concerns. For these customers, an e-mail address or a Web site where customers can post their complaints works well. However, be warned that upset customers can use your site to vent their emotions in much more outrageous and angry ways than they probably would if a human being with a gentle voice were listening. You may also be subject to spamming, which occurs when a group of unhappy customers fills your Web site with their diatribes.

Developing customer satisfaction programmes

Your ability to nip a complaint in the bud is directly related to your level of communication with the customer. Customers who feel that your company is genuinely interested in making things right are more co-operative, understanding, and less likely to flee at the first mistake. One way to try to catch complaints in the early stages is by using satisfaction surveys at each point of contact with the customer. That way, the complaint is focused on a specific process or product. This system makes it easier for you to correct the situation quickly, without having to spend a lot of time trying to understand what the customer is complaining about.

Here are some suggestions for effective ways to deal with complaints:

- Never treat a customer like a number. Always find a way to personalise any solution to a complaint.

- Let the customer do the talking first. Acknowledging that the customer's perception of the situation is the reality, whether it's right or wrong, is best. Accept what the customer is saying without interruption.

- Hear the complaint in full before asking clarifying questions. Be sure that you ask the most important question: *What can we do to make this better?*

- If the customer is particularly angry, you can diffuse that anger by showing that you understand their point of view. Then immediately shift from the problem to a discussion of solutions. You're looking for a win-win situation.

- Be sure to follow up with the customer about a week later to make sure that everything turned out the way you planned and the customer is satisfied.

Also, remember that many customers don't overtly complain when they're unhappy – they suffer and fume in silence. These customers are particularly difficult for a company to deal with because you don't know they're unhappy. To help reduce the number of your customers who are suffering in silence, you have to stay in contact with your customers at all times and solicit feedback at every point of contact. A recent research project found five dimensions on which customers judge their satisfaction with your company:

- How reliable your company is about providing customers with what they want.

- How knowledgeable and courteous your employees are and whether or not they inspire customers with a sense of trust and confidence in the company.

- The appearance of your facilities and whether they convey a sense of pride in the business.

- How much attention you pay to your customers as individuals.

- How willing your company is to provide prompt, quality service.

Winning them back

Sometimes, no matter how hard you try, you lose a customer. Maybe you lose that silent customer who doesn't like to complain but just goes somewhere else. Before thinking about winning your customers back answer the question, 'Do you want to win them back?'

Losing customers costs your company a lot of money. Take a look at Figure 16-1 to see what we mean.

What Does it Cost to Lose Customers?		
Accounts lost	2,000	167 accounts every month
	x 1,200	Average revenue per account
	£2,400,000	Total lost revenue for the year
Profit lost	x .12	Profit margin
	£280,000	Total lost profit
Account closing costs	£20	Per account
	x 2,000	Number of closed accounts
	£40,000	Total costs to close accounts
	£280,000	Total profit lost
Total costs	£280,000	Total profit lost
	+ 40,000	Closing costs
	£320,000	Annual cost of losing customers

Figure 16-1: Your company suffers when you lose customers.

As you can see, the amount your business loses is no small potatoes! Very few growing businesses can afford to lose that much money.

Think of winning back lost customers as a challenge to help make your business better. After all, they stopped buying from you for a reason. If nothing else, you at least want to communicate with customers to find out why they haven't come back. You may not be able to change their minds, but you may learn something valuable about how you're treating certain customers.

Sometimes, the blunt approach works best: *Is there anything we can do to bring you back?* Offering your customers a discount on a future purchase may nudge them to reconsider.

The key to minimising the number of customers you lose each year is to stay in contact, so that you can spot problems before they cause disgruntled customers.

Chapter 17

Focusing Your Efforts: Marketing Planning

. . . .

In This Chapter

▶ Focusing on key principles of marketing

▶ Preparing to do a marketing plan

▶ Deciding on your target market

▶ Doing market research easily and quickly

▶ Understanding the five Ps of marketing

. . . .

*M*arketing is required wherever the customer or consumer has a choice. You have to have good products and services, and you must also be able to present the benefits and advantages on offer in the best possible ways – the ways that engage the interest of the customers or consumers, ensuring that they buy from you and not from someone else. And you need a marketing plan. Whether this plan is a short set of notes, or a long and detailed document, you need to set out clearly your marketing aims and objectives; who you're going to target, and how; and how you're going to measure your marketing success or failure.

Sergio Zyman, marketing wizard and former chief operating officer of the Coca-Cola Company, asserts that marketing is about 'coming up with plans and taking actions that get more people to buy more of your product more often so the company makes more money.'

Marketing is not only everything you do to make your customers aware of your products and services. Marketing also includes the features and benefits of your products and services, packaging, how you deliver the product, the promotional mix, logistics, and after-sale customer service. Marketing is also about the presentation of your company: How your receptionist greets visitors, how the telephone is answered, and the demeanour of your staff.

Marketing Today

In recent years, marketing has become much more complex, disciplined, and expert. Mass marketing still relies on extensive advertising and promotion campaigns to maintain high levels of brand awareness, value, and identity. Mass marketers now develop their marketing approaches and strategies to provide benefits and value to individual customers and consumers, as well as the market as a whole. Additionally, people don't respond to advertising the way they used to. The cost of television advertising has fallen drastically, while marketing on the Internet is much cheaper and has grown sharply. And postal advertising (junk mail) generates £67 billion of business each year in the UK alone (whatever we think of it as it drops through the door).

Today, branding and brand loyalty are critically important.

- ✔ *Branding* means creating a recognisable image of your company. For example, suppose that you produce performance tyres for cars. When a potential customer needs that type of tyre, if the name of your company and brand comes immediately to their mind, you've been successful at branding.

- ✔ *Brand loyalty* means that customers regularly seek out your products and services first because they've had a positive experience with them.

The only way to rise above the cacophony of competing products and services is through the brand you create. Branding today is not about creating an image that may or may not be real. Branding's about conveying the philosophy and character of the business. To convey that information, you must be market driven, not marketing driven. In other words, you must understand the needs of your customers and use marketing strategies and tactics that respond to those needs. For example, David Beckham is one public figure who understands the value of branding. The former England football captain has, through extensive media and public relations coverage, ensured that he, his wife, and family, all carry a *brand value*. This brand has enabled him to maximise returns on all of his business ventures – clothing, merchandise, public appearances, and other commodities ranging from razors to hair gel.

Key Principles of Marketing Today

Here are the three fundamental principles of marketing in today's global, technology-driven marketplace:

1. **Customers are an asset of your company that actually grows in value over time.** Firstly, you wouldn't have a business without customers. Secondly, customers become more valuable because they refer potential new customers to you and they tend to buy more from you over time. Thirdly, customers give you input and insight into new markets and new products. Finally, the cost to maintain a customer may decline over time, while the cost of acquiring a new customer keeps rising. (Refer to Chapter 16 for more about the importance of customers.)

2. **Think of quality as a competitive strategy for your company.** Today, customers expect a certain level of quality, so you won't stand out in the crowd if the level of quality your business provides simply meets those expectations. You need to go beyond the standard and be absolutely fanatical about quality in every area of your business.

3. **No matter what kind of business you have, it's a service business.** Today, the boundaries between industries are eroding. Product-focused businesses are adding service to their mix, while service-type businesses are developing new products to be able to sell more to the customers they have. The result? Businesses that are a mix of products and services. For example:

   - Civil engineering contractors now undertake to manage access and egress effectively, as well as conducting environmental restoration after the project has ended.

   - All of the major supermarket chains now offer a home delivery service, provided that you order the groceries online.

   - Thomas Cook, the travel agency and tour operator, sells luggage items, clothing, and other branded merchandise.

So, whether you are in project work such as civil engineering, offering products for sale, or providing a service, you can always find additional marketing and business development opportunities.

A Step-by-Step Approach to the Marketing Plan

A marketing plan is really just one part of your overall business plan. Like a business plan, a marketing plan is a living guide to your plan for starting and building customer relationships for life. This plan contains your marketing goals and the strategies and tactics you'll use to achieve them. But don't think that you can write one marketing plan that will be good for the life of the business (or even for a year for that matter). Your plan will evolve with your business, your customers, and the market.

The starting point for your marketing plan is that it must be compatible with your overall strategic approach (if you're not sure of this, refer back to Chapter 4). If your core strategic approach is seeking cost advantage, then make sure that your marketing concentrates on this, and on the price and value advantages that accrue as the result. If your core strategic approach is driven by branding and differentiation, then make sure that your marketing concentrates on quality, value, and exclusivity – anything that you want to be associated with your brand. And if you're concentrating on niches, make sure that you present the benefits of your products and services in ways that are of value to the particular niches you serve.

Preparing your plan

Before you sit down to outline your marketing plan, do a few things in preparation to make your job easier. Include all the members of your management team as well as key front-line employees in your planning effort. The more input you get from all the functional areas of your business, the more effective your plan will be. A kick-off meeting is probably a good place to start. At the meeting, you can share ideas and assign duties that individuals or teams can undertake. But be sure to regularly meet as a large group to make sure that everyone is on target. And don't forget to include the customer in your planning! Ask some of your best customers to give you feedback on your marketing ideas. If possible, invite them to a meeting to let them know that what they have to say is important. Here are some tips for getting started:

- **Brainstorm a list of possible marketing strategies and tactics.** This list will help you see all the possibilities before you narrow down your choices. You need to have a good understanding of which strategies have been successful and which ones haven't. You can do that by looking at other companies in your industry. Your goal is to collect as many strategies and tactics as you can. At this point, don't worry about whether they're feasible for your company. You can judge feasibility after your list is complete.

- **Try to think like your customers.** Look at your company, its products and services, and its employees from the customer's perspective. In other words, look objectively at your business.

- **Know your competition as well as you know your own company.** Look at what your competitors are doing right and what they're not doing that maybe you should be doing. Can you think of ways to improve on what your competitors are doing?

✔ **Begin analysing your options and ranking them.** On your list of marketing strategies, eliminate the tactics that are obviously not possible for your company at this time. Perhaps they cost more than you have in your budget or maybe they simply aren't appropriate for your customers. This step is where your understanding of the customer comes into play. You need to choose strategies that not only meet the customers' needs but also find customers where they're most likely to be. For example, if your customers aren't regular television watchers, you probably don't want to waste money advertising there.

Now you can begin to write your marketing plan.

Writing your plan

Technology has changed the way you market your business. Today, you can market to your customers for a lot less money than you used to. Technology lets you create professional-looking brochures, business cards, advertisements, and reports as easily as you write a letter. Anyone can set up a dazzling Web site within minutes that can reach customers anywhere. Access to this technology means that more people and more businesses are marketing in a variety of new ways to their customers – so your business must stand out from the crowd. Therefore, you need a plan that contains strategies and tactics that will help you achieve that goal.

Your marketing plan can be as elaborate as a complete 50-page Business Plan or as spartan as one paragraph. In fact, starting with one paragraph that says it all is a good idea. Many very experienced marketers suggest that approach because it forces you to keep your plan focused and to identify the key components. A good one-paragraph marketing plan has the following seven components:

1. **Purpose:** What is the marketing plan supposed to accomplish?

2. **Benefits:** How will your products and services satisfy the needs of the customer?

3. **Customer:** Who is your primary customer and what is your strategy for building long-term relationships with that customer?

4. **Company:** How will the customer see your company? Remember that customers are some of the many people who contribute to positioning your company in the marketplace.

5. **Niche:** What is the niche in the market that your company has defined and will serve?

6. **Tactics:** What specific marketing tools will you use to reach the customers?

7. **Budget:** How much of your budget will you allocate to this effort?

Here's an example of how all this information goes into a paragraph that gives you the essential points of your marketing plan:

> The purpose of the marketing plan is to create awareness for ABC Strategies Corporation, which will provide flexible, responsive, and expert management consulting services to technology companies through direct contact with the customer and via the Internet. The niche that ABC will serve is the small, growing, technology company. The customer will see ABC Strategies as a high-quality, expert, management consulting firm providing advice and guidance in response to the precise needs of each customer or client. Initial marketing tactics will include half-day workshops and advertisements in technology publications. Ten per cent of sales will be applied to the marketing strategy.

Defining Your Target Market

Your *target market* is that segment of the marketplace whose needs your product or service is going to satisfy. To put it another way, the target market is those customers who are most likely to purchase your product. Why is it so important to target a specific market rather than try to hit the whole market at once? The answer is very simple. Marketing to customers is a very costly undertaking for any business, so you want to be sure that you reach the customers who will actually buy from you. Furthermore, when you're introducing a new product or service, you want it to catch hold quickly, and the easiest way to ensure that popularity is to go after the people or businesses most likely to purchase.

The customer is not always the end user of the product or service. If you use intermediaries (distributors, retailers, and so on), then, strictly speaking, they are your customers because they're the ones who pay you. But you do need to understand your end users. Because you're supplying the product or service, you need to give them what they want. You also have to be able to convince retailers or wholesalers that they'll find a market for the product you're selling to them.

The term customer doesn't refer only to consumers. It also includes business-to-business transactions. We use the term *customer* to include both groups of people.

Forget technology for technology's sake

Industry is moving so quickly that businesses, in their effort to stay ahead of their competitors, often come up with new products or services that aren't based on real demand in the market. Instead, innovations are based on some great new technology that the company's engineers have developed. For example:

✔ Many organisations have automated telephone response systems, while those who ring up simply want to be able to speak to someone about their own personal and individual concerns.

✔ Sony has a history of technologically superior products that failed. The most notorious is the technologically superior Betamax video cassette system which people didn't buy because they preferred the universally available VHS products.

✔ By the industry's own standards, Apple continues to develop both hardware and software that are superior to others on offer. However, the industry standard remains the Windows operating system.

Remember that any technological innovation has to deliver benefits that are of value to your targeted customer groups. While people with technological expertise or interests may admire technological innovation, the response from your customers determines whether or not such innovations are successful.

Realising that you have more than one kind of customer

In your search for your target or primary customer, you'll find that several other types of customers may eventually buy from you. One quick and easy way to help you see the big picture when you're considering all the possible customers for your products or services is to create a *customer matrix*. A customer matrix is simply a table that compares all the categories of customers you've identified across several characteristics or variables. The typical characteristics used to compare customers are the benefits that customers seek from your products and services, the distribution channel you use, and the marketing strategy that's appropriate for that customer. Of course, you can add any other type of comparison category that you want. These three categories, however, will get you started.

Table 17-1 shows an example of a customer matrix.

Table 17-1	Customer Matrix for ABC Strategies Corporation		
Broad Customer Description	*Benefit*	*Distribution*	*Marketing Strategy*
Rapidly growing technology companies	On-call guidance through rapid growth phase	Direct, on-site to the customer	Referrals, trade journal promotion, seminars
Start-up technology companies	Low cost consulting as needed	Online via the Internet – e-mail and online chat	Direct mail, workshops, university programmes, links with other business Web sites
Established technology companies	Use expertise of ABC for specific projects	Direct to the customer	Referrals

Notice that each customer has different benefits that are important. What this matrix really tells you is that you define customer categories by the benefits to the customer. So, for example, the needs of a rapidly growing company are greater and more frequent in terms of management strategies than are the needs of either the start-up venture or the established company. Chances are that you won't reach all your customers through the same distribution channels. In Table 17-1, start-up ventures with limited resources are most easily served via the Internet. Likewise, it follows that if you're reaching different customers through different marketing channels, then you're probably also going to use different marketing strategies and tactics to create awareness and get them to buy. You can decide which type of customer you're going to target first; and from there, how you're going to develop your business.

After you've decided who your potential target customer is, you need to define that customer or create a *customer profile*, which is an in-depth description of the customer.

Defining your customer

Before you do some market research (covered in the following section), find out what others have said about your customer. You can use freely available data, your own resources, or else specialist market research organisations to provide more detailed information. Such organisations conduct random samples of the population in an effort to provide companies like yours with the data you need to make decisions.

You can segment a market in four different ways. These methods are guides for you, but don't forget that the best way to understand and define your customers is to get out there and talk to them.

- ✔ **The benefits of the product/service:** Market research can tell you which types of customers are seeking such things as very high quality or convenience, for example, and are willing to pay for it. If that's what you're selling with your products and services, then you want to know about these customers, because they're your most likely buyers.

- ✔ **Location of your customers:** Customers in different locations have different buying habits, and different needs and wants. Naturally, then, the location of customers will also affect your distribution and marketing strategies.

- ✔ **Psychographics:** When you look at the personality traits, lifestyles, and behavioural patterns of customers, you're looking at *psychographics*. Psychographics are very important in deciding which types of marketing tactics will catch your customers' attention.

- ✔ **Demographics:** Demographics are the most common type of segmentation. Good market research firms can tell you, down to the precise locality, what people buy, when they buy, how much they buy, and how much they earn. These firms also can give you information on the standard characteristics of your customers, such as their sex, age, disposable income, ethnicity, and so on.

Whichever approach you use, the overall objective is to ensure that you know and understand your customers in as much detail as possible.

Market Research Made Easy

Smart researchers always identify the information they need before they go out to talk to customers.

Here's a list of the kinds of information that you probably need. Of course, you can modify this list and add to it to suit your specific needs.

- ✔ What do your potential customers typically buy?

- ✔ How do they hear about products and services?

- ✔ How do they like to buy your particular type of product or service?

Some useful sources of information

Take a look at some sources of information on industries and specific markets from government and private sources. Others have collected this data – known as *secondary data* – for you to use either for free, or in return for subscriptions or membership fees. In all cases, discovering what has already been written about your target market enables you to ask better, more informed questions when you go out to talk to customers. For example:

✔ Government sources such as the Department of Trade and Industry (www.dti.gov.uk), and the Central Statistical Office (www.statistics.gov.uk) have a range of useful general information on population clusters and other demographic issues.

✔ Employers' associations and trade federations carry extensive general marketing and customer information databases.

✔ Information is available from the national press, especially *The Financial Times, The Times, The Telegraph,* and *The Economist.*

✔ Regional development agencies and business links have specific information, often very extensive, concerning their areas. Check out the Business Link Web site at www.businesslink.gov.uk.

✔ University libraries and electronic databases such as those at Harvard (www.library.hbs.edu/), the City University's Cass Business School (www.cass.city.ac.uk), and the London School of Economics (www.lse.ac.uk), which carry research projects and the associated databases, and which can be bought by all interests.

✔ How often do they buy?

✔ How can your company best meet their needs?

✔ Where in the order of priority of your customers' needs and wants do your products and services come?

✔ Is this a faddish or transient purchase, or are you offering regular products and services?

✔ How many customers are in the target market?

✔ How long is the market likely to last?

Make sure that you collect data that gives you a sense of trends in the market and the level of demand for the product or service you're offering.

Finding the information

Primary data is all the information that you personally (or your team) collect about your potential customers. You get this information through observing or talking to customers, suppliers, distributors, and anyone else who can help you better understand your customer and the market.

You can gather data in a myriad of ways, some more effective than others, and some more expensive than others. We cover some of the more common data collection methods in the following sections.

Postal surveys

If you've bought a new car recently, you've probably received at least one questionnaire from the manufacturer and/or the dealer asking you how you bought the car and what you like or don't like about it. The good thing about postal questionnaires is that you can reach a lot of people relatively easily and quickly. This technique, however, does have problems. Firstly, the response rate, even with follow-ups, is small, at around 15 per cent. Secondly, you don't achieve any interaction with the respondent, so the information is pretty basic and not nearly as helpful as methods in which you have the advantage of seeing non-verbal communication and clarifying responses.

People mistakenly believe that developing a questionnaire is a pretty simple task, but they couldn't be more wrong. However, if you use the very proven methods for questionnaire design, you enhance the chances that you'll get more accurate responses and lessen the opportunity for biasing the outcomes. Here are a few hints to improve the quality of your questionnaires:

- Start with the statement 'The purpose of this questionnaire is . . .'
- Keep the questionnaire as short as possible and use lots of white space so that it's not intimidating.
- Start with easy questions and lead up to more complex questions.
- Ask demographic questions (age, income, and so on) last, when you're about to lose the attention of the respondent.

 Realise that most people tend to increase their income by one category and decrease their age by one category, so take these factors into account when examining responses.

In terms of valuable information gained, we rank postal surveys towards the bottom of the list as tools for customer data gathering.

Phone surveys

We rate phone surveys right down there with postal surveys in terms of popularity with the respondents. Essentially, a phone survey is taking the questionnaire you were going to post and asking those same questions over the phone. Think about how you feel when a telephone salesperson interrupts your dinner (the most popular time to call) and wants just a couple of minutes of your time. Of course, that couple of minutes always turns into at least

10 or 15, and by then, your dinner is cold, and you wouldn't buy from that company if they paid you to!

We highly recommend that you avoid phone surveys at all costs.

Interviews

You can conduct interviews by phone or in person. We favour in-person interviews because you get both verbal and non-verbal feedback. The way a person physically responds to your questions tells you a lot about whether they're being honest in their answers, for example, whether they smile or frown, their tone of voice, and the words that they use.

Interviews are more costly and time-consuming than postal or phone surveys, but they have the highest response rate (nearly 100 per cent) and provide the best chance of getting accurate responses. Start by targeting specific groups of customers and then engaging their interest in giving you the information that you need. You can either do this by arranging your outlets to find customers for you to interview, or you can find and contact customers yourself. Decide what the specific purpose of your interview is, and then design the questionnaires accordingly. Remember that you need the customers' co-operation, so if you're going to ask customers to give up a portion of their time for you, then at least give them a cup of tea and biscuits!

In an interview situation, you have the ability to clarify responses, carry on a discussion so that the respondent can elaborate where necessary, and ask open-ended questions (that require more than a yes or no answer) more easily.

You need to use a designed questionnaire for interviews to ensure that you consistently ask the same questions of every interviewee, if that is important to you. We highly recommend interviews as the best source of primary data on customers.

Focus groups

Focus groups are a way to reach several customers at once to gain insight into their needs or to test an idea on them. You bring together a group of six to ten customers and often enlist the aid of a group facilitator trained to conduct focus groups. You may even want to videotape the session so that you can review it more carefully later.

Suppose that you're introducing a new type of herbal tea to the market. You may choose to do a blind test in which you serve the participants several unmarked drinks, one of which contains your new herbal tea. Then ask the participants to rate the drinks and discuss what they like and don't like about the product. Focus groups are great ways to introduce new products and services and to find out the characteristics of the actual customer who will buy.

Be aware of the *would-buy/will-buy* conundrum. Always remember that you're trying to establish the characteristics of the people who *will* buy your products and services, and the conditions under which they'll buy them. You don't want a generally favourable response along the lines of, 'Yes, I would buy this, it looks quite nice.' If you go to the time and expense of setting up a detailed study, make sure that you target it specifically.

Mix and match

No rule says that you can't do a combination of the preceding methods to achieve a level of information that satisfies you. Researchers often start with a postal survey. From the survey respondents, they select those that match the criteria they've developed and do interviews with them. Researchers may then group the interviewees into focus groups for further study.

Remember that the goal of your research, whatever methods you choose, is to understand who your customer is and how, what, and when they buy. Any method that gets you credible, reliable marketing data along those lines will work.

Guessing at how much you'll sell

The hardest question facing anyone introducing a new product or service to the market is 'How do I know how much I'll sell?' Unfortunately, there's no totally accurate way to get the answer. You have to triangulate (come at it from three different directions) to get to a number that seems to make sense. No one gets this number right all of the time.

Here are some tips to help you get as close as possible to the real demand for your product or service:

- ✔ **Look at substitute products.** If your product or service isn't unique, or one of a kind (and most aren't), then you may be able to find an existing product, study its demand patterns, and extrapolate that information to your own situation. Choose a product that uses your distribution channel. Remember that the number of intermediaries a product goes through to reach the customer affects the final price.

- ✔ **Talk to industry experts.** The people who deal with your type of product or service every day in the market have a good handle on demand, so talk to distributors, retailers, suppliers – anyone who deals with your category of products or services.

> ✔ **Conduct market testing.** Many companies, particularly those dealing with consumer products, try to conduct market testing in areas where the population is diverse, and supposedly representative of the population of the country as a whole. The purpose of testing in this way is to try to get a microcosm of the response that supposedly would occur if the product or service was made available across the whole country.

Add to this mix your own experience and understanding of the customer and the market, and you've probably done the best you can to predict demand.

You Can't Be an MBA without Knowing the Five Ps

All marketing texts refer to the four 'Ps' of marketing (product, price, place, and promotion). But it has always seemed a little odd to us that the four Ps never include the most important 'P' of all in the mix – people! If you don't understand the customer, all the rest is just a waste of time. The customer determines the price, how you deliver the product, what the product looks like, and how you promote it. That sounds pretty important to us.

Because we spend a good bit of this chapter on the fifth P – people – here's a look at the other four.

Focusing on the product

Your product or service is really a bundle of features and benefits to the customer that include such things as quality, service, warranties, options, characteristics, and so on. One of the most important results of your marketing efforts is that customers will be enticed to buy because of the features and benefits you offer. Now, if you take our advice and include customer input when designing your product or service, you have a major advantage on the product side of marketing. The fact that customers help to design your products and services is, in and of itself, a strong marketing message about your company.

Conveying the intangible benefits of your products and services is also important, including such things as quality, convenience, reliability, and innovation. Intangibles are the principal source of differentiation for most products and services today.

Don't forget positioning

You need to position not only your product or service but also your company. One helpful tactic is to write a positioning statement that explains how customers see your company relative to your competitors. Here's an example of a good positioning statement.

> The customer will see ABC Strategies as a high quality, expert management consulting firm providing effective solutions to the problems faced by customers and clients at all times.

After you've written your statement, test it on your customers to make sure that they believe this position about your company. If you find that you're off track, go back and revise your positioning statement and test your customers again.

Packaging and labelling make a difference

The way you package your products says a lot about your company, particularly if you're selling consumer products. Packaging needs to reflect the culture of your company, the nature of the product you're selling, and the channel through which you're selling it.

Anyone who visits a Tesco supermarket can instantly recognise their own-brand 'value lines', because of the distinctive blue and white packaging. Packaging for consumer products needs to grab the attention of the potential buyer quickly. In an attractive way, the packaging also should give buyers the information they need to make a purchase decision.

Giving your product away can be a great pricing strategy

Did you know that you can make money by giving your product away – for free! When you think about it, many supermarkets do this (or at least appear to do it) through their policies of BOGOF – buy one, get one free. Airlines are also effectively giving their services away for free by giving discounts for regular users of services (air miles and frequent-fliers' clubs).

Spiral Frog, the Internet music company, is proposing to provide people with free and legal downloads of music of all kinds. The company expects to be able to pay for the service through its ability to attract advertising.

With all these initiatives, the overriding purpose has to remain your ability to relate the price you're charging to what customers are willing to pay. And if your product or service has no value, you won't be able to charge a price low enough to make it attractive!

What about price?

No matter what else you do right, if you don't price your product or service correctly, it won't sell in enough quantity to allow you to make a profit and survive. Customer price tolerance determines where that price should be. But the customer isn't the only arbiter of price. Here are some other things to consider:

- Top brands in any sector normally command the highest prices.

- You can usually command a higher price if demand for your product or service is greater than you can supply.

- If you're distributing a product or service that people will buy no matter what it costs, then you're free to charge more. For example, electricity, gas, and water all fall into this category.

- You may have to hold your price down if you have a lot of competition. In this case, if you can show intangible benefits to your customers, they may pay more for your product just to get those benefits that they can't get from your competitors.

- You can usually charge more for added features, but only if customers perceive them as valuable. They won't pay for things they don't need or want.

- If you're introducing new technology or product and service ranges, you will probably want to charge a higher price initially and then bring it down as competitors enter the market.

- If you successfully position your product among higher-priced items, you may be able to command a higher price.

The strategy that you use to price your products and services may change over time depending on where they are in the product life cycle. Figure 17-1 and the following list explain the various strategies used at particular points in the product life cycle.

- **Cost-based pricing** is based on simply adding a profit margin to the cost of producing the product. Of course, you also need to consider how competitors are pricing their products, and also market demand.

- **Sliding on the demand curve** is a strategy in which you introduce a product at a high price and then, as technological improvements let you achieve economies of scale, you reduce the price. This strategy enables you to maintain an advantage over competitors.

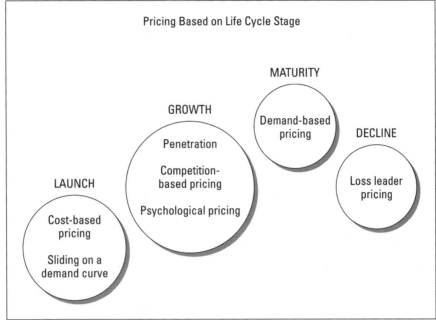

Figure 17-1:
Pricing
based on a
product's
life cycle.

- ✔ **Skimming** is a strategy that you can use when you have a product that no one else has. You can maintain the higher price until competition forces the price down.

- ✔ **Penetration** is effective in a very competitive market with similar products when you need to gain quick acceptance and broad-based distribution. Penetration involves introducing the product at a very low price, producing very minimal profit. Then the price is gradually raised as customers accept it. This strategy requires huge expenditures for advertising and promotion.

- ✔ **Demand-based pricing** focuses on finding what customers are willing to pay for the product.

- ✔ **Loss leader pricing** has you pricing certain products and services below cost to attract customers to other products in the line.

Choose a strategy that reflects the type of customer you have, your costs related to the product, and the competitive environment.

The budget: A real guessing game

For your marketing plan, and ultimately your business plan, you need to consider how much of your budget you should allot to promotion.

Many businesses use the 'percentage of sales' technique, which is based on how much, on average, businesses in your industry spend on promotion. Average percentage of sales in your industry is really only a benchmark for your company. For example, if you're trying to differentiate yourself, you may be doing things that your competitors aren't, and that additional effort affects your promotional budget. In such a case, the benchmark may not apply. In thinking about the budget, you also must figure out how much you have to spend to achieve your marketing goals. In general, consumer products require a much greater promotional budget than other types of products.

If you have a start-up or young business with limited resources, be especially careful about designing your promotional mix. Thinking creatively about how to promote your products and services is even more important in such a situation. Chapter 18 can help you discover some advertising tactics.

Place is more than a location

In marketing terms, *place* has to do with where your customers find your products and services. Having a good product or service isn't enough; you need to get it to customers in the manner that is best for them, whether that's a retail outlet, mail order, direct from the manufacturer, or via the Internet. Just because your business is located in a certain place doesn't mean that customers will logically seek that location when they're looking for your product. Talking to your customers tells you where they want to find your product or service. Doing anything other than what the customer expects is a recipe for disaster.

Promote, promote, promote

The purpose of the promotion part of your marketing plan is to firmly establish the identity and vision of your company in the customer's mind. Promotion is, perhaps, the most creative and important aspect of marketing and includes personal selling, public relations, guerrilla advertising (using limited resources and creative methods), sales promotion, and publicity.

You can't plan an effective promotion strategy if you don't know your customers. Talk to your customers! Doing so will pay big dividends and save you a lot of time and money. You can find out all about promotion in Chapter 18.

Putting It All Together

After you consider all the important parts of your marketing plan, it's time to organise all the data you've collected. Use the following brief outline, but feel free to modify it to better suit your particular business.

1. Purpose of the marketing plan

    a) Target market

    b) Unique market niche

    c) Business identity (how customers perceive the business)

2. Marketing tools

    a) Advertising and promotion

    b) Plans for free publicity

3. Media plan

    a) Plans for use of TV, radio, and print media, if appropriate

    b) Costs of each medium based on usage rate

4. Marketing budget

    a) Individual and total costs itemised

    b) Marketing costs as a percentage of sales

5. Public relations

    a) Gaining newspaper, media, and journal coverage

    b) Getting good stories out to the public

Chapter 18

Looking at Advertising and Promotion

. . . .

In This Chapter

▶ Advertising where it pays

▶ Publicising and promoting your company

▶ Getting attention through special events and initiatives

▶ Using guerrilla marketing

. . . .

*E*veryone needs to advertise. Whatever your line of business, and however good your products and services, people cannot take advantage of what you have to offer unless they know who you are and where to find you. And, as more organisations, products, and services come into the market place, it is not enough simply to advertise – you have to think of ever more creative and inventive ways of selling yourself if people are going to notice you, rather than all of the other alternatives.

Marketing is based on the combination of the substance of what you have to offer, with how you present it to best advantage to the groups of customers you target. This chapter deals with presentation. We look at advertising, publicity, promotions, special events, and sponsorship. We also look at how to use *freebies* – give-aways and take-aways – to best advantage. Finally, we look at what has come to be known as *guerrilla marketing* – using a combination of creative and highly individualised ways of getting your message across.

Advertising doesn't always work – or at least, not in the ways you may intend. A saying in the advertising industry is: 'Nothing shows up bad products as well or as quickly as good advertising.'

For example, the Ondigital television service launched by ITV in 2000 was advertised and promoted so effectively that the manufacturers of the digi-boxes and aerials could not keep pace with demand. Or, at least, not at first.

The first customers quickly found that reception through the digiboxes and aerials was bad, or the digiboxes jammed up altogether. Customers discovered that new programmes and alternative choices were not going to be forthcoming; and when Ondigital's final promotion – lower league football – was brought on-screen, the venture's fate was sealed. All by excellent advertising!

So when you come to advertise and promote your business, products, and services, make sure that what you present and what you deliver are the same. And while true that if you under-promote yourself, you sell yourself short; it is also true that if you over-promote yourself, you'll very quickly have scores of dissatisfied customers.

The Basics of Advertising

At its heart, advertising is communication. More specifically, advertising is non-personal mass communication intended to encourage potential customers to buy a company's products or services. Why advertise? For one thing, companies lose, on average, 25 per cent of their customers *every* year. This loss creates a continuous need for companies to encourage new customers to buy their products.

Companies spend billions of pounds each year to advertise their products and services for reasons other than attracting new customers and clients. Here are some of the key objectives of advertising:

- Improve brand recognition.
- Persuade potential customers to buy from you rather than from a competitor.
- Generate sales leads.
- Promote special events and sales.
- Improve the image of the business.
- Increase the quantity of items purchased.
- Increase the amount spent per order.
- Maintain your existing customer base.

The right advertising viewed by the right people at the right time and place can and does achieve all the goals in the preceding list. However, you have no guarantee that the right people will see your ad, nor that they will see it at the right time and place. Indeed, getting the right message to the right people at the right time and place is critical to advertising success, and it is central to the focus of advertising agencies and clients alike.

Running a successful advertising campaign

Collectively, advertisers spend billions, and advertising agencies work countless hours putting together advertising campaigns. And even after all the money has been spent and the hard work put in, some campaigns clearly work better than others! So to give yourself any chance of a successful campaign, make sure that you start with your core strategic position (see Chapter 3 for how to work out your core strategic position).

The approach is simple: If the source of your business is low cost or good value, reinforce this strength with your advertising. If you concentrate on branding and high added value, reinforce the benefits to customers of using your products, services – and brand. And if you concentrate on narrow sectors of the market, then constantly drive home the benefits of value to those niches.

Advertising can be expensive, and can be an incredibly easy way to waste money if you don't do it properly, target it effectively, or integrate it into a proper campaign. You can easily lose a lot of money and have nothing to show for it. So make sure that you structure your advertising and make it work hard and effectively.

Plan your advertising efforts and make sure you attend to the following steps:

1. **Understand why you're advertising.**

   Are you trying to create a good feeling about your company among people that view your advertisement? Are you trying to get them to buy more of your products? Are you trying to convince people that you've got product quality at the very top of your list of priorities? Your advertisement needs to be developed *after* you understand why you're advertising, not *before*. Always use the following statement at the start of planning any advertising campaign: 'The purpose of this advertising campaign is . . .'

2. **Develop a budget.**

   Before you advertise, decide how much money you can devote to the effort and create a budget based on this estimate. And after you decide on a budget, stick to it. Avoid the temptation to load your campaign full of unnecessary extras at the last minute. Make sure that you know what you're budgeting for. If you pay an agency to do your advertising, ensure that they know precisely what you expect from them. And never forget the hidden extras – for example, repeat inserts in printed media, and the costs of postage for mailshots.

3. **Calculate your break-even point.**

Figure out how much advertising you can afford based on the medium you select (such as television or newspapers) and the size of your budget. If you're going to advertise in multiple markets or media, then recognise that increasing your efforts in one area requires you to decrease them in another.

4. **Choose a target market.**

Who are your most likely customers or clients? These people are your number one priority in your advertising campaign.

5. **Place your advertisement.**

Although designing an effective advertisement is not necessarily an easy task, placing the ad is generally quite easy. The media place a very high priority on advertising sales. As a result, most media outlets have made placing ads simple and provide ample customer service to help you through the process.

6. **Evaluate your response.**

Closely monitoring the results of your advertising campaign to find out whether it had the desired effect is incredibly important. These results tell you almost immediately whether you've taken the right approach. The results also reveal whether you should continue with a particular ad or whether you should dump it and move on to something else.

7. **Adjust and repeat as necessary.**

After you have the results of your advertisement, you can adjust your ad – including the design of the ad and where and how often it runs – and then repeat Steps 1 to 6. A positive change tells you that you're on the right track; a negative response tells you that you've got your work cut out for you and need to rethink.

The ultimate measure of success of any advertising campaign is whether it attracted people's attention, and interested them in your organisation, products, and services.

Deciding on the best place to advertise

The answer to the question, 'Where's the best place to advertise?' is simple: Advertise where your potential customers are. If your potential customers are buyers of cutting-edge computer equipment, chances are you'll find them surfing the Web or reading a variety of computer magazines that cater to their particular tastes and interests. If your potential customers are children, the Saturday cartoons are guaranteed to draw them in. If you spend your advertising budget in places where you have no potential customers, you're wasting your money.

The following are usually highly effective places to advertise:

- ✔ **Internet:** Internet advertising is growing fast; however, its overall effectiveness is still uncertain. In particular, people have to be able to find your Web site, which normally means that you must co-ordinate Internet advertising with more traditional forms – just so that people know where to find you in the first place.

- ✔ **Newspapers:** Although newspapers have traditionally been the first resort for many advertising campaigns, their popularity is declining with the advent of 24-hours-a-day, all-news television stations and the proliferation of the Internet. Having said that, Ryanair in particular run very effective advertising campaigns using newspapers as their main traditional media.

- ✔ **Magazines:** Magazines are terrific places to advertise because they're typically already targeted to specific audiences. You can choose from magazines covering cars, sewing, news, stereo equipment, sailing, and much more. Each magazine has its own unique demographic of readers just waiting to read your ad!

- ✔ **Direct mail:** With direct mail, you can either target mass markets, or you can target individuals. This medium is best used as an integrated part of a wider marketing or advertising campaign.

- ✔ **Radio:** Different radio stations have different kinds of listeners. A station that plays classical music has a very different listener profile to a station that plays alternative rock. Once you have a pretty good idea of who your prospects are, you can target them through the selective use of radio advertisements.

- ✔ **Television:** Different television programmes have different kinds of viewers. Advertising can easily be shown at specific times and days of the week, depending on the demographics of the anticipated audience.

✔ **Outdoor signs:** Hoardings, the sides of buildings and buses, football stadium walls – all are examples of outdoor advertising at its best. If you can put an ad on it, you can bet that someone already has.

✔ **Street sellers:** Street sellers are used especially by charities in big cities both to promote general awareness of the cause that they represent, and also to generate income for themselves. This form of advertising is best used in conjunction with other forms of marketing and promotion, rather than in isolation.

Keeping your ads on the level

We know that *you* wouldn't intentionally create a deceptive or misleading advertisement. But the history of advertising is full of examples that are both misleading and fraudulent. The Advertising Standards Authority (ASA) is charged with monitoring advertising in this country and taking action against companies that break the law – something that happens quite regularly.

According to the ASA, all advertisements have to be 'legal, decent, honest, and truthful.' You may not do either of the following:

✔ Engage in a representation, omission, or practice that misleads consumers.

✔ Engage in a dishonest or untrue representation, omission, or practice.

✔ Misrepresent the properties and benefits of your own products and services.

✔ Misrepresent the properties and benefits of the products and services of your competitors.

Unfair or deceptive advertising is strictly prohibited in any medium. Whether it takes the form of a radio or television commercial, a Web site banner ad, a newspaper advertisement, or any other variation on the theme, advertising must tell the truth and not mislead consumers. Advertising claims can be considered misleading if you leave out relevant information or if the claim implies something that's simply not true. For example, an advertisement for a new car that claims the transaction can be completed with 'no deposit' may be misleading if significant and undisclosed charges are due at contract signing.

And making a claim of performance in your advertising isn't enough – claims must be substantiated, especially when they involve health, safety, or performance. The type of evidence required for proper substantiation of advertising claims depends on the product itself, the nature of the claims being made, and what experts in the field believe is required. For example, if your advertisement offers specific figures supporting a claim – 'tests show that nine out of ten consumers are happier using our products' – you must have evidence that clearly shows that nine out of ten consumers really are happier using your products.

Keep in mind that sellers are ultimately responsible for claims they make about their products and services. Additionally, third parties, such as retail outlets and mail-order companies, also may be held liable for deceptive advertising if they participate in the preparation or distribution of the advertising or are aware of the deceptive claims. If you're a retailer who sells products manufactured by someone else, make sure that you check any claims that they make before you offer them for sale.

You also need to be absolutely clear about the following:

- ✔ Disclaimers and disclosures must be clear and conspicuous. That is, consumers must be able to notice, read or hear, and understand the information. Still, a disclaimer or disclosure alone usually is not enough to remedy a false or deceptive claim.

- ✔ Demonstrations must show how the product will perform under normal use.

- ✔ Refunds and/or replacements must be given to dissatisfied consumers provided the customer has a good reason.

- ✔ Advertising directed at children is a controversial area and raises special issues. For example, evidence shows a direct relationship between the promotion of convenience foods, sweets, crisps, and high-sugar drinks, and the onset of the obesity crisis. However, this evidence has to be balanced against the fact that none of these products are illegal or made misleading claims. Ultimately, you must be prepared to accept responsibility for this part of your advertising if it applies.

Using Publicity and Promotion

You can get the attention of your prospective customers in other ways besides spending all your money on advertising. In fact, for many companies, advertising is a small part of the marketing mix. For these companies, publicity and promotion are the most effective way to get the word out about products and services.

Publicity and public relations

Publicity and public relations (PR) relate to messages communicated through the media about your company or your products or services because of perceived news value. Publicity is all about attracting the attention of your potential customers by first attracting the attention of the media – newspapers, magazines, radio talk shows, television news, Web sites, and similar media outlets.

Good publicity and PR is worth its weight in gold because when a potential customer sees, hears, or reads the media story, the perceived credibility of the message is higher than an advertisement. Why? Because your potential customer tends to believe that the media is unbiased and therefore is more apt to tell the truth about your company, products, or services.

For example, if potential customers encounter gushingly positive reviews of your studio's latest film in their newspapers, magazines, and radio talk shows, that publicity probably has a much greater impact on increasing attendance figures than does your advertising campaign. On the other hand, if the reviews are negative, no amount of advertising is going to save your film. Advertising is a powerful tool, but the right publicity at the right time and place can have even more power.

As you can imagine, all kinds of ways – some traditional and some not so traditional – are available to attract attention to your company or product. Here are some of the most common methods of getting publicity:

- **Media appearances:** Have you ever watched *The Oprah Winfrey Show* and wondered how she finds all those interesting people to interview? For the most part, these interesting people found Oprah through their publicists. Publicity on a popular, internationally broadcast show such as *Oprah* can have an incredibly positive impact on a business and on the sales of its products and services. Members of the media are always looking for interesting people to interview; contact your local newspaper, call in to a radio talk show, or get your company featured on a local television news show. It might not be *Oprah*, but it will put you in touch with thousands of people in a moment.

- **Press conferences:** If you want to get your message out to a lot of people at one time, call a press conference. If your story is sufficiently newsworthy (perhaps your researchers just invented a new flavour of chocolate), you'll have newspaper, radio, and television reporters falling all over themselves to cover it. Send out a press release and make an event of your announcement. If you have any friends in the media, invite them to attend. Generate some buzz!

✔ **Feature stories:** Many magazines and newsletters, particularly those produced by professional associations and local lifestyle publishers, get stories from experts in various fields. If you're an author who just wrote a book on dieting and you want to get some good publicity, try writing an article on holiday weight loss tips for a lifestyle magazine. In the process, you can plug your book and your Web site. Find the magazines most appropriate for what your company does or produces, and offer your services. You'll make a busy editor *very* happy when you do.

✔ **Opinion pieces:** Many newspapers and magazines invite readers and guest columnists to submit articles offering a particular point of view; and you can always approach people directly with your own ideas. Guest columns are in all of the national newspapers and most trade press and journals. Be aware of this opportunity, and use it when appropriate.

✔ **Web sites:** Web sites aren't always the best forms of publicity, but we include them in this list because they can reach thousands of people at little cost. If you use your Web site as an advertising, publicity, and PR medium, make sure that the links are clearly sign-posted and attractively presented – otherwise, people will simply log-on for what they wanted, and then move on.

✔ **Press releases:** *Press releases* are written summaries of some newsworthy bit of information about a company, its products, or services, written in a way that's instantly digestible by the news media. Most companies send out lots of press releases all the time, particularly when they introduce a new product or service, or when they want to announce a particular achievement or milestone. If you're not using press releases, then start doing so today. Create a list of media – both local and national – and start sending away. One story is all it takes to get your company the attention it deserves.

Promotion: Conveying information

Whether you advertise or not, the bulk of your marketing money and effort probably goes into creating and distributing promotional materials. *Promotion* is the conveying of information about your company and its products and services. And although most promotional materials are written or printed, they also take the form of CDs, DVDs, and Internet presentations.

Make sure also that you maximise the opportunities presented by the following promotional materials:

- ✔ **Sales letter:** A sales letter is a written appeal to a customer to consider buying a company's products or services. The sales letter may contain information about the products or services, as well as special offers for buying sooner rather than later. A sales letter is often accompanied by brochures, product sheets, or other promotional materials.

- ✔ **Brochures:** Brochures can take the form of a couple of simple pieces of paper, or they can be slick, full-colour, multi-page marketing pieces or reports. Brochures generally present detailed information about a company, product, or service.

- ✔ **Product sheets:** Got a product? Then you've got to have a product sheet to go along with it! A product sheet is a one-page (often front-only, but sometimes front and back) description of a product along with a photo and key specifications. A product sheet is complete enough to answer your customers' initial questions without overwhelming them with detail.

- ✔ **Publicity photos:** Publicity photos give your customers (and the media) an idea of what you and your products look like. Generally, publicity photos are accompanied by other promotional literature – perhaps a brochure or press release.

- ✔ **CDs/DVDs:** Brochures, product sheets, and publicity photos are static, but CDs and DVDs are dynamic, so they can convey much more information than a simple piece of paper. And with the advent of audio and video presentations on the Internet, you can easily maximise this opportunity when appropriate.

- ✔ **Promotional kit:** A promotional kit is simply a folder that contains some or all of the preceding items in this list. A promotional kit for your company's latest disposable camera, for example, might contain a sales letter, a brochure, a product sheet, a publicity photo, a DVD, and a working sample of the camera. The purpose of a promotional kit is to generate interest and sales by giving your potential customers an in-depth look at your product.

- ✔ **Web sites:** More and more companies are transferring their promotional materials to their Web sites for a couple of reasons. First, doing so costs little or nothing because you've already invested the money to create the promotional materials. Second, your Web site is available 24 hours a day, 7 days a week.

As with all company information, tailor the use of promotional, publicity, and PR material specifically for its intended recipients. Establish what kind of materials they want, and then provide them. And make sure that they are fully up-to-date!

Considering Special Events, Sponsorships, and Merchandise

If you really want to attract attention, special events and promotions have the potential to do just that. For example, when BMW really wants to attract the attention of its potential customers, it invites them to attend the Ultimate Driving Experience, where they can drive the company's new model cars, accompanied by skilled driving instructors. As BMW says, after you spend a day driving its cars, 'your biggest challenge will be saying good-bye'.

Special events

Special events provide a unique forum for potential customers to view, touch, and actually try out your company's products before they commit to buying them. In some cases, a company's involvement may be a bit more subtle, with little or no specific mention of products or services that the company pro-vides. For example, the launch of a new music album may be sponsored by a drinks company; a television soap opera or drama may be sponsored by a food company; or a theatre production may be sponsored by a bank. In each case, the goal of these kinds of special events is to raise the awareness of com-panies and their products and services in the eyes of potential customers.

Here are a couple of examples of common special events:

✔ **Trade fairs:** Every industry has trade fairs. Trade fairs attract a lot of attention from potential buyers. Also, people from the industry turn up to trade fairs, just to make sure that they're not missing something or losing out to a particular initiative from a competitor! Trade fairs allow companies to show off their products and services to both potential cus-tomers and the media. And you also hope to do at least a bit of business while you're there!

✔ **Demonstrations:** If you've ever been to a supermarket where someone was cooking and handing out food samples, you've experienced a mar-keting demonstration. Demonstrations allow consumers to experience and try products and to make an informed decision about buying them.

Sponsorships

Many companies sponsor public events to improve their public image while attracting potential customers in the process. Football games, town shows, festivals, charity walks, and more are all events that need sponsorship to help further their cause. And these sponsorships can help companies reach their desired audiences. The practice of sponsorship is presently expanding much further. Cash-strapped public services now seek money from other sources to such an extent that there are sponsored wards in NHS hospitals; sponsored research programmes in universities; sponsored canteens and refreshment services in schools; and sponsored transport for the disabled and disadvantaged.

Merchandise

Have you ever been to a sporting event where the home team gave away hats, flags, or T-shirts? Have local estate agents left you calendars with their address and phone numbers on them? Have you ever received a pencil or pen with the name of your local plumber? These are all examples of company merchandising, and merchandising is a more or less universal form of general advertising and promotion.

Merchandising exists to serve the dual purpose of getting something into your hands that you'll regularly use, and sending you a marketing message on that item by emblazoning it with the company or product name. Each time you use the item, you receive a small dose of advertising.

Here are some of the more popular items of merchandise:

- Pens and pencils
- Mugs
- T-shirts
- Mouse pads
- Baseball caps
- Balloons
- Calculators
- Shoulder bags

If you decide to go down this route, set a budget in advance and make sure that you can measure the returns on your investment. For example, good quality T-shirts can be reproduced relatively inexpensively; on the other hand, you want to make sure that people will actually wear it! Always evaluate in advance the purpose of giving people branded merchandise in this way, to make sure that your money is spent wisely and well.

Do *not* buy cheap, inexpensive-looking items! Each of these items is a reflection of your company. If the items that you hand out to represent your company and its products are shoddy, that's the message that you communicate to your customers and prospects. Get the best-quality items that your budget can support.

Going Undercover with Guerrilla Marketing

Guerrilla marketing is a combination of taking the most creative and innovative approaches to advertising and publicity that you can, combined with a disciplined understanding of the effect that publicity and promotional initiatives have. According to Jay Conrad Levinson, author of *Guerrilla Marketing for the 21st Century*, this approach can be summed up as

Achieving conventional goals, especially profits, with unconventional methods, such as investing energy instead of money.

Levinson has developed five new rules that reflect the guerrilla marketer's view of the world:

- ✔ **The 10/30/60 rule:** According to Levinson, you should invest 10 per cent of your marketing budget in talking to everyone in your marketing universe, whether or not they match your customer profile. Use another 30 per cent of your marketing budget to convince people who match your customer profile – your prospects – that they should become your customer. Devote the last 60 per cent of your marketing budget to marketing to your current customers, producing the most profits at a lower cost per sale.

- ✔ **The 1/10/100 rule:** This rule says that £1 spent communicating with your own staff is equivalent to £10 spent communicating with the trade, which is equivalent to £100 spent communicating with your customers. In other words, your employees can be the most cost-effective way to transmit your marketing message to your prospects and customers.

- ✔ **The rule of thirds:** According to Levinson, you need to spend one-third of your on-line marketing budget on designing and posting your Web site, one-third on marketing the site offline, and one-third on improving and maintaining your Web site, keeping it entertaining and fresh.

- ✔ **The rule of twice:** This rule says that remaining truly competitive on-line is going to cost you twice as much as you think it's going to cost.

- ✔ **The rule of the ruler:** Although you can delegate the marketing function to others in your organisation, you cannot delegate the passion and the vision that you feel for it. To ensure marketing success, take command of the marketing process and keep a close eye on it, regardless of who is in charge.

Chapter 19

A Special Relationship: Selling

....

In This Chapter

▶ Trying relationship-based selling

▶ Using the person-to-person approach

▶ Looking at both sides of telesales

▶ Making sales online

▶ Selling to other businesses

....

*P*ersonal selling and direct sales are techniques in which one person approaches another person and pitches the benefits of a product or service with the purpose of making a sale – a business process that's been around for centuries. Throughout time, the personal selling process has basically remained unchanged:

1. Prospect for customers.

2. Prepare an approach.

3. Make your approach.

4. Present and demonstrate.

5. Handle objections.

6. Close the deal.

7. Follow up.

In years past, salespeople often focused on maximising the amount of product that they sold – to the detriment of building long-term relationships with their customers. Today, however, salespeople and the companies they work for have begun to realise that building relationships with customers offers tremendous advantages. Customers are happier, salespeople sell more, and the company's bottom line improves. Personal selling presents truly a win-win situation all round.

In this chapter, we explore the shift from the old style of selling to the new style of selling. We explain person-to-person selling, and the good and the bad about telesales. We take a look at selling on the Internet and selling to other businesses. We show you why companies that build relationships instead of only sales goals are more likely to prosper.

Forget the Hard Sell

Used car dealer. Slowly say those words to yourself. What picture comes to mind? For many, you can't find a better example of the worst style of selling than a used car salesperson. Aggressive, pushy, and focused only on making a sale – any sale – *now*! What happens two months from now, or two weeks, or even two days from now isn't important. That salesperson is absolutely *not* going to let you walk out of the dealership without putting the hard sell on you.

This old-style approach to selling is called *transaction marketing*. Why? Because it focuses on individual sales, or *transactions*. In transaction marketing, buyers and sellers usually have no ongoing relationship with one another, and communications are limited. The primary goal is a short-term one: Sell something and sell it now. What? You don't like that pink Skoda? How about if we repaint it for you? What do we need to do to get you to buy this car right now?

Plenty of salespeople are still out there who concentrate only on transactions. And that situation's really no surprise because most salespeople sell on commission and are expected to sell a certain number of units each month, week, or day. If they don't make their goals, not only will they not make the commission they hoped for, but they may be disciplined by their supervisor or manager.

Many salespeople and the companies that employ them (including car dealerships) are trying a new approach. This new approach is based on *relationships*, not transactions. Indeed, more and more companies every day are discovering that creating long-term relationships with clients and customers can pay off – not only in increased sales but also in decreased marketing costs over the long term. And these results mean a much healthier bottom line.

Creating bonds, one step at a time

If you want long-term business relationships with your customers, you have to build them one step at a time.

For example, the financial services sector in the UK has undergone a radical transformation in recent years. The transformation began with designating bank cashiers as 'salespeople'. As customers were making their transactions and paying their bills over the counter, they'd be asked if they wanted a savings review, home insurance, or anything else. The cashiers were required to do this, whether or not they wanted to.

This approach didn't work. Customers had called in to pay bills or make withdrawals. Going about their daily business, they hadn't thought in advance if they wanted a savings review.

Accordingly, the banks and financial institutions introduced telesales (see the later section 'Telesales: Good or Bad?'). This worked better, but wasn't ideal.

So finally, the banks and financial services' institutions began to introduce expert and dedicated financial advisers. The retail branches and telesales were limited to making sure that customers were aware of the expert advice available, and then leaving the financial advisers and individual customers to make their own relationships.

Step by step, the companies arrived at a more or less ideal and effective working relationship; and step by step, the customers at last got what they wanted, and at times that suited them – not just the banks and financial institutions themselves.

In relationship-based selling, the focus is on

- Building a long-term relationship with the customer
- Selling the benefits of the product or service
- Providing dedicated customer service
- Being totally committed to the customer
- Talking to the customer continuously

What happened? Why the change in emphasis from transactions to relationships? Customers today have an incredibly wide variety of products and services to choose from, more than ever before. In addition, customers have almost unlimited choices when deciding from whom to buy their products and services. With an ever-increasing array of resources available for all products and services, the range of customer choices has skyrocketed.

But with all this choice comes a problem. If everyone is providing the same products for about the same price, how do you decide on one company to buy from? Increasingly, people are basing their decisions on relationships. People prefer to buy from companies with which they have relationships. They want companies that show they care about their customers through their commitment to their customers, their superior customer service, and the importance they place on maintaining a relationship instead of simply selling a product.

Contrast the typical picture of the used car dealer to the way that Toyota approaches the selling of its Lexus line of luxury cars. Suddenly, everything is customer-focused. Customers may make several visits to the showroom or dealership before deciding to buy. Everything is concentrated on reassuring the customer that what they're getting in return for their expensive purchase is what they require from it – not just a sale to the dealership. People who buy the cars will tell their friends that they have full confidence in the dealership itself. And this is a critical part of marketing and selling!

How do you change your company's sales approach from transaction-based to relationship-based? Here are the six keys to building relationships with your clients and customers that you can put to work in your organisation:

- **Build trust.** The first step in developing long-term relationships with clients and customers is to build trust. Trust is the glue that holds business relationships together and the catalyst that makes them stronger and deeper over time. When a supplier honours his commitment to sell you 1,000 cases of Merlot wine at a price of £100 each – even though his costs have increased and he'll make far less money as a result – he builds the kind of trust that makes for strong, long-term business relationships.

- **Build confidence.** Everyone needs confidence in their relationships, business or otherwise. If you're making high value sales, you need to spend part of your sales effort on ensuring that the potential customer or client has confidence in you that you'll deliver what you say when you say it.

- **Create bonds.** Long-term business relationships depend on the creation of bonds between organisations and people. Bonds arise when organisations and people find that they have mutual goals and interests, and they decide to work together to take advantage of them. As time goes on and the relationship matures, the bonds become increasingly stronger.

- **Be empathetic.** Being empathetic means that you see a situation through the eyes of another party. If you're empathetic, you have an understanding of a person that goes much deeper than you ever get by focusing only on a transaction. Empathy is a key building-block in relationships and an emotional link that builds trust between parties.

Everyone loves to get a good deal. However, a responsibility is attached to this scenario. Especially, you still have to look after your staff properly. If you load up all of your empathy on the side of the customer, your own people will feel let down. For example, the Virgin Organisation takes the view that it's only through full empathy with the staff that empathy with the customer can be achieved.

✔ **Encourage reciprocity.** Sometimes, you have to give a little to get a lot. *Reciprocity* is giving something up to get something that you need, such as offering a 20 per cent discount – as long as the customer signs up for the product or service today. Effectively structured, reciprocity is a key part of ensuring successful and profitable business transactions. For example, many companies give you some kind of reward if you introduce friends to them; and some supermarkets and department stores give additional loyalty points and discounts after you spend a certain amount of money with them.

✔ **Follow up.** If someone buys from you, make sure that you follow up their custom. Ensure that they're satisfied with their purchase; and if not, establish where the faults lie, and take immediate remedial steps. If a customer didn't make a purchase, have a quick follow up to find out why this was the case. You can gain additional information to use as a part of developing your future sales efforts.

Person-to-Person Selling

Person-to-person selling is a subset of the overall category of selling called direct sales. Direct selling is the sale of a consumer product or service in a face-to-face manner away from a fixed retail location. What makes person-to-person selling special is its unique system of selling in which salespeople take on two key roles:

✔ **Distributor:** A distributor's job is to buy products from the parent company and sell them directly to the public, usually friends, relatives, and work associates. Every time you sell an item, you make a profit.

✔ **Recruiter:** If you're a recruiter, your job is to sign up other distributors to work for you. Every time your distributor sells an item, you receive a percentage of the profit made by that distributor.

As a person-to-person seller you have two key ways to make money. You can sell products as a distributor, or you can sign up new distributors and take a cut of their product sales. Signing up new distributors creates a *downline*, that is, all the people whom you sponsor into the sales programme, as well as the people *they* sponsor, and so on. An *upline* is a distributor's sponsor, as well as the other sponsors above him or her in the organisation.

Direct selling (including person-to-person selling) offers a number of benefits to those who decide to try it, including the following:

- ✔ Direct selling is a good way to meet and socialise with people.

- ✔ Earnings are in proportion to efforts.

- ✔ Direct selling offers flexible work schedules.

- ✔ Direct selling is a good way to earn extra income – although usually not a lot.

- ✔ Direct selling is a good way to own a business.

Be warned! If you go down the direct sales route, remember that most people don't make much money out of it, so don't commit to it full-time. According to Amway, the American kitchen products company and direct sales pioneer, the average income per salesperson is £50 ($88) per month – before expenses! Don't put your life on the line for this kind of return.

Telesales: Good or Bad?

If you've ever had your dinner interrupted by a telephone sales call (and who hasn't?) then you know just what the main problem with telesales is. Nobody likes these calls, whether they're from home improvement companies, double-glazing contractors, or the financial services sector. Telesales conjures up an image of rooms full of low-paid employees working their way through lists of people as fast as they can.

As the result of practice and perception, the public view of telesales is largely negative. However, for companies that get it right, telesales is a very effective tool for business development, when properly targeted and directed. Table 19-1 shows the advantages and disadvantages of telesales.

Table 19-1: The Advantages and Disadvantages of Telesales

Advantages	*Disadvantages*
The personal contact of telesales can build long-term relationships if done properly.	Telephone salespeople have a bad image.
Telesales is much more cost effective than face-to-face selling.	Telephone salespeople may have to make many calls to find a customer.
Telephone salespeople can speak with far more prospects each day than can a salesperson doing face-to-face selling.	Potential customers find saying no easier when they're talking to someone on the phone rather than face to face.

Two distinctly different kinds of telesales exist: *Inbound*, or *passive* (the kind that most consumers seem to like) and *outbound*, or *active* (the kind that most consumers seem to hate).

Inbound telesales

If you've ever called a company on a free-phone number to place an order for a product or service, then you've participated in inbound (or passive) telesales. Inbound telesales is a particularly effective and fruitful sales technique because people generally call only when they're ready to place an order to purchase your product or service. They often call as a result of advertisements, catalogues, radio or television advertising, your Web site, or other forms of advertising that your company uses.

Here are some ways to use inbound telesales to your benefit:

- ✔ Order taking
- ✔ Customer services and complaint management
- ✔ Ticket sales
- ✔ Web site call processing
- ✔ Surveys and questionnaires
- ✔ Dealer location
- ✔ Seminar registration
- ✔ Reservations

Although many companies run their own inbound telesales operations, others outsource these operations to call centres that are specifically geared to handle the task of inbound telesales. Such call centres are often less expensive than hiring in-house staff, buying telecommunications equipment, and leasing phone lines. Another benefit of these call centres is that the individuals working there are generally specially trained for the task. Many call centres can offer your customers 24-hours-a-day, seven-days-a-week service.

Outbound telesales

Outbound telesales is the active kind of telesales. In outbound telesales, salespeople make phone calls to prospects (potential customers), make a quick sales pitch, and then try to sell them a product or service. If they can't make a sale, telephone salespeople at least find out whether there's enough interest to turn the prospect over to a full-time salesperson to make a more sophisticated sales pitch.

Here are some ways to put outbound telesales to use for you:

- Sales lead generation
- Customer service
- Appointment setting
- Customer surveys
- Sales campaigns
- Database updates
- Customer care and retention
- Follow-up calls

Just as some companies specialise in *inbound* telesales for other businesses, some companies specialise in *outbound* telesales. If you decide to outsource your outbound telesales, be sure that the company you appoint has a good reputation in the industry. Also confirm that the company has specific experience selling the kinds of products and services that you offer for sale. Ask for references and check them.

So is telesales good or bad? It depends on which end of the phone you're on and whether you're receptive to the message that the salesperson has been ordered to give you. Unfortunately, because of overzealous outbound telesales companies, many consumers consider telesales calls to be bad news. Until the telesales companies target their efforts much more effectively, people will simply continue to hang up whenever their phones ring at inconvenient times.

Selling on the Web

Selling on the Internet has come a long way. Not so long ago, experts were predicting the imminent demise of the high street, and retail and shopping centres; everyone was going to do all their shopping online. Boo.com, the online footwear retailer, asserted that it would supply shoes to customers anywhere in the world from its warehouse in Sweden – and if you could buy shoes on the Internet, what possible reason could you have for going to old-fashioned shops at all? Of course, all these predictions turned out to be nonsense. Indeed, the big retailers have expanded their operations over the last five years, opening new shops and taking on extra staff. And sales at retail outlets (bricks and mortar shops!) continue to grow. Occasional retail downturns are blamed on the weather, interest rate rises, increases in charges for gas and electricity – but not the Internet.

In order to be effective, you need to have a clear understanding of what your customers and potential customers want from an Internet facility. Your Web site itself needs to be easy to use. You need a system of order numbers, or a secure credit and debit card payment facility. Your products and services must be delivered in ways that offer a clear and alternative advantage to mainstream wholesale and retail. And people must be able to contact you directly whenever they need to.

Having said that, for companies that have 'got it right', Internet sales have caused substantial and sustainable business development. For example:

✔ Argos uses Internet presentations and offers to support its catalogue, mail order, and retail operations.

✔ Tesco presently generates £400 million worth of sales through Tesco.com, its online operation. This makes it the company's largest performing single outlet in the UK.

✔ Amazon has generated a successful and sustainable business through large volumes of sales of books, CDs, DVDs, and other related products.

✔ e-Bay, the online auctioneers, has developed a real alternative to show-room sales, second-hand shops, and traditional auctions.

✔ Ryanair and EasyJet make virtually all of their ticket sales through the Internet; indeed, both companies make it inconvenient and more costly to book other than online.

Serving the e-shopper

The shake-out of failed Internet companies over the recent past has left behind those that are able to make a success, using the Internet as a business medium. The main lessons that anyone who seeks to be effective in selling on the Internet are as follows:

✔ You need advertising, public relations, and other media coverage in the traditional world, so that people know who you are, what you do, and the benefits and value that your products and services bring to the customers that you serve.

✔ You need helplines that customers can reach whenever they need or want.

✔ You must have an Internet presence that reinforces any physical presence; and/or a physical presence that reinforces any Internet presence.

✔ You must be able to deliver something over the Internet that is of value to the customers that you seek to serve – and judging by the crowds at supermarkets and other retail outlets on a Friday evening or Saturday morning, sitting at the computer is no – or not yet – one of them.

However, there are substantial business reasons why these companies, and others like them, have been so successful and effective in generating continued retail and sales activities, including:

- ✔ Argos and Tesco continue to operate their traditional, familiar retail outlets in full, and as the core of their business. Tesco has opened new retail outlets alongside the development of its Internet operation, including Tesco Metro and Tesco Local in town and city centres. Internet sales are a by-product of their physical presence, and a development alongside their physical presence. The volumes of sales are generated largely through the enduring confidence that Tesco's physical presence has built up over many years.

- ✔ Amazon and e-Bay ensure extensive and continuous media coverage through priority attention to public relations. Amazon reinforce their good public relations through low prices and assured delivery dates. e-Bay ensure that all stories, including frauds, are fully covered in the news media and on television and radio. e-Bay take the view that all publicity is good publicity, and open coverage of fraud and failure, and what they do to repair the situation, reinforces and develops public confidence in using the service.

- ✔ Ryanair and EasyJet reinforce their brands, and especially their unique selling point of very low fares, through extensive and concentrated advertising and billboard campaigns. Ryanair's newspaper advertisements (including one featuring Pope John Paul II) have a history of controversy, recognition, and identity – leading to increased sales.

Selling to Other Businesses

The nature of selling to other businesses has changed dramatically over recent years. The change is not so much a shift from transaction selling to relationship selling, because businesses have long depended on developing strong relationships with business customers to promote sales. The change has resulted mostly as a result of the mass computerisation of the ordering process and the widespread use of the Web for e-commerce applications.

Business-to-business sales remain heavily dependent on personal selling because this builds a personal, as well as professional, relationship between the two organisations. You can reinforce this effort with e-mail and Internet presentations, both in terms of general awareness raising, and also in terms of the speed of response you can generate.

The Internet

The early focus of commerce on the Internet was on retail sales to individual consumers. This focus is beginning to change as software and security evolve to a point where companies can do business with each other as safely and securely as traditional invoicing systems. You can establish convenient systems whereby the ordering of parts and components can be generated automatically through an e-mail request, and an invoice sent out at the same time. Additionally, most Web sites now contain pages under the headings of 'trade enquiries', 'business partners', 'business associates', and 'suppliers' – and, of course, 'contact us'. All these developments mean that more information is available more readily for all suppliers and business partners, so that contact can be accurately directed.

Other electronic sales and ordering systems

The purpose of any electronic sales and ordering system is to deliver all of the accuracy required in terms of volumes, quality, and deadlines of the traditional billing and invoicing process, but with extra speed and no postage costs. Costs are reduced in terms of the numbers of staff required to work in sales, support, and other back office functions; and flexibility and responsiveness to customer demands are increased.

Businesses can experience major benefits from electronic sales and ordering systems. For example:

✔ Matalan, the UK good value clothing retailer, developed a system in conjunction with one of its suppliers whereby the latest catwalk designs could be copied, made, and in the shops within first days and subsequently hours of the fashion shows. Previously, the fashion industry had produced expensive and exclusive designs that sold for many months at premium prices, before the mass retailers and clothing outlets were able to copy and distribute them. The Matalan system, worked out and designed with its suppliers, speeded up the whole process and increased sales.

✔ Campbell's, the soup company, completely revamped its order processing system after finding mistakes in up to 60 per cent of all the orders received by phone or fax. Because of these errors, the company's sales teams were spending up to 40 per cent of their time clearing up the mistakes to provide customers with the products that they really wanted. In addition, delays in the internal operating system resulted in a time lag of

48 hours between receiving the order and getting it out. By renovating its order processing system, Campbell's was able to reduce order turn-around time to between 3–6 hours, and the number of mistakes from 60 per cent to 2 per cent.

Any electronic sales system is only fully effective if you target a specific purpose, and design and implement the system with that particular purpose in mind. Your fundamental organisation and business drive is to produce and deliver products and services as efficiently and effectively as possible, and when customers require them. Don't contemplate anything that doesn't support this, or you'll experience problems. For example:

✔ A supermarket re-ordering system meant that by the time that perishables with a short-term shelf-life were delivered to outlets, they had to be sold at a discount or else thrown away because they weren't arriving until the end of the 'best-before' date.

✔ A hospital re-ordering system was producing the same volume of antiseptics and bandages on the last day of a month, whether or not the hospital actually required them. If the hospital ran out of these stocks early, the system had no flexibility for early re-ordering.

✔ A white goods manufacturer introduced an electronic sales invoicing system that was fully accurate, but wasn't quick enough to process sales and purchase orders. Consequently, the company suffered serious cash flow problems, until it discarded the system and went back to manual operations until a better system was delivered.

Supplier-managed stock control

In order to be effective in selling, you must have a stock of products and services available for sale, and so you must ensure that you have effective stock management in place. However, the costs associated with carrying large volumes of stocks have led many companies to address their supply side and seek alternative ways of managing this effectively.

Many companies and organisations, especially large and complex institutions, require large quantities of different items, and so use lots of time, space, and staffing in stock processing and stock management. In such organisations, the process of ordering, receiving, and stocking is continuous and can be expensive. This situation has led many organisations to consider alternative approaches to sales, purchases, ordering, and re-ordering of stocks. In particular, a current favourite is outsourcing the whole stock management process to dependent or even wholly-owned individual suppliers, responsible for managing stock volumes and ensuring that the right quantities are delivered when required to the parent organisation.

The great strength of this approach is that it enables the parent organisation to concentrate on its core and primary tasks, whatever these may be. It also enables the subsidiary or dependent organisation to specialise and concentrate on what it does best – supplying the parent or dominant organisation.

Despite the advantages, be aware of the following:

- ✔ Vauxhall, the UK subsidiary of General Motors, outsourced the production of a range of thousands of essential components to a subsidiary, Unisys. For a time, the relationship worked well. However, the contractual arrangement went wrong when Vauxhall tried to reduce the payments to Unisys at a time when the cost of the production of components was rising. Unisys called in the receivers and ceased trading for a time. Vauxhall had to provide a substantial cash injection, and increase the payments that it made to Unisys in order to ensure that its supplies were maintained.

- ✔ British Airways contracted out the whole of its catering supplies for its long-haul routes to Gate Gourmet Ltd, a specialist supplier of airline food and other industrial catering products. Problems arose when British Airways was unwilling to put up the prices that Gate Gourmet needed to charge as the result of increased raw materials, ingredients, and staffing costs. Again, the consequence was that the supplying company was unable to continue to do business with the main institution. This particular relationship was damaged further when Gate Gourmet experienced a strike by all of its 600 workers following a proposal to restructure the firm and cut costs.

Both Vauxhall and British Airways have found a way of managing their stock control, purchases, sales, and re-ordering processes. Any such relationship must be based on the assurance of continuity of supply from both sides, as well as mutual trust, and assurance of mutual benefit: A genuine partnership. Otherwise, either the supplier won't be able to guarantee deliveries, or else the dominant organisation may use its position in its own narrow interests, rather than those of the business as a whole – and the customers, who ultimately ensure the success and well-being of both companies. Another firm may supply you with components, but you cannot abdicate the responsibility for the whole of the supply side, or you risk letting down your customers.

Part V
The Last Pieces of the Jigsaw

'It used to be called 'The Economic
Miracle' in the boom days.'

In this part . . .

*I*n this part, we take a look at a variety of other important business topics not covered in the preceding four parts. We discuss manufacturing, distribution, and service – and how technology has had a major impact on each — and we explore the most important concepts of risk management. We also reveal the secrets of successful negotiation.

Chapter 20

Manufacturing and Distribution: Technology Makes the Difference

- -

In This Chapter

▶ Understanding how technology has changed production processes

▶ Concentrating on your stock

▶ Purchasing the right amount at the right time

▶ Looking at distribution as a competitive advantage

- -

Sometimes, you have to look to the past to find the right road to the future. We have to go back nearly 200 years to find a time when manufacturing was more like it is today than ever before. That's because 200 years ago, manufacturing was essentially a craft industry that produced products to customers' specifications. Quality was important, and people received exactly what they wanted when they wanted it.

But over time, the population grew, customers began to value and demand standardised products, and manufacturers began to find more products to produce. As a result, manufacturing evolved from customisation to mass production. Instead of remaining the holistic undertaking that it was, manufacturing became a separate entity that was set apart from the other functions of business. Any input that manufacturing used to get from the customer now came from marketing, finance, and management.

Western manufacturers finally embraced the concept of total quality in the 1980s, after years of stinging defeats to Japanese manufacturers who had made quality the number one issue during the previous two decades. Western companies finally adopted such principles as total quality management (TQM), and just-in-time (JIT) manufacturing (see the later section 'Getting what you need just in time'). As a result, manufacturing again became a significant contributor to the overall performance of companies. Furthermore, over the past decade, manufacturing productivity has increased substantially to the point where businesses now often have excess capacity that they can use to partner with smaller businesses that have compatible products, or else expand into new markets.

The combination of higher productivity and increasing small business entry into manufacturing can be attributed to three factors:

- The recognition that flexibility is essential and that companies need to focus on their core competencies and outsource any capability that they cannot easily do themselves.
- The strong commitment to total quality in both products and processes.
- The emphasis on *agile manufacturing* or flexible manufacturing systems.

Throughout all the changes that manufacturing has undergone over the past 50 years alone, not until the end of the 20th century did we see a return to the idea of giving customers exactly what they want when they want it.

And none of these achievements can happen or be sustained without technology, and without the expertise to use it to best advantage. This chapter explores all these changes in greater detail.

How Technology Has Changed the Production Process

The impact of technology on manufacturing processes is vitally important. Understanding this can help you recognise what's possible for your business, and whether you choose to manufacture products yourself or find someone to do it for you.

What do customers want today? They want superior quality, excellent service, on-time delivery (or sooner, if possible), and the specific features and benefits they're interested in. Now, how are traditional manufacturers with standard mechanical, assembly-line processes supposed to meet those demands? If they're going to stand any chance at all, then technology has to be capable of delivering both superior quality, and also individual specifications when required.

Technology has changed the face of manufacturing in a variety of ways. Here are a few of them:

✔ Using technology to improve your products, processes, and services gives you a strong competitive advantage in the market over companies that do not use technology in that manner.

✔ You can use technology to improve quality – in the design of products, in the accuracy of specifications, and in the accuracy of assembly processes.

✔ If your company develops a new process or product technology, it becomes something like an incubator for the new products that you can develop from that technology. That same technology may also help the many other companies that supply you with your materials and production needs.

✔ Technology allows your company to reduce costs, increase process speed, and better track performance in the various critical areas of your business.

✔ Technology allows your company to improve productivity, reduce wastage, and vary the speed of the overall production process according to demand.

✔ Using technology allows you to set up *manufacturing cells*, essentially tiny product manufacturing teams that are fully responsible for the complete production of a product. In this way, you can reconfigure your manufacturing capability as needed.

✔ Technology allows you to develop new products faster, and to redesign your existing products more quickly and more in line with specific customer demand.

Making your company more agile

The rapidly changing global business environment has made agile manufacturing an absolute necessity, not just an attempt to adopt the latest business fad. *Agile manufacturing* or *lean production* is about responding quickly and effectively to changes in demand, preferences, expectations, and opportunities. The customer decides what is produced, when it's produced and how much is produced, and the company responds.

The process is as simple as that, but it does bring additional commitments. Customers still want their products and services delivered at their convenience. So lean and agile production demand speed and flexibility of working as a direct consequence.

For example:

- Levi Strauss can tailor their jeans to the customers' precise body shape and measurements, but the customers still want their clothes quickly.

- Dell Computers manufacture and deliver computers directly to order, which means that they have to be capable of being assembled in minutes.

- Marton Office Furniture is only manufactured to order and to precise specification, and the company guarantees a 48-hour response; so the work has to be completed rapidly.

- The retail fashion industry has to be able to get catwalk designs into the shops within 24–48 hours of the fashion shows taking place.

Today, the perceived value of a product is directly related to the knowledge, information, and services bundled with it. These new products are called *knowledge-based products* and include things such as mobile phones, drugs and pharmaceuticals, and mid-range to top-of-the-range cars. Each delivers more than their primary purpose (in these examples, making calls, curing an ailment, and getting about). The great thing about producing products that have more value than only their tangible value (their features) is that they give you an opportunity to create long-term customer relationships which are essential to long-term business survival. For example:

- The phone comes with games, Internet, radio, and music download capability.

- The drugs and pharmaceuticals come with preventative as well as curative properties.

- The car comes with satellite navigation, rain sensitive wipers, automatic headlight beam adjustment, and speed and cruise control.

To become an agile or lean manufacturer, you need to do several things:

- Create a team that consists of your employees, your suppliers, and your customers, so that everyone is in this together. Get your customers involved so that you gain full understanding and agreement about likely delivery deadlines and product and service volumes that they may require. This system reduces the times when customers drop onto you from out of the blue (although if they do simply drop on you, you still have to deliver!).

- Try to stick with a core technology that allows you to produce a variety of products. This approach is much less expensive and more efficient than creating something completely new each time.

✔ Strive to use common parts on several different products. Doing so saves design time on the parts you build and permits you to buy in volume on the parts you get from your suppliers.

✔ Wherever possible, use off-the-shelf components instead of designing from scratch. Why reinvent something that someone else has already designed very well?

✔ Talk to your suppliers about designing the parts you need or modifying their parts to work in your products. If they see your products as viable new markets for their parts, they'll want to help you succeed.

Becoming an agile manufacturer requires a fundamental re-think of your production planning approach. You're planning for flexibility and responsiveness rather than assuredness; and you're planning to respond to customer demands, rather than to meet production targets.

Let a robot do the work: Automation

One obvious effect of technology on manufacturing is the use of robotics and intelligent machinery to gain productivity, flexibility, and quality. This effect is particularly relevant for repetitive tasks and quick set-ups. Here are three examples of how automation is used in different situations:

✔ **Stock tracking:** Bar coding technology has certainly lightened the load for businesses that track stocks. Bar codes contain all the information about the product, whether it's a consumer product or a part for manufacturing. The bar coder allows you to capture production information without having to manually enter it into a computer. This technology saves a tremendous amount of time and decreases the chance of error that so often occurs with manual data entry methods.

✔ **Instruction, fabrication, and assembly:** Computer-generated manufacturing has made it possible to programme a machine to produce exactly the part you want much more quickly and accurately than it ever could by hand. Manufacturers who've invested in these state-of-the-art machines now have computer screens on the factory floor so that workers can access designs, instructions, and manuals and then make decisions about modifications, all with a few keystrokes. They can also enter order status information, which can then be accessed by marketing, finance, and any other departments within the organisation.

Increasingly, workers in all manufacturing sectors require the capability to access a virtual library of information as they pursue their particular tasks. They need to be able to do this quickly and accurately so as to be able to respond immediately to any sudden changes in specification that may be required of the particular products.

✔ **Access to data:** The ability to move data around quickly from one function, department, division, or site to others is also important to effective manufacturing processes. If your designers are in Leeds but your factory is in Southampton, you can easily transfer designs and other information, and get the modifications that you need very quickly.

✔ **System compatibility:** If you enter into partnerships with your customers and suppliers, then all systems have to be fully compatible. The last thing you need is for information to be made totally illegible just because you've chosen to stick to your present systems, or have forgotten to ensure that systems are compatible.

Making sure technology works for you

Technology encompasses more than automation, robotics, and computer-aided equipment, or solving problems with technology. Technology is an enabler that makes being more productive, performing better, and achieving higher returns on investment possible.

Technology is a means to an end, not the end itself. At its best, technology helps you achieve your company's goals. At its worst, it can introduce a level of complexity not required to accomplish those goals. Never be blinded by the sheer capability, complexity, or intrinsic excellence of the technology itself. Always ensure that you evaluate technology on the basis of what it can do for you in terms of improving the quality, efficiency, and productivity of your manufacturing processes. Never introduce technology just because it is fashionable or state-of-the-art.

Most important of all, make sure that your staff are fully trained to operate the technology. Having unproductive staff, simply because they have been inadequately trained to operate the technology, is very expensive. Having technology that isn't being used to full capacity is also very expensive.

Finally, make sure that you design and implement technological advances because they're going to be of value to you in the future. Many managers and organisations make the mistake of introducing new technology because it will produce some marginal advantage to today's activities. If at all possible, you need to be looking at technology from the point of view of enduring contribution to the long-term future of the organisation, and not simply an immediate (and often notional) cost saving today.

Designing your production process

So many manufacturers devote the majority of their budgets to new *product* development and don't think about how important new *process* development is.

In today's market, the way you manufacture a product is often the critical element, perhaps even more so than the product itself, because your innovative process is probably what gives you a competitive advantage in the market.

Today, you have to be prepared to plan for anything from long run production processes, to producing limited batches, and even *single unit build*. The single unit build process means that a product goes through a series of tasks and operations while remaining inside the manufacturing cell. Contrast that process with the way companies used to do manufacturing: Centralising tasks and operations and then sending multiple products through the process assembly-line fashion. The purpose of this older method was to maximise the use of expensive equipment. Now you need to balance demands for mass products, while at the same time being able to deliver individualised items when required. Additionally, you need to be very aware of the costs incurred in stockpiling and storage.

All manufacturing processes need careful design. Remember – your intention is to produce the right volume and quality of products for your customers, when they need them. Pay particular attention to the following:

- ✔ If desirable, set up a supplier just-in-time system. We discuss just-in-time in the section 'Getting what you need just in time', but essentially you want to make sure that your supplies arrive when you're ready to use them so that you don't have to store raw materials.

- ✔ Train all of your employees in as many of the tasks and duties required as possible so that you have a fully flexible and responsive workforce, and so that people can be moved from one task to another as required.

- ✔ Reduce the *set-up time*, which is the time it takes to get the right equipment ready for a particular product, from hours to minutes.

- ✔ Design your manufacturing plant at the same time that you're doing product development so that the product flow from one task to another is smooth.

Stock: Too Much, Too Little, or Just Right?

Stock is those materials and goods that you hold for manufacture or sale. Every business has stock of one type or another because meeting customer demand in a timely fashion is vital. However, stocks are costly to maintain, so you have to create a delicate balance of raw materials, work in progress, and finished goods. The following sections look at some of the costs of storage.

The hidden costs of storage

Many business owners don't realise that the hidden costs of storage can amount to as much as 25 per cent of the base cost of the stocks. That's a substantial amount. Some of these costs are:

- **Financing cost:** This is the interest paid on money borrowed to purchase the stocks. Most businesses can't afford to pay cash for stocks, so they finance it. It's an expensive way to do it, but a fact of life.

- **Insurance costs:** You need to protect your stock from fire, damage, or theft.

- **Obsolescence:** This is the cost of stocks that are no longer marketable or usable.

- **Opportunity cost:** This is the loss of use of the money that's tied up in storage.

- **Staffing cost:** All stocks and storage need staff to make sure that they're maintained in a useable condition as and when required.

- **Premises costs:** All stocks have to be stored somewhere, and if you choose to do this yourself, you have to pay for premises and make them secure.

Do everything possible to reduce these costs. In the section 'Getting what you need just in time', we talk about just-in-time purchasing to help reduce storage costs. But another way you can manage stock is by tracking it.

Tracking stocks

Keeping track of stocks has really been helped by technology, specifically bar-coding technology. Consider these three methods of monitoring your stocks:

- **Perpetual stocking system:** These systems are based on keeping a running count of items used or sold via an electronic point-of-sale device such as the ones used in your supermarket. As materials are purchased, their bar code information is scanned into the system; as the materials are used, they're deducted from the stocks held. With this system, you have immediate access to the status of your stocks.

✓ **Physical count system:** You probably won't physically count your stocks if you have a sizeable business. But most businesses still do some physical stock checking to look out for errors in their electronic system. Of course, to make the physical counting manageable, you need to get your storage system as simple as possible.

✓ **A combined storage system:** Some companies use a combined system of perpetual and physical stock management. They do physical counts on less commonly sold items that they carry in small quantities, and they use a perpetual system for the majority of their items.

Companies need to understand the amount of resource that can be tied up in stocks and storage systems, and they need to make sure that this resource works as effectively as possible at all times.

Purchasing: When, Where, and How Much?

When purchasing raw materials or goods for resale, you need to consider three very important factors: Quality, quantity, and timing. We define quality materials as those that meet the company's specific requirements, which means that level of quality will be different for every company. Quantity purchased always depends on demand by the customer and your ability to manufacture, based on your plant, equipment, and staff. Timing is about making sure that you're using plant, equipment, and staff to their full capacity and that space (such as a warehouse) is used only when necessary. This section discusses the supply side of production and how to make it more effective.

Getting what you need just in time

Materials management is a very important part of manufacturing. The goal is to have the raw materials you need when you need them – not before, not after, but right when you need them, or *just-in-time* (JIT). The benefits of JIT are many:

✓ You can improve your cycle and delivery times.

✓ You use material only when you need it.

✓ You can reduce stock and storage levels, and thereby reduce space needs.

- ✔ You can improve quality.

- ✔ You improve cash flow by paying only for what you need when you need it.

- ✔ You ensure that staff are targeted at effective activities rather than stock and storage management.

- ✔ Raw materials are turned into finished products as quickly as possible.

If your company is producing a single product in high volume, use the *continuous flow* version of JIT. In this version, the amount of raw materials needed is placed at the start of the process and moves through the process as needed.

If you're producing a variety of products, you can use the JIT version called *kanban*. Kanban in Japanese means 'visible record' and actually refers to the signal cards used to move bins full of parts through the process line. For example, the process starts with bins full of parts. Then, when the part bin nearest the task being completed is empty, it moves to the source of supply, and the next full bin moves forward. In this way you don't build up storage queues. Also, defects are caught and corrected and therefore not passed along the line.

If you're considering using JIT, make sure that you have the five primary components in place:

- ✔ Know your customers. Know what their requirements are, because they determine the time to delivery and the actual production process.

- ✔ Set up your production so that at each point along the line you're completing a task. Each task needs to take about the same length of time so there's no waiting.

- ✔ Make your supplier a central part of the process so that you don't need warehouse materials – your supplier does the warehousing and gets materials to you exactly when you need them.

- ✔ Attend to every aspect of your production process. All production and manufacturing processes only deliver finished items at the speed of the slowest element. If you experience a hold-up on the supply side, then make sure that the components are delivered a little bit in advance.

- ✔ Make sure that you have no logistical problems that can hold up production. For example, make sure that you're not losing money because your components are caught in traffic jams. If necessary, consider opening a night-time delivery facility, so that stocks arrive when the roads are less crowded.

Choosing the right suppliers

Finding suppliers for whatever you need isn't hard. The trick is to find the good ones. The first decision you need to make is whether to use one supplier or multiple suppliers for each of the components or materials you require. Getting your materials from more than one source has an important advantage. If something happens to your supplier, you have a backup. But here are also a couple of good reasons to use a single supplier for materials:

✔ You'll probably get better service and attention.

✔ The supplier may combine your order with those of other companies so that you can all benefit from a volume purchase.

You need to take an active and informed view of how you're going to structure your supply side. You don't want to become dependent on one supplier, but on the other hand, you don't want to miss out on advantages that may be present if you do place the bulk of your business with one supplier. When the time comes to select among suppliers, here are some questions to ask:

✔ Can the supplier deliver what you need, when you need it?

✔ If you use this supplier, what will your freight costs be?

✔ What kinds of services does the supplier offer?

✔ How well does your supplier know the product line he or she is selling you? Can he or she answer all your questions to your satisfaction?

✔ What kinds of guarantees can the supplier offer, and what are the supplier's maintenance and return policies?

Check every aspect of your proposed relationship with the particular suppliers. You need to compare prices, service levels, regularity and frequency of deliveries, and the supplier's ability to vary volumes and specifications at short notice if needed. All of these details form the foundation on which an effective and enduring relationship with suppliers is built.

Distribution: A Great Way to Compete

Distribution comprises all the ways that you get the product to the customer. Logistics is the physical aspect of production – transporting the manufactured product to the customer. New approaches to manufacturing, in which flexibility and responsiveness are central, have led to new distribution strategies that are more compatible with the fast-changing marketplace. This section looks at some of the major changes in distribution strategy today.

Some new distribution strategies

Technology once again has provided new solutions to old problems, and it has opened the door to great opportunities to innovate in distribution. Here are four changes taking place right now in distribution:

- ✔ Companies are adding value wherever they can find it, and speed of delivery is one key area. Manufacturing companies now offer product replacements, upgrades, and maintenance and after-sales functions as a matter of course; and again, each has to be delivered quickly when demanded. Indeed, if you don't deliver quickly and effectively, you must have a very good reason otherwise customers will simply use your competitors who do provide these services. Some companies outsource these services to specialist providers.

- ✔ Companies are shifting to broaden their position wherever possible. For example, if you serve specialist niches, consider how your products might be modified or re-designed to be distributed in new markets. Or you may want to introduce *add-ons* – accessories and other features that are compatible with your core products and that complement their appearance and value to the customers. And again, additional features have to be capable of quick and effective delivery.

- ✔ You may be able to appeal to new types of customer by redefining or re-branding your existing products. For example, Sony historically provided high value, high cost products; however, the company was able to enter the good value market by introducing a range of products under the brand name Aiwa, in spite of the fact that it was using the same components as in its core range. Sony was able to make this effective by ensuring that the Aiwa range was available in the outlets used by those who sought good value.

- ✔ Companies rejuvenate old or ageing products all the time. If something has lost its fashionability or currency, consider how you can re-present or rejuvenate it. For example, all of the English pub chains have transformed their core business – the sale of alcoholic drinks for consumption on the premises – through introducing branded soft drinks, meals and bar food, and tea and coffee.

So if you're going to take advantage of any of these distribution opportunities, you need to do the following:

- ✔ Analyse and evaluate your value chain. Your *value chain* is a representation of all of your activities, assessing where in your processes value is added, gained, and lost. When you assess your activities for value added and lost, make sure that you do so from the point of view of your customers and the operating environment as well as your own internal activities. And concentrate on speed and effectiveness of distribution as a source of major potential advantage and added value.

✔ Look at how you can combine products and services in your business so that you can add value for your customers. If you're in manufacturing, don't overlook the services you can provide your customers.

✔ Find new customers to serve with your products. Make sure that a proportion of your sales effort is directed at potential, rather than actual, markets (Chapter 16 has more about finding new customers).

✔ Look at your products in a new light and see if you've missed some ways to use them. (Do you know what Arm & Hammer did with baking soda? It turned baking soda into a deodoriser for refrigerators – and a toothpaste!)

A note on logistics

The relationship between manufacturing and product value enhancement through service improvements means that many companies use specialist logistics and delivery firms to provide fully flexible distribution.

You need to be able to guarantee deliveries to your customers when and where they require them, so you need a very reliable logistics firm. You may need the logistics or delivery firm to store your products before transportation. And if you have specialist products to deliver, such as frozen food or delicate components, then you want to be certain that the logistics or distribution firm you choose can manage every aspect of the delivery of these items.

Here are some questions that you need to ask any potential logistics or delivery companies:

✔ Can the logistics company do what you need it to do when you need it?

✔ What are the costs involved?

✔ What kinds of services does the logistics firm offer?

✔ Is the logistics firm used to dealing with your types of products? This information is particularly important if you have special packaging needs.

✔ What kinds of guarantees does the logistics firm supply?

Chapter 21

The Ins and Outs of Risk Management

··

In This Chapter

▶ Understanding risk

▶ Managing risk

▶ Looking at risk and insurance

▶ Using employee training to avoid risk

▶ Developing workplace safety rules

··

Most people are optimists. Plenty of businesses fail every year, but most people think that their business won't be among the statistics. Natural disasters – earthquakes, hurricanes, tornadoes, floods – happen, but they certainly won't happen to us. And even if they do, we'll be all right. Robbery, theft, arson, embezzlement, fraud – these crimes are happening all around us, but somehow most people like to think that they'll come through it all untouched by business disaster, with their customers, their businesses, and their investments intact.

Unfortunately, the world is a risky place, and bad things really do happen to even the most well-prepared, good-hearted, and competent businesspeople. The question isn't, 'Will something bad happen to my business?' Instead, the question is, 'Will I be prepared *when* something bad happens to my business?'

In the past ten years, the number of businesses in the UK having risk management policies in place has risen from 30 per cent to over 90 per cent. So at least the first step has been taken – understanding that bad things can, and do, happen, and that they can happen to anyone, at any time, anywhere.

You need to work on the basis that, at some point in its lifetime, *your* business will experience some sort of misfortune. And you have no way of knowing exactly what kind of misfortune will befall your company, nor will you know when and where it will hit. When a hurricane hit south-east England in

1987, it left ten people dead, many injured, and more than £1 billion worth of property damage. The UK has a history of bad weather – as everyone knows! Yet nobody had insured for this eventuality – it simply did not enter their thinking.

This chapter is all about risk and how to manage it. You find out how to develop and implement an effective risk management process, as well as how to identify and act on potential vulnerabilities. You discover the many different kinds of insurance available to businesses today and see how to train employees to avoid or even eliminate risk altogether. Finally, you get some advice about how to implement safety rules for the workplace.

The Basics of Managing Risk

The key to dealing with risk – whether natural disaster, theft, property damage, or personal injury – is to anticipate it and to have a plan for dealing with it. *Risk management* is the process of understanding and anticipating risks and then taking steps to minimise their impact on a business and the people within it.

Here are the five basic steps for managing risk:

1. **Identify potential risks.**

   The possibilities for loss are almost endless. What risks is your business exposed to? You need to consider, loss of or damage to property and equipment; computer crashes and loss of data; financial risks; loss of sales income; rises in costs (of electricity and taxes as well as supply side charges); fraud; vandalism and violence; and court case judgements on employment, product, and service issues.

2. **Assess and prioritise potential risks.**

   If your business is located in Bognor Regis, chances are, you won't have to worry about getting earthquake insurance. You may, however, want to prioritise the purchase of insurance in the event of a flood.

3. **Select the right risk management tools to deal with each potential risk.**

   Develop a risk management process and plan with specific strategies for dealing with risk in your business. In some cases, prevention is the right course of action. In other cases, employee training may do the trick. Sometimes, you may simply have to buy insurance to cover your risk. We explore some of the different risk management tools available to you later in this chapter, in the section 'Insurance: Shifting the Risk'.

4. **Ask specific and detailed questions about every aspect of your business.**

   Get everyone to assess and itemise the things that could conceivably go wrong in their own particular domain. Make sure that everyone knows about the risks, and understands the potential for things going wrong.

5. **Evaluate the results of your risk management strategies and revise or renew them as appropriate.**

   Periodically revisit your risk management process, strategies, and plans and ensure that they still provide the desired protection to your business. If they are, terrific – keep on doing what you're doing. If they aren't, don't hesitate to adjust your strategies or plans where necessary.

By following these steps for managing risk in your business, you'll be prepared if the unthinkable occurs. And, unfortunately, the unthinkable occurs to businesses just like yours more often than you've ever imagined.

Managing Risk (Before It Manages You)

You *can* – and need to – manage risk. Many insurers make the development of a risk management plan a condition of granting insurance coverage. No risk management process can prevent every possible risk from occurring, but a good risk management process can minimise the financial loss to a business, as well as help prevent injuries and death.

Developing a risk management process

Developing a risk management process takes the concerted effort of one or more employees over an extended period of time, and it must be done properly. Here are seven steps for developing a risk management process that really works:

1. **Get the commitment of top management.**

   For a risk management programme to work over the long haul, you must have the support of top management.

2. **Assign one person to lead your risk management efforts.**

   One person should have ultimate responsibility for your organisation's risk management process. Such a policy ensures accountability and prevents finger pointing if something goes wrong and the business is not prepared.

3. Establish a risk management committee.

Employee input is essential. Employees must participate in the risk management process by helping to identify risks and by taking actions to minimise their potential impact on your organisation. The committee can also track risk and employee injury trends and take action to reduce risks and injuries. Make sure that the committee includes a broad cross-section of employees from all levels and all parts of the organisation.

4. Create an emergency action plan.

If the unthinkable – a fire, an explosion, a natural disaster – happens, will all your employees know exactly what to do and where to go to protect your organisation's property and themselves from damage or destruction? An emergency action plan ensures that they do.

5. Establish a formal self-inspection programme.

Is your workplace safe? Are you sure? Establish a self-inspection programme to identify potential safety hazards and to take action to make repairs or corrections. Use members of your risk control committee to conduct inspections throughout your organisation.

6. Establish an accident and incident investigation programme.

The best organisations learn from accidents and incidents, and they use this information to help prevent future accidents and incidents. Appoint someone in your organisation to look into every accident and incident to determine what you can learn from and change following the mishap or occurrence.

7. Develop a training and education programme.

Train your employees to identify hazards, prevent injuries – to themselves and to others – and respond appropriately in case of emergency or disaster. A strong training and education programme can accomplish those goals.

These steps are the basics of establishing a strong foundation of risk management in your organisation. You may wish to do even more. You may want to use the expertise of consultants who specialise in this field as you go through the process. Whatever you decide to do, don't forget that sufficient foresight and planning can help prevent losses and reduce risks. A formal risk management process greatly reduces your exposure to risks and undoubtedly saves your organisation time, money, and loss of employee productivity.

Conducting a vulnerability analysis

Before you can manage the risks that your organisation is exposed to, you need to understand specifically what they are. The goal of a vulnerability analysis is to assess the probability and potential impact of different risks.

Make sure that you cover each of the areas that follow in full detail. And when you conduct a vulnerability analysis, make sure that you concentrate on people's attitudes as much as actions – the last thing that you want to occur is an accident, disaster, or emergency simply because, while you understood fully that it *could* happen, you assumed that it *wouldn't* happen.

Step 1: List potential risks

First, list all the potential risks that could affect your organisation. Make sure that you consider:

- ✔ Risks that could occur on the premises
- ✔ Risks that could occur in the immediate environment

As you consider the different risks that could possibly occur, think in terms of each of the following areas.

Corporate attitudes: What are the corporate attitudes to risk? Where do these come from? Are these attitudes adequate and concerned; or are they complacent to the point of mortal danger? Consider potential risks as the result of

- ✔ Complacency
- ✔ Arrogance
- ✔ The attitudes of one dominant personality
- ✔ The attitudes of one dominant stakeholder group
- ✔ Unwillingness to face reality

Human error: What potential risks is your business exposed to that would be the result of employee error? Are your employees trained to work safely? Do they know what to do in an emergency? Consider potential risks as a result of

- ✔ Poor training
- ✔ Poor maintenance
- ✔ Bad decisions

- ✓ Supervisory attitudes and pressures
- ✓ Carelessness
- ✓ Misconduct
- ✓ Substance or alcohol abuse
- ✓ Fatigue

Business: What kinds of risks does your organisation face that are uniquely business risks? The risks that a business faces can be quite different from the risks that an individual faces. Consider potential risks as a result of

- ✓ Malpractice
- ✓ Embezzlement
- ✓ Product liability
- ✓ Fraud
- ✓ Loss of a key person
- ✓ Errors and omissions
- ✓ Construction defects
- ✓ Worker injury and death
- ✓ Non-performance

Historical: What types of risks have your community, your premises, and other business facilities in the area faced in the past? Consider potential risks as a result of

- ✓ Fires
- ✓ Severe weather
- ✓ Hazardous material spills
- ✓ Transportation accidents
- ✓ Floods
- ✓ Hurricanes
- ✓ Terrorism
- ✓ Power cuts

Geographic: What can happen as a result of the facility's geographic location? Consider potential risks as a result of proximity to

✔ Flood plains and coastal tidal surges

✔ Companies that produce, store, use, or transport hazardous materials

✔ Major transportation routes and airports

✔ Nuclear power plants

Technological: What could result from a process or system failure? Consider potential risks as a result of

✔ Fire, explosion, or hazardous materials

✔ Safety system failure

✔ Telecommunications failure

✔ Computer system failure

✔ Power failure

✔ Heating or cooling system failure

✔ Emergency notification system failure

Physical: What types of risks could result from the design or construction of the premises? Does the physical layout of the premises enhance safety or detract from it? Consider potential risks as a result of

✔ The physical construction of the facility

✔ Hazardous processes or by-products

✔ Facilities for storing combustibles

✔ Layout of equipment

✔ Lighting

✔ Evacuation routes and exits

✔ Proximity of safe areas

Environmental: What types of risks could result from the present ways in which the environment operates? Consider potential risks as a result of

✔ Terrorist attacks

✔ Transport breakdowns

✔ Breach of security

✔ Robbery

✔ Loss of key suppliers

✔ Loss of key customer bases

Step 2: Estimate probability

Rate the likelihood of each risk's occurrence by using a simple scale of 1 to 5, with 1 as the lowest probability and 5 as the highest.

Step 3: Assess the potential human impact

Analyse the potential human impact of each potential risk – the possibility of death or injury. Assign a rating of the Potential Human Impact, again by using a 1 to 5 scale, with 1 as the lowest impact and 5 as the highest.

Step 4: Assess the potential property impact

Consider the potential for property losses and damage. Assign a rating to potential property impact, again by using a 1 to 5 scale, with 1 being the lowest impact and 5 being the highest. Consider potential risks as a result of

- Cost to replace
- Cost to set up temporary replacement
- Cost to repair

Step 5: Assess the potential business impact

Consider the potential loss of market share. Assign a rating to the potential business impact, by using a 1 to 5 scale, with 1 being the lowest impact and 5 being the highest. Consider potential risks as a result of

- Business interruption
- Employees who are unable to report for work
- Customers who are unable to reach your premises
- The company being in violation of contractual agreements
- Imposition of fines and penalties or legal costs
- Interruption of receipt of critical supplies
- Interruption of product distribution

Step 6: Assess internal and external resources

Assess your resources and ability to respond. Assign a score to your internal resources and external resources by using a 1 to 5 scale, with 1 being the lowest impact and 5 being the highest. The lower the score, the better. To help you do this, consider each potential risk from beginning to end and evaluate each resource that you need in order to respond. For each risk, ask these questions:

✔ Do we have the needed resources and capabilities to respond?

✔ Will external resources be able to help us quickly, or will they have other priority areas to serve?

If you do have the needed internal and external capabilities to respond, move on to the next assessment. If you don't, identify what you can do to correct the problem. For example, you may need to

✔ Develop additional risk management procedures

✔ Conduct additional training

✔ Acquire additional equipment

✔ Establish mutual aid agreements

✔ Establish agreements with specialised contractors

Step 7: Add the scores

Total the scores for each potential risk. The lower the score, the better. Although this is a subjective rating, the comparisons help determine your risk planning and resource priorities.

Taking action

After you've assessed your risks and prioritised them by their urgency, you need to take action to reduce risks or to eliminate them entirely. Consider these four basic strategies when selecting risk management tools. Keep them in mind as you decide what strategies you'll pursue to implement your risk management goals.

✔ **Shift the risk.** One way of shifting the risk is to make sure that your insurance cover is adequate for every eventuality. However, you need to make sure that the risks and responsibilities are made clear when you use subcontractors, or when you outsource specific activities. Consider that you'll be held liable, or else make sure that your insurance covers the actions of subcontractors and outsourcing partner organisations.

✔ **Avoid the risk.** By identifying and correcting a hazardous situation – say, for example, by repairing the brakes on a company delivery van – you can avoid a potential risk altogether.

✔ **Reduce the risk.** Although you can't entirely avoid some risks, you can reduce them. Training employees in the proper techniques for lifting heavy objects substantially reduces the incidence of back injuries and the resulting lost productivity.

✔ **Assume the risk.** In some cases, an organisation may decide to bear the financial burden of a risk. By self-insuring for workers' compensation claims, for example, or by paying higher premiums on insurance policies, organisations assume all or part of a risk of loss.

Whatever you do, do *something*! After you've determined a potential risk of injury or loss, you have to take action by shifting, avoiding, reducing, or assuming the risk. Don't waste time hoping that the risk will go away if you ignore it. It won't.

Insurance: Shifting the Risk

When you buy insurance, you shift the risk of loss to a third party, in this case an insurance company. The insurance company, in essence, is betting that you won't suffer a loss. It hedges its bet by collecting a sufficiently high premium to make money even if you do suffer a loss at some point. Insurance is essential in modern business, and you need to be covered against every eventuality. Make sure that the coverage is sufficient to cover all potential losses or damage.

Take a close look at your organisation and determine the full range of risks that you've identified (see the section 'Conducting a vulnerability analysis', earlier in this chapter). Make sure that you buy insurance that shifts the risk of loss, and covers everything in full.

Here are the most important kinds of insurance to have and maintain for your business:

✔ **Liability insurance:** If someone is injured or has property damaged or destroyed while on your premises or while using your product or services, your organisation may be sued for unlimited damages. Liability insurance protects your organisation from these kinds of financial losses. If you rent your office or manufacturing space, your landlord probably requires you to carry a certain amount of liability insurance as protection from liability claims.

✔ **Property insurance:** Natural disasters such as floods and storms wreak millions of pounds worth of property damage every year. But an estimated 70 per cent of all business property losses happen not as a result of natural disasters, but because of employee negligence, errors, or lack of planning. Property insurance generally covers the risk of property loss due to fire, smoke, wind, and other sources of damage or destruction.

- **Business interruption:** If a fire, flood, or other disaster forces your business to close until you can repair or rebuild your facility, business interruption insurance covers you for the risk of lost sales.

- **Professional and occupational liability:** Professional and occupational liability insurance covers businesses that give advice and deliver professional services, as well as conducting activities. So, as well as organisations overall, doctors, lawyers, consultants, accountants, and stockbrokers are among those who need malpractice insurance in case their clients are injured – physically or financially – as a result of the company's work.

Other, more specialised forms of insurance may also be appropriate for your situation. If you're not an expert in the insurance industry, find a qualified insurance broker who can explain and recommend different kinds of insurance to you, as well as how much coverage to buy. A reputable broker also can search the insurance market for you to get the best coverage at the best price.

Training Employees to Minimise Risk

Full employee involvement is critical for any company looking to reduce its risk of loss. Employees not only can proactively identify and remedy potential risks but also can train others to do the same. The result is a much safer workplace, with improved employee morale and productivity.

Safety

Safety training needs to cover all potential risks and hazards at the workplace. The Health and Safety at Work Act 1974, and specific industrial and materials handling regulations, require that specific actions are taken where appropriate or required. All safety training must cover the following areas:

- Diseases and illnesses

- Industrial illnesses and injuries

- Correct lifting techniques and manual handling

- Ergonomics, which is the relationship between staff, equipment, and the operating environment

- Forklift truck and other specialist equipment training

✔ Electrical safety

✔ Office security

✔ First-aid and cardio-pulmonary resuscitation (CPR)

✔ Fire drills, evacuation plans, and other emergency drills

✔ Machine safety

✔ Use of specialist equipment and clothing

✔ Use of cleaning materials

✔ Cleaning machinery, and other equipment and technology

When employees follow the safety rules that you establish, they help your organisation avoid and reduce the risk of injury, property damage, liability, and other risks to your business. This compliance, in turn, results in a healthier, more productive workforce.

Security

All organisations can make their premises, activities, systems, and procedures as secure as possible by attending to security issues. Every company and industry is different, so your approach needs to be tailored specifically. Security training always needs to cover the following:

✔ The handling of incoming packages

✔ Computer and information systems

✔ Access to petty cash

✔ Access to corporate and capital finance

✔ Relationships with third parties

✔ Access to confidential staff information, product and service information, and financial information

Make sure that these issues are covered in company manuals and at the induction and orientation stage. Your employees need to know and understand what your company expects from them, and what they can, and cannot, do.

Finance

Your organisation needs to be aware of the potential for theft and fraud and how to minimise the risk by attending to the following issues:

- ✔ Managing expenses

- ✔ Managing access to corporate finance

- ✔ Being clear about arrangements for share trading and capital dealings

- ✔ Managing relationships with customers, clients, and suppliers

- ✔ Identifying possible and potential conflicts of interest; for example, where members of staff do things for the advancement of their own careers, which may not be in the interests of the organisation as a whole

- ✔ Confidential organisational information

- ✔ Employees taking on other work without the organisation's knowledge

If employees understand what you require of them in relation to these issues, nothing should go wrong – except as the result of negligence or conspiracy. As well as training people in these areas, your organisation needs active monitoring and auditing systems to ensure that rules are being followed and standards met. Normally, if employee malpractice in these areas is proven, it's a cause for summary dismissal, as long as you've followed procedures.

Bullying, victimisation, discrimination, and harassment

The risk to organisations of bullying, victimisation, discrimination, and harassment going unchecked is the unlimited damages paid to those who prove they suffered from this behaviour. General employee morale is also damaged when these matters are going on, and nobody does anything about them. Make sure that people are trained in each of the following areas, and that they know how to behave towards each other at all times:

- ✔ Race, ethnic origin, and religion

- ✔ Sex and gender

- ✔ Disability

- ✔ Age and seniority

- ✔ Job title and status

- ✔ Modes and forms of address

- ✔ Ways of raising serious issues, such as theft, fraud, and bullying

- ✔ Whistle-blowing, or how to report wrongdoing to the correct authorities

Tips for getting your risk management message across

Training employees is both an art and a science. You want to communicate your important messages in an engaging and entertaining way, but you also want to make sure that your employees retain your messages over a long period of time and modify their behaviour in a positive way as a result.

You can make your training sessions much more effective by following a few simple tips:

✔ **Tailor your presentation to meet the needs of your audience.** Many companies and organisations have standard video or computer presentations on risk management that they give to all employees, whatever their occupation. If your company takes this approach, be advised that employees ignore the parts that don't apply to them and eventually ignore you altogether. To ensure that every employee listens to your messages and takes them to heart, customise your presentation to the exact needs of your audience.

✔ **Use graphics, charts, and photos to reinforce key messages.** A picture, especially of the results of environmental damage to businesses, really is worth a thousand words in the minds of your audience. Simple but compelling graphics, charts, and photos can help the members of your audience relate to your message.

✔ **Use colour.** Colour has been shown to accelerate learning. Use colour in your presentation liberally, as well as in any study guides or reference manuals that you hand out as a part of your training.

✔ **Hand out copies of all your presentation materials.** Before you start your presentation, hand out a copy of your presentation materials to each participant with extra blank pages or room in the margins for employees to take notes.

✔ **Encourage audience questions and participation.** Instead of simply lecturing your audience, get them involved in your presentation. Encourage them to ask questions and ask them to share their own personal experiences with workplace hazards and safety, theft and fraud, security scares and alerts, and any other matters that may arise. Not only will participants be more engaged in your presentation, the rest of the group will also find the training to be far more interesting and relevant.

Each of these areas is bound by law. The penalty for bullying, victimisation, discrimination, and harassment is normally dismissal. Transgressions in each of these areas normally mean that your organisation will have to face either a court case or an employment tribunal. You must take steps to ensure that everyone knows how to conduct themselves at all times, as well as provide the basis for positive attitudes and a harmonious place of work.

Chapter 22

Playing the Negotiation Game

• •

In This Chapter

▶ Getting ready to negotiate

▶ Exploring the critical elements of any deal

▶ Warming up

▶ Knowing how to play the game

• •

*Y*ou're looking for a new location for your business, and can't afford more than £3,000 a month to rent office space. You call an estate agent who finds the perfect location for £3,500 a month – £500 more than you can manage. Will this negotiation be easy or difficult?

If you need the premises badly enough, you'll find the extra £500 from somewhere. On the other hand, if the estate agent is under pressure to get the premises rented, you're more likely to be able to beat the agent down to what you can afford to pay. And don't forget the human elements – if you or the agent is in a good or bad mood, and how you get on with each other at a human level, all affect the outcome of the negotiation. This example is just one of hundreds of situations in which business owners, managers, and MBA students must negotiate for something they need or want. In this chapter, we explore the nature of negotiation and give you some tips for doing an effective job of negotiating in any business situation. Anyone can find out how to negotiate effectively by following the guidelines provided in this chapter. It just takes planning, practice, and patience.

Getting Ready to Negotiate

Negotiating is an important part of every business relationship, whether with suppliers, distributors, employees, partners, or customers. Negotiating is also an important part of your life in general. Consider the following scenario: It's Monday morning. Before leaving for work, you and your spouse agree on who is going to take the children to their after-school clubs. You probably have to negotiate to decide who's in the best position to take on that task.

Maybe you each have something you need to do at that time. Whose task is more important? Who can change what has to be done?

You arrive at your office, and your colleague wants to discuss fitting two new projects into your already overburdened schedule. Will that discussion require some negotiating skills? Are you predisposed to take on more than you can handle? An employee asks for a pay rise that's far beyond what your budget allows. How can you satisfy your employee's needs and the company's needs at the same time? Is that a negotiation?

As with all aspects of business and management practice, you can find experts in the field, so you can always hire professional negotiators when you need them. Clearly, however, using a professional negotiator to handle your every negotiation is an unrealistic notion (especially when you stop to think about how many times a day you find yourself in mini-negotiations). Obtaining a negotiator for very important negotiations that may mean life or death to your business, however, is important. So you need to have both the expertise to carry out negotiations, and also the wisdom to know when you need the help of experts.

Every business person, manager, and MBA student needs to understand the basics of negotiating so that you can handle whatever situations come your way.

The first thing to understand is what you want from a given negotiation, and what the other party wants. The four main outcomes are:

Win-win

- The issue is important to you.
- You value your relationship with the other party.
- You have enough time to search for an approach that satisfies everyone.

Win-lose

- The issue is important to you.
- Preserving your relationship with the other party doesn't matter.
- You have the time to beat the other party down.
- You can't use a win-win solution because the other party will take advantage of you.

Lose-win

- The issue isn't important to you.
- You value your relationship with the other party.
- You are under time pressure and want to finish quickly.

Lose-lose

> ✔ The issue is relatively unimportant to both parties.
>
> ✔ You may build a relationship based on mutual suffering. Time and/or transaction costs are primary considerations.

Is winning everything?

Although it would be nice if both parties could win in every negotiation, win-win situations are not often possible. In fact, sometimes you may even choose to lose. Why would you go into a negotiation planning to lose? Remember the many times a day you face negotiations, most of which are probably low-level issues. Because the rewards for these low-level issues aren't great, working to come up with a win or a win-win situation isn't worth your time and effort. Or, you may choose to lose something, knowing that a bigger issue is going to come up fairly soon which you'll need to win. In other cases you may have to be seen to win; and other cases where you're seen to lose, to reinforce and underpin perceptions that you're a reasonable person, prepared to give and take.

The whole field of negotiating is very complex, and you need to be aware of the consequences of winning and losing in every situation. If those consequences aren't great, why waste time? If the consequences are serious, however, make sure that you gain the outcome that you require.

Negotiations cost time, effort, and resources (including money). You must weigh those costs against the benefit gained by winning.

When it comes to negotiating with customers, never engage in a fight. You know the saying: 'The customer is always right'. So you may lose when the customer demands satisfaction – even when the customer is wrong. We know of several retailers who accept returns from customers even when the customer obviously didn't purchase the item at their shop or obviously has used the item. The retailers maintain such a policy because they want satisfied customers to tell others about their positive experiences. If a retailer loses one disgruntled customer just to win a negotiation, the loss of that customer can translate into a loss of nine customers – the number of people to whom the disgruntled customer tells the tale of woe. Of course, if the same customer pulls this trick on a regular basis, the time may have come to get rid of the customer by letting him or her lose the negotiation. The cost of retaining this person as a customer is greater than the loss of his or her business.

Some basic rules of negotiation

You can find many great books about how to negotiate, but they all contain some very basic rules that are true in every negotiation:

- Never say yes to a proposal the first time you hear it, even if it's too good to be true – *especially* if it's too good to be true.

- Never negotiate with yourself. Some people, faced with silence after making an offer, feel the need to fill the space with their chatter. Often they raise their price or justify the other person's point of view. At that point, they may as well end the negotiation because they've lost any power they had.

- Don't be afraid to say no. Provided that you understand the consequences of saying no and walking away, this is a very powerful negotiating ploy.

- Understand the psychological and behavioural issues and rituals present in the situation. If, as the result of letting someone have a rant of their own, you get your own way – then let them rant!

- Deal only with the person who can make the decision. When you buy a car, the salesperson often claims that he or she must talk with the manager. That move only gives the two of them a chance to renegotiate the deal. Control the situation by making a deal only with the person who can say yes or no.

- Everything is negotiable, even if it's in writing in contract form. Don't be intimidated by professional-looking documents with 'iron-clad' terms.

- Don't always trust the other party's actions. If the other party arrives late to the negotiation or appears disinterested, don't assume that this behaviour reflects a lack of interest. The other party just wants you to think that.

- If you can't control your temper or emotions, let someone else do the negotiating for you. Yelling and screaming never ends up with a good deal.

- Don't talk about the deal in hallways or lifts. You just never know who's listening.

Critical Elements of Negotiation

To understand what really goes on in a negotiation, you need to know about the critical elements of any deal: Power, time, and information. To the extent that you can control these three factors, you'll be successful in your negotiating efforts. Consider our example at the start of the chapter: You want to negotiate some office space, but the price is too high. Power enters the picture when office space is in short supply and the estate agent can easily find another renter. Time becomes a factor when you must be out of your present location within two weeks. Finally, information plays a role when the estate agent knows more about your needs and your timing than you know about the agent's. The next few sections look at each one of these factors in more detail.

Knowing where the power lies

In any negotiation, the first thing you need to d understand is the power that you have, and how you're prepared to use it. Your opponent also has power. You need to know what are acceptable and unacceptable uses of that power, the extent of your authority, and the boundaries within which you must operate. Never make deals or agreements outside your power, authority, or sphere of influence.

Several types of power come into play in negotiating situations. The following sections look at each type individually.

Sometimes you have legitimate power

Your position determines your legitimate power. As director of a company, you have legitimate power to make decisions in a negotiation, so letting people see you as capable of carrying out that role is important. If the other party involved in a negotiation is the director of another major company, you must see that person as a peer and equal. Do not give your opposition more power than that to which they're entitled because you'll weaken your position in the negotiation.

You have the power to reward

Reward power is the ability to offer rewards to the other party for agreeing to something you want in the negotiation. This power greatly resembles an incentive system you may use with your employees to get them to be more productive. Be sure that you reward only those behaviours that you're looking for. If you reward everything, the reward loses its value to influence.

You also have the power to punish

We don't encourage you to use coercive power in a negotiation setting because doing so probably won't lead to a win-win conclusion. People don't like to feel that they're doing something because they must. A far better power tactic is to get them to do something because they want to; then they will see the rationale and the benefit of doing it.

You may be an expert in some area

As an expert, you have a particular skill or knowledge that the other party doesn't have. That additional knowledge gives you a certain amount of power and allows you to deal in a less emotional way. In any negotiation, define what expertise you have that may give you power in the negotiation. You have no doubt seen instances where a lawyer's reputation and expertise have allowed them to win over a jury even when the evidence pointed in the opposite direction. Of course, part of that is the next type of power: Charisma.

You may simply be charismatic

Yes, charisma – that certain something that some people have that attracts others to them – can play an important role in a negotiation. Charisma often intimidates and distracts the other party. One person may be in such awe of the person sitting across the table that he or she immediately loses any power they may have had.

Time is on your side

The minute that your opponent knows that you're in a rush, you give them a tremendous advantage. They'll spin things out to the point at which you're seriously stressed; you then come under great pressure – from yourself – to settle with them because you have other more pressing things to attend to.

In early 2007, the cabin crew staff of British Airways announced that they were going on a series of strikes. The issue was sick pay, staff bonuses, and working hours, each of which British Airways wanted to change. The ballot held by the staff and their trade union attracted an 86 per cent response, and 96 per cent of those balloted favoured the strike action. The first strike was due to take place at the end of January. In response, British Airways first tried to state that the cabin crew staff had no grievances, and then broke off talks. British Airways then briefly threatened to use management and agency staff to try to run some kind of a service during the strike days. To each of these responses, the staff and their trade union simply held their position. They waited the matter out until immediately before the first of the strikes was due to take place. They wanted to retain the power of time on their side; and they did. And, as very often happens in these and similar circumstances, a resolution to their mutual problems occurred in the final moments before the deadline.

When you go to the bargaining table, remember these tips:

✔ Be patient and try not to reveal your deadline.

✔ Understand that *everyone* has a deadline no matter what picture the other party paints for you.

✔ Be prepared that you probably won't achieve a negotiated agreement until the last possible moment.

PEARL OF WISDOM

Peter Bennett-Jones: Six rules of negotiation

Peter Bennett-Jones is an agent who represents some of the UK's major entertainment stars, including Rowan Atkinson, Lenny Henry, Harry Enfield, and Barry Humphries. In order to maximise the position of his clients, he has to undertake extensive negotiations with large and powerful media, entertainment, and sponsorship companies. Here's how he sets out his position:

✔ **Be prepared:** 'I go into a negotiation pretty certain about what I want to come out with, and knowing exactly what the other half wants, because successful negotiating is not going to come out of confusion.'

✔ **Straight and open dealings:** 'Maybe if you ask for things in a very polite way, people are slightly bamboozled. But I don't think I am deceptive and I believe bluffing should be kept for poker. I hate aggression – it gets you nowhere. A deal works when both parties think they have got a good deal. I have never walked out of a meeting, although I have got cross a couple of times. If people think they have to scream and shout and get angry, it's gone wrong, it's broken down.'

✔ **Build up a good relationship:** 'I actually really like all the people I negotiate with on a regular basis. I may not be so keen on the dark forces behind them but I enjoy their company, which is why face-to-face always beats the phone. Going for the jugular from the word go is a waste of time. Some agents do conduct things like that but the loss of goodwill that such a move involves outweighs the benefit. You can hold anyone to ransom on one occasion, but if next time you want something more complex, it makes life harder.'

✔ **Detail is all**: 'I am a great believer in pen and paper. Putting down in writing is important to me. But you'll never get an American agent to agree to that. That suggests an attempt to avoid the awkward issues that will come back and bite you later.'

✔ **It isn't just price that matters**: 'Price is one element of the equation, not the key thing. If you make price the dominant factor, you are likely to slip up elsewhere. Get a long-term commitment on a deal if possible, and remember the importance of piggy-backing other concessions to achieve what you want. That way you can plan properly. Never do anything in a hurry – which is the converse of the way the City works – short-term, turning a buck. Think long-term. People like John Cleese and Ronnie Barker have forty years in them.'

✔ **If all else fails, be prepared to walk away**: A television executive who deals with Bennett-Jones says: 'He will walk away. That's very clever. But if he doesn't get what he wants, he just says no.'

Source: Adapted from 'The Secrets of a Negotiator' - *Management Today* (May 2000).

Information is the key

In essence, negotiation is about gathering information so that you can reach a decision and achieve a resolution. Each party strives to give only information that's absolutely necessary, and each party attempts to gather information from the other side that will help them gain an advantage in negotiating a resolution. Information is particularly important if you're trying to achieve a win-win solution – always the best way to go. The information is necessary because you must understand everyone's interests in order to satisfy those interests.

To gain information you need from the other party, try to appear a bit confused about what the other party says. Asking for clarification on something forces the other party to restate the demand in another way. Maybe that new statement will provide a piece of information that you didn't have.

Remember that the other party is trying to do the same thing with you. Three tips that should help you are:

- Control the information you give and watch carefully how you word what you say. Give only as much as you have to and then stop talking.

- Practise active listening. Take notes and attempt to find patterns in the other party's arguments that will lead you to an understanding of what they really want and why.

- Watch the other party's non-verbal cues carefully. More than 70 per cent of communication is non-verbal. For example, if you note that while you're speaking, the other party is sitting with arms folded in a closed position, this position may signal that he or she is not receptive to what you're saying. On the other hand, if the other party leans forward when you speak, you're saying something of interest.

Before You Start the Negotiation

Before you start a serious negotiation, you need to prepare thoroughly. Here are the three steps you need to take before you enter into any serious negotiation. Know and understand in full:

- Your own position.
- The other side's position.
- The things that you can agree on; and the things that you cannot agree on.

Ask yourself the following questions in full detail before entering into any negotiation.

Step One: What's my position?
- What do I want from this negotiation?
- Why do I want it?

> ✔ Who besides me is interested in the outcome?
>
> ✔ What should I propose? What should I not propose?

Step Two: What's the other side's position?

> ✔ What does the other side want from this negotiation?
>
> ✔ Why do they want it?
>
> ✔ Who else is interested in the other party's outcome?
>
> ✔ What will the other party probably ask for?

Step Three: What do we agree on?

Put the answers to Steps One and Two together and compare.

> ✔ On which points do we agree, and on which do we differ?
>
> ✔ What do I get if I do it their way?
>
> ✔ What do they get if they do it my way?
>
> ✔ What are my alternatives?
>
> ✔ What are their alternatives?
>
> ✔ How is each issue of the negotiation likely to be resolved?

If you compare the two points of view in detail, you may be surprised at how much you do actually agree on! Answering these questions means that you won't finish up arguing over things that you do agree on; you'll concentrate instead on those areas of difference.

Playing the Game

Playing the negotiation game is much easier if you know the rules and you think about how you're going to play before the game starts. Seasoned negotiators recognise the natural sequence of activities that take place during a negotiation. The reason the sequence is 'natural' is that it makes sense; the order is logical. When you don't follow the sequence, negotiating becomes more difficult. The simple sequence has four parts.

1. **Set the stage and know the players.**

   Creating an environment conducive to a good negotiation is important. Often this environment is a neutral playing field so that one side doesn't have the home advantage over the other. You also want to spend some time in non-negotiation chatter to put everyone at ease and to establish procedures for the negotiation process.

2. Get to know each other's interests.

Most negotiations start with the parties stating their positions. These position statements reflect a win-lose attitude and do not open the door for other negotiating strategies. You must get beyond position statements to find out what the other party really wants. Where many ways exist to satisfy an interest, you have the potential for a mutually beneficial outcome.

3. Revisit those interests with new proposals.

After you understand each other's interests, you can begin to develop proposals that meet them. Don't worry about making a proposal complex and legally correct at this point. You merely want to establish agreement on the fundamental points of the negotiation.

4. Construct a winning agreement.

The final stage of the negotiation is where all the hard work happens, most probably running up against a deadline. Now some trading, bargaining, compromising, and swapping are needed to beat the agreement into a form that is acceptable to both sides. Each time you reach agreement on a point, having both parties acknowledge that point of agreement is a good idea so you feel that you've accomplished something and can move forward.

If you don't know what you want, don't play

One of the biggest problems people have in negotiations is that they don't know what they want to have achieved when the negotiation is over. How do you successfully negotiate when your target keeps moving? If you can't define a goal for the negotiation, then don't negotiate.

Become a more effective negotiator by considering the following tips:

- **Go with a plan.** Negotiating for something important to you is not the time to 'wing it'. Set some objectives that you want to achieve, and understand what you're willing to give up to make things work.

- **Put yourself in the other person's shoes.** Always work out the other party's interests and needs. Ask questions and try to see things from the other person's point of view.

- **Be an effective listener.** You always discover more by listening than by speaking. In fact, one thing that can hurt you in a negotiation is talking too much, because you give away too much information. Always let the other party begin the talking.

✔ **Focus on the issue, not personalities.** Remember, you're trying to find a win-win solution.

✔ **Never threaten or intimidate.** Explaining your point of view is necessary, but subtle threats about what will happen if the other party doesn't accept your proposal only serve to alienate the other party. In addition, you're less likely to achieve an amicable solution.

✔ **Remember that patience is a virtue.** That saying is certainly true in a negotiation. If your opponent gets the idea that you're in a hurry, they'll spin things out. If it takes a bit more time to get to an agreement that satisfies everyone, then so be it. And if you have a deadline to meet, then begin the negotiations as early as you possibly can.

✔ **Know what to do if you can't come to agreement.** You need to know whether you can afford the luxury of walking away from a negotiation. If you've defined an acceptable back-up strategy, you're in a better position to walk away from a bad situation.

Ending up with a good deal

A negotiation is successful to the extent that it achieves the goals set by the parties involved. In other words, both parties in the negotiation must define what success means to them. The next few sections look at some signs of a good outcome.

It beats your other choices

Working on an agreement with the other party must be more valuable than your best alternative to the negotiation or negotiating doesn't make sense. Your back-up option should be a good one, but the outcome from a negotiated deal should have much greater value because you put a lot more effort into it.

It makes everyone happy

To get someone to accept your deal, you must satisfy their interests, at least in part. If you don't, you'll cause resentment and the person may cause trouble for you the next time you have to negotiate something. If you get your own way on all the main issues, and can be magnanimous, then make sure that your opponent receives everything that they asked for, or is of value to them, outside the main issues.

It's the best solution among many

Generating more than one solution to the situation and then choosing the best from among all the alternatives is an important step in negotiating. So, wherever possible, have a range of solutions in mind and when the time arises during the negotiation, raise them all in general terms, and see which ones appeal most to your opponent.

No one is taken to the cleaners

Everyone has to come away from the negotiation feeling that, given the circumstances, the achieved outcome was the best possible end. If both parties don't clearly understand the rationale for the outcome, an optimal outcome was not achieved.

No one is humiliated

Always remember that the worst injury that you can cause to anyone is to their pride! If you come away from a negotiation not only having won, but also having humiliated your opponent, you'll store up resentment, and they'll be back to get you if they possibly can. Concentrate on the issues, not the personalities involved. That way, even if you don't like your opponent as an individual, the question of humiliation never arises.

Everyone knows who does what and how

After you've reached an agreement, ensuring that both parties understand what they have to do – and when – is important. Coming up with some action steps is a good way to make sure that both parties carry out the agreement in the way that everyone expects.

Part VI
The Part of Tens

'And to deliver the goods, I bought the postage online—a new company called "Rocket Deliveries".'

In this part . . .

Every *For Dummies* book ends with top-ten lists. Here, we present tips that can help you to quickly become an effective participant in *any* organisation. We show you how to avoid the most common mistakes that managers make, the best ways to market your products and services, and how to improve your cash flow. We also point you in the direction of ten free business resources, and give you ten more books to read!

Chapter 23

Ten Mistakes Managers Make

*E*veryone makes mistakes – and managers are no different than anyone else. The trick is to learn from your mistakes, to avoid them in the future, and to help others in your organisation to avoid them, too. Here are the ten biggest mistakes that managers make, and that you, as a budding MBA student, can avoid.

Forgetting Who Pays the Bills

Unfortunately, the very nature of management often means that managers spend little or no time with customers. Their primary job is to direct the work of other employees and budget and allocate staff and other resources. For many managers, this means spending lots of time in staff meetings, employee training sessions, and other internal activities.

This isolation from the customer – the person or company that buys your products or services – can create real problems in an organisation, especially when managers and employees forget that their job is to serve the customer, and not the other way around. Managers have a long list of people with whom they have dealings, and customers and employees both need to be at the top of that list. Customers are at the top because they pay the bills, and employees share the top position because they directly serve customers.

Neglecting the Details

If you're a manager with employees who take care of running your business on a day-to-day basis, that doesn't mean that you can completely divorce yourself from the operation.

Every truly professional manager knows and understands where the organisation is going and every part of the operation required to make the organisation's vision and strategy a success.

This doesn't mean that you need to get overwhelmed with detail, or meddle in affairs that don't concern you. It does mean that you need to have a full working knowledge of every aspect of the organisation, and especially of those small but important details that can, and do, cause serious problems from time to time.

Getting Caught Up in the Red Tape

Red tape, or unnecessary bureaucracy, can be very restrictive for a company. Any organisation can refuse something, stating: 'It's against company policy,' and any individual can refuse to do something, stating: 'It's not my job.' Of course, you have to have rules, procedures, and regulations, and you have to have boundaries that groups and individuals operate within. However, these rules and boundaries must work in your favour, and must never become a barrier to progress. So each time you find yourself unable to do something simply because of company policy or divisional boundaries, attack those boundaries. Making sure that everything works in the interests of the organisation, its staff, and its customers, is a continuous process – and managing your way through the rules, regulations, and procedures is no different. Keep them up-to-date, and make sure that they work for you, not against you.

Not Setting Clear Goals with Employees

If you don't know where you're going then how will you know when you get there? This simple question is at the heart of setting goals with employees. Managers set the vision in an organisation that everyone strives to achieve.

Goals are nothing more than the steps people take to achieve the organisation's vision. Not only that, but goals act as tangible, measurable milestones for employees to measure their progress. Goals give people something to strive for – making their jobs more interesting and fulfilling. As you achieve goals, the organisation moves closer and closer to the vision of its leaders.

Managers who fail to set clear goals end up with employees who are confused about their priorities and what is important. So, make sure that everyone knows and understands what's expected of them and how, when, and where their work is measured for success or failure.

Forgetting What Being a Worker Is Like

One of the most common complaints about managers is that, somewhere along the way, they've forgotten what it is like to be an ordinary employee. They forget how hard it is to deal with unruly customers, colleagues, and suppliers on a daily basis. And remember how you used to feel when your manager imposed jobs on you at the last minute!

Employees aren't your servants, or your children. The next time you have to inconvenience an employee, first put yourself in their shoes and then consider just how important what you have in mind is to the organisation. Anyone will understand if you ask them to work an occasional evening here or there, or if you need to squeeze one more year out of that old computer before your budget will allow you to buy your employee another. But if these inconveniences become habitual, then something is wrong, and you need to step back and work out what it is, and how to put it right.

Talking More Than They Listen

Effective communication is a critical ingredient in any organisation. And communication is a two-way process – effective communication means talking *and* listening. And good managers do much more of the latter than the former. Just because a manager is a manager doesn't mean that he or she has a monopoly on experience and knowledge. The simple fact is that you can find talented individuals in every possible job in an organisation – from the bottom rung of the corporate ladder, to the top. Failing to hear all those good ideas because you're busy promoting your personal agenda is a *big* mistake. In fact, many business owners and managers make it a practice to hire and surround themselves with people cleverer than themselves. That's how they become better at what they do.

The next time you sit down with an employee to have a discussion, make a conscious effort to listen – *really* listen – to what he or she has to say. You may be pleasantly surprised at what you hear.

Failing to Delegate

One of the biggest mistakes a manager can make is to fail to delegate in one or both of the following ways:

- ✔ The responsibility for getting a task done.
- ✔ The authority to get a task done.

Managers who fail to delegate overload themselves with work, keep their employees idle and frustrated – and become micro-managers. Managers who fail to delegate miss out on opportunities to develop their employees' skills and expertise; and they cause themselves stress by overloading themselves with tasks that ought to be carried out by someone else – at the end of the day, they still have their own workload to get through.

So, concentrate on what is important to you. Make sure that you give authority and responsibility to your employees for particular tasks. Make sure that they keep you informed of progress, and come to you whenever serious problems occur. In that way everyone benefits – you get to concentrate on your priorities, and the staff have rewarding and fulfilling working lives.

Communicating Too Little, Too Late

Communication is the lifeblood of any organisation. And as the speed of business continues to increase, making sure that barriers to communication within organisations are dismantled and discarded, and that a culture of communication is created and rewarded, is increasingly important. Information is power, and far too many managers hoard information and give it out to their employees only when it suits their purposes, if at all.

If you're going to process information effectively, everyone needs to know what's important and where the priorities lie. So make sure that your communication systems are full and comprehensive, covering everything that is of value and importance to all your staff. Use every means at your disposal – face-to-face, notice boards, meetings, and the intranet. And this must apply to external matters concerning products, services, and markets, and internal matters relating to staff, business, and organisation development.

Not Showing Employees They Care

A major part of the motivation and inspiration of employees relates simply to showing them that you care. You can show that you care through the following:

- ✔ Active understanding of everything in which employees are involved, especially the problems and issues that they have to address and tackle.
- ✔ Active understanding of a job well done, and personally thanking the employees for doing it.
- ✔ Active understanding of when problems and issues arise and fully supporting the employees as they try to resolve them.

If you forget to show you care and become remote and distant, employees will withdraw their involvement with you. This situation means that problems and issues are raised more slowly, are more serious when they're finally raised, and take a lot more effort and resources to put right.

Make sure that you know, understand, and trust your employees, as the basis on which they'll know, understand, and trust you. Interact with employees, ask questions, and make sure that you know and understand where the pressures lie.

Taking Work Too Seriously

Of course, work is serious. As manager or business leader, you have to produce the right products and services, and employ people to ensure that they're made and delivered according to customers' needs.

You need to make sure that you create the right environment in which all of this work is possible – and you have no need to be overbearing or a bully. Create a positive, safe, and happy working environment, so that not only do people want to do their jobs to the best of their abilities, but they also actively look forward to coming into work in the first place!

When people say that they hate their jobs, what they actually mean is that they either hate their manager, or they hate their colleagues! Clashing with a manager or colleagues is the largest single cause of people leaving their jobs. So create a friendly, open and productive atmosphere, where everyone gets along professionally, personally – and with their work. By doing so you remove any reason why people could conceivably hate working at your organisation. Create a harmonious working environment – and watch people fight their way in! (For more about creating a harmonious working environment, see also *Managing For Dummies* by Richard Pettinger, Bob Nelson, and Peter Economy, published by Wiley.)

Chapter 24

Ten Creative Ways to Market Your Products and Services

. . . .

In This Chapter

▶ Using your imagination

▶ Making customers take notice of you

▶ Keeping your promises

. . . .

*I*f you want to be noticed, you've got to be creative. Mass marketing and promotional campaigns must have a creative edge. And if you're promoting to niche or narrow groups of customers and clients you have to tailor your efforts to their precise needs and wants. You can't push products and services down people's necks anymore; you have to persuade them that you're serving their needs. This chapter can help!

Focus on Your Existing Customers

You may be asking yourself how you can make money by focusing on your existing customers. Well, the truth is that you'll bring more money to the bottom line by finding more interesting ways to serve your existing customers than you ever will spending money trying to find new customers. For most businesses, the old rule of thumb that 20 per cent of your customers bring in 80 per cent of your revenues is true. So talking to your existing customers and finding ways to build on the products and services you sell to them makes sense. They trust you; that's why they buy from you – so make sure that you build on that trust and never ever lose it.

Tell an Interesting Story

You have to develop creativity, both in yourself and also your staff, so that when particular events do happen, such as a new product or service launch, you can find an interesting, exciting, or curious angle on which to build.

If you make a major achievement in your field or market, make sure that you get maximum possible coverage so that everyone knows about it! An achievement by one of your employees, new uses for your products and services, an event such as a merger, or industry award that happened within your company – all of these are newsworthy events, and you can use them to maintain and develop an active interest by your customers in your company.

Become an Expert

Every company has some kind of expertise for which it is known. For example, McDonald's is known for burgers and the fact that no matter where you go to a McDonald's, you'll find the same level of food quality.

This happens because McDonald's has ensured that its presentation is consistent throughout the world. It has standardised a large range of its products; any local variations are just that – local. As it has grown, the company has used its physical and financial resources to ensure that everyone knows and understands that they'll get exactly what they expect. McDonald's have very few customer complaints about their food or services.

If people believe that you're an expert in your field, whatever that may be, they'll beat a path to your door.

Use the Internet

Put simply and succinctly, you need an Internet presence to enhance your marketing activity. Keep your Web site fully up-to-date, so that visitors know what you are offering now, not what you used to offer some months ago!

As you develop your Internet expertise, make sure that you have arrangements with search engines such as Google, so that when prospective customers and clients type particular key words relevant to your business, your name comes up as early as possible. Make contact with the sales and marketing staff of the search engines that you intend to use, and come to agreements with them so that you get as high up the ladder as possible. If you can generate home page pop-ups or toolbar banners, so much the better – everyone (allegedly) hates them, but industry research shows that they are an excellent way to raise awareness of your business. For more on using the Internet as an effective marketing initiative, see *Digital Marketing For Dummies* by Ben Carter, Frank Catalano, and Bud Smith published by Wiley.

Make the 'Wow' Factor Work for You

Today's customers are overwhelmed with advertising to the point that they don't pay full attention to it anymore. So you have to find ways to get their attention. What is the one thing about your business, product, service, or organisation that makes people say 'Wow' – that really makes them sit up and take notice? For example, Ryanair and EasyJet make an immediate impact through the huge differences in the low-cost fares that they offer. The price difference between Ryanair and EasyJet, and their competitors is the 'Wow' factor that works for them. So find whatever excites people – and work on it.

Give Your Product Away

So, you want to make a lot of money and you've got a great product. Why not give it away to customers? No, we haven't lost our minds; we're serious. That's how Netscape started, and Microsoft as well. This strategy isn't new; Gillette, the razor company, followed it years ago. They gave away the razor knowing that their customers would continue to come back to them to purchase the blades, the consumable part of the product. You need to decide what you must sell and what you can give away. Every company has something it can give away, even if it's a 90-day free trial. Giving your product away is the quickest way to get customers to try out your products and services. The big consumer products companies such as Procter and Gamble know this because they spend millions each year to give samples of new products to customers.

Build Relationships, Not Sales

The nature of marketing has changed radically as a result of mass customisation and technology that have made it possible to reach individual customers and give them exactly what they want, when they want it. To be successful today, you need to build long-term relationships with your customers and interact with them in ways that will make the relationship better for both sides. This means knowing and understanding the basis on which successful customer relationships are built in your sector and industry. You want customers and salespeople to interact as people, so that when the time comes to purchase new products and services, the customer wants to deal with someone he or she knows. In your business, look for ways to build long-term relationships and the sales will follow. Chapter 16 has more about building customer relationships.

Integrate All Your Marketing Activities

Integrating your marketing activities isn't a new idea – however, it's amazing how many companies and organisations don't do this! If you're running a poster campaign, make sure that this is integrated with direct mail, television campaigns – and any other marketing that you're using. If you're sending out letters to particular customers introducing new products and services, make sure that the customers receive them before you follow up with a direct sales call.

Flexibility and responsiveness are vital parts of integrated marketing activities. Make sure that if you get sudden requests from customers for sales meetings, you're able to respond at their convenience, not yours.

In these ways you present a fully integrated marketing and presentational front, and you build on the confidence that your customers already have – rather than diluting this confidence through a lack of integration.

Make Follow-Up Part of Your Strategy

However good the marketing of your products and services is, never forget the after-sales part! Make sure that you know and understand what customers need and want from you after they buy your product or service; and make sure that, when they do call you, they get the full level of after-sales service that you promise in your promotional literature, and that they expect as the result of being your customer.

Focusing on the follow-up is especially important with product and service guarantees. Make sure that you honour these guarantees whenever required.

In 2006, the UK travel insurance sector was found to be selling policies to customers that would only pay out under a very limited set of circumstances. This led to many of the companies within the sector getting a bad reputation. Any company that gets a bad reputation will find customers taking their business elsewhere.

Follow the Ten Golden Truths of Customer Care

Customer care is an integral and critical part of effective and creative marketing. Academics Roger Cartwright and George Green did extensive research into best practice in customer care across a wide range of industrial and commercial sectors, and public services. They came up with some simple rules to follow. Make sure that the following golden truths are known and understood by all of your staff.

- Gaining a new customer costs far more than retaining an existing one.

- Unless you recover the situation quickly, a lost customer is lost forever.

- Dissatisfied customers tell more friends about their bad experiences, than satisfied customers tell about their good ones.

- The customer isn't always right but how you tell them that they're wrong can make all the difference. Remember that, ultimately, the customer pays your wages.

- Always welcome complaints – then address them in full, because they allow you to improve your products and services.

- Never forget that the customer has a choice.

- Treat customers within the organisation (the other departments to which you yourself provide supplies or services) exactly the same as you do those from outside.

- Listen to customers and clients to find out what they want from you.

- Believe in your products and services (how can you expect the customer to if you don't?).

- If you don't look after your customers, somebody else will.

Chapter 25

Ten Best Free Business Resources

In This Chapter
▶ Using government resources
▶ Reading the trade press
▶ Going back to school

*B*usiness owners, managers, and budding MBA students have plenty of opportunity to take advantage of free resources, contacts, and information available both within the business environment and also the wider community. By building on these contacts effectively, you not only hone your business skills, knowledge, and expertise, but the contacts may lead to even further opportunities.

Department of Trade and Industry (DTI)

As the government department responsible for trade, employees, business, and consumers, the DTI is an excellent source of information, advice, and guidance, provided that you know what you want from them in the form of contacts and expertise. The DTI has information and databases on everything from trading regulations to providing introductions to potential joint venture and business partners (if, for example, you're considering expanding overseas). The DTI can put you in touch with sector specialists able to provide specific information and statistics on markets, locations, products, and services. If you're on the point of opening up in new locations, the DTI can provide introductions and lists of contacts for you. You can find out more from www.dti.gov.uk.

The Internet

Use the Internet effectively, and you have as much excellent and up-to-the-minute information as you could possibly want or need! However, you don't want to simply surf the net for the sake of it – focus on the specific tasks you want to accomplish, or the particular things you need to find out. Make your questions and searches as specific as possible.

The following Web Sites are excellent and effective starting points for anything concerning business and management:

- ✔ www.ft.com (Financial Times)
- ✔ www.bbc.co.uk (BBC)

Professional Associations

Everyone belongs to something! And in all but the smallest of organisations, employees belong to all sorts of different professional bodies and associations depending on their professions and occupations. Simply by using Yellow Pages or an Internet search, you can find professional bodies for accounting, administration, human resources, and marketing, and they all have local branch networks. Make sure that you know who in your company or organisation belongs to professional bodies and associations; and make sure that people go to the meetings, and return with new ideas and inspiration.

Business Links

Business Links are non-governmental organisations that exist across the United Kingdom. Their purpose is to provide support for all of the organisations in their neighbourhood. Business Links provide resources, advice, and guidance, with particular reference to the locality. You can find your local Business Link either through Yellow Pages, or else via the Internet. Take a bit of time to get to know the Business Link staff, and to give them the chance to get to know your business, and your specific needs and wants. The Business Link can then tailor its services and expertise to your own specific requirements.

Trade Press

The sheer volume of business and trade magazines, journals, and periodicals produced means that nobody needs to be ignorant about anything! Concentrate on those sources that are going to provide the most valuable information for you. Naturally, choose sources from your own sector and/or profession – and those of your customers and clients. Not many people read the trade press of their customers and clients – so make sure that you do to stay ahead of your competitors!

Visits

When you or your staff visit other organisations, you will of course have your own very specific reasons for doing so. But you can also use the visit as an opportunity to come back with ideas for improving your organisation, or examples of something that the other organisation does better than you. Make sure that you log the ideas, circulate them, and follow them up. This is an excellent and substantial – and free – contribution to organisation, collective, and individual development.

Advisory, Conciliation and Arbitration Service (ACAS)

ACAS are a publicly-funded body that delivers advice and guidance on all aspects of human resources and employee relations practice. ACAS also provide conciliation, mediation, and arbitration services if you have serious staffing problems.

So make sure that you know your local ACAS official. Take a look in Yellow Pages for their number. Local, regional and national contacts are posted on their Web site. You can at any time call the helpline on 08457 47 47 47 or visit the Web site at www.acas.org.uk. Make sure that you use the ACAS advice and guidance to support you in setting the highest possible standards, so that you never have to use their problem-solving services for your company!

The Chamber of Commerce

Every community of any size has a chamber of commerce where business people come together to share ideas and work for a better community. Chambers of commerce gather a lot of information about their communities and can help you identify your competitors and those businesses that can help you succeed. Their events are also a great place to network, which is the subject of the next item on our list of top ten free business resources.

Network, Network, Network

One of the best free resources for business people is *networking* (meeting people with common interests) at any event or situation in which you find yourself. Letting other like-minded people know your interests can result in finding the people and other resources you might need to move your business forward. Be confident and approach people you don't know. In situations like business events and trade shows, you need to make the effort to meet new people to really benefit from others' expertise. You never know when you're going to meet that one person who'll make a difference to your business.

First show an interest in the other person and what he or she does, which naturally leads to a discussion of your own interests.

Colleges and Universities

Colleges and universities are a great source of help for businesses. In addition to their libraries and activities that put you in touch with the latest trends and technologies, they can supply you with students to work as work experience in your business. The work experience programmes in colleges and universities are a win-win situation for the students and the businesses involved. The students get experience for their CVs that they wouldn't have had otherwise, while the businesses get free or good value staff and the cutting edge education and ideas that the students bring to the business.

In addition, many colleges and universities have outreach programmes, which require students to work in particular localities, industries, or sectors, to help community businesses meet their needs.

Chapter 26

Ten Steps to Improve Your Cash Flow

*Y*ou have to have payments coming in for your business to survive. However, because every business is different, every business needs its own approach to cash-flow management. If you only get paid irregularly, you still have to pay your invoices, salaries, and any other bills regularly. So one of the most important duties for any manager is to make sure that the cash flow is as positive as possible. In this chapter we share ten ways of managing your cash flow so that it's as effective as possible in your particular set of circumstances.

Require Immediate Payment

Wouldn't it be nice to run a *cash business*, one where your customers paid you in cash when they purchased their merchandise or services? While relatively few businesses today run solely on a cash basis, many do require immediate payment by way of cash, cheque, or credit card when an item or service is purchased.

If you can, you demand payment at the point at which you provide goods and services. However, in practice, this situation is rarely possible, though some organisations (such as supermarket chains, department stores, and travel companies) do get most of their money at this point. If your business doesn't fall into one of these categories, you have to require payment as soon as possible.

If you can get paid in advance, so much the better. Many businesses require deposits, retainers, and other forms of advance payment as a normal part of doing business. Building contractors take deposits before they start work, authors receive advances before they start writing, and consultants may be paid a portion of their fee before they set foot in their client's building.

So, if you can, it is definitely worth your while to require payment on delivery, or even advance payment. Don't forget: Happiness is a positive cash flow. For more on cash flow, see Chapter 13.

Encourage the Use of Credit Cards

Have you noticed that most online shops require customers to provide payment at the time of the transaction, and that payment is generally made by credit card? Not only do you get more sales if you accept credit cards because they're so easy and everyone is used to paying with them, but you get your money more quickly than if you simply send out an invoice. Of course, you have to pay your credit card company or bank a small fee for the privilege, but most companies find that the additional sales that credit cards generate more than make up for the fee.

Don't Pay Sooner Than You Have To

Every invoice has a due date. Though some businesses may require payment 30 days after delivering an invoice, others may require payment in only 15 days or less. *Always* pay your bills on time, but don't pay your bills sooner than you have to. If your supplier has agreed to finance your purchase for 30 days for *free* (which is exactly what is happening when you're sent an invoice with payment required in 30 days), then you can take full advantage of this free loan. By waiting to pay until payment is due, you have the benefit of your cash for longer, and you improve your cash flow.

Make Sure that Your Invoices Are Correct

Many companies simply reject invoices that have mistakes in them. And if an invoice is rejected, it won't be paid, and it may not even be returned to you. After all, the company you invoiced is also taking advantage of the preceding tip (don't pay sooner than you have to). And by sending an invoice with a mistake on it, you're giving that company a way to extend the payment time.

Be sure that your invoices are absolutely correct before you send them out, and make sure that they're addressed to the right place *and* the right person. When invoices go to the wrong place or to the wrong person, they tend to sit around unpaid or, worse, simply get thrown away. If you want to get paid sooner rather than later, double check all your invoices before they go out, and make sure they're going to the right person at the right place.

Invoice upon Delivery

Unless you have compelling reasons for doing otherwise, invoice every customer upon delivery. If you don't, you're effectively giving your customers a certain number of 'free days' – using your own resources for the customer's initial use of your product or service.

Of course, many large organisations choose to send out batches of invoices on particular dates of the month. Be aware that you can, if you choose, affect your cash flow positively by taking the invoice upon delivery approach.

Invoice More Often

If you provide a service or deliver goods under contract over a long period of time, you may send out invoices after so many units have been delivered, or after a set period of time – say, a month – has elapsed. If you're in this particular situation, an easy way to improve your cash flow is to increase your invoicing frequency. So, if your current agreement requires you to invoice monthly, you could renegotiate it to allow for invoices twice a month, or perhaps even weekly.

The more often you invoice your customers, the better the impact on your cash flow. The payments are smaller, but you get your money sooner.

Give Prompt-Payment Discounts

A *prompt-payment discount* is when you allow a customer to decrease a payment by some set percentage – 1 per cent for example – for paying an invoice within a specific period of time, usually 10 or 20 days. Offering a prompt-payment discount to your customers can be a powerful incentive for them to accelerate their payments to your organisation, thus improving your cash flow. In many cases, this positive impact on cash flow exceeds the small amount you lose in offering the discount.

Set a Cash Budget

Few businesses have steady cash flows that remain the same from day-to-day, week-to-week, and month-to-month. Where a business may go for days or even weeks without receiving any payments from clients and customers, another week can unleash a veritable torrent of cash and cheques. As a result, many businesses check cash in and out of the business on a daily or weekly basis. Matching your projections for the month against what actually happens is a good way to find problem areas.

A *cash budget* or *cash flow forecast* is an estimate of a company's cash position for a particular period of time. By using your current cash position as a baseline, you can estimate all cash inflows (sales) and outflows (expenses) during whatever time period you specify – say, a month – to determine a projected cash position at the end of the period. By checking your cash over the course of several months or more, the cash budget tells you when cash will be abundant, and when it will not. You can then use this information to ensure that you pay your own bills at times when cash is most abundant.

For more on cash budgets, see Chapter 12.

Manage Your Expenses

Cash flow is nothing more than the net result of the money that comes into your organisation less the money that goes out. The less money that goes out, the better your cash flow. And when you do have to spend your company's hard-earned cash, the timing can have a major impact on your cash flow. One way to reduce the amount of money that flows out of your organisation – and to improve cash flow at the same time – is to manage your expenses.

As we said in the preceding section, try to ensure that you pay your expenses only when you have plenty of cash. Always try to get the best possible terms for major purchases; and always be prepared to negotiate on things like finance charges, deferred payments, and monthly repayments, so that your own cash flow is as little affected as possible. Of course, you may have to pay a bit extra for these arrangements, because you tend only to get discounts for things like annual payments on advance; but on the other hand, less money is going out of your organisation on each payment occasion, so your cash flow improves.

Manage Your Income

When was the last time that you took a close look at who owes you money, how much they owe you, and how far overdue their payments are? If you aren't keeping a close eye on your income, you're missing an opportunity to improve your cash flow.

Some customers don't pay on time – indeed, some don't pay at all. If a customer is a day or two late with making a payment, that's not a problem. However, bills that remain unpaid for weeks or even months become a problem – and you're effectively underwriting this lack of payment.

Make sure that you have a system in place for chasing up unpaid bills and invoices. Always start with friendly reminders, and never threaten sanctions until you've exhausted all other avenues. If you do threaten sanctions or legal action, make sure that you follow it up; and make sure that you never ever deal with those customers again.

Chapter 27

Ten Best MBA Books

*E*ntrepreneurs, pioneers, managers, and MBAs are nothing without knowledge, understanding, awareness, and expertise. So, as well as practising and immersing yourself in your activities, you have to read. The books in this chapter are, in our minds, essential reading – and they're the tip of the iceberg. Books can help you to keep abreast of developments, and to be inspired by the experiences of others.

Our book list comes in two halves. The first five books cover the basis of knowledge and understanding that's been developed by business and management experts over time; and the second five are stories of excellence and expertise in action – apart from the final book in this chapter, which examines what happens when things go wrong!

Management Challenges for the 21st Century, Peter F Drucker

Peter Drucker is the leading expert in the whole field of management. He died in 2005, still writing, advising, and consulting. *Management Challenges for the 21st Century* (HarperCollins) clearly outlines the constraints under which present and future generations of business leaders and managers are going to have to work. In particular, Drucker deals with the need for leadership expertise, and an entrepreneurial and pioneering spirit in everyone, whether business owner, director, entrepreneur, or corporate manager. The book outlines the need to be able to lead, direct, and influence change; to manage knowledge workers (such as people in training and education) and their expertise; to produce top quality products and services; and to identify and maximise the opportunities afforded by technology.

Thriving on Chaos, Thomas J Peters

If Drucker is the greatest management guru of them all, Peters is certainly the most colourful! *Thriving on Chaos* (Alfred A. Knopf/Pan) was written in 1987, before the Internet, telecommunications, and technological revolutions, and yet the main messages of the book remain completely contemporary. The title is the key – there are no certainties in business and management, and so in order to prosper and profit you have to be able to embrace disorder and chaos, uncertainty and change. According to Peters, to be effective, your priorities need to be what he calls '*total customer responsiveness*', as well as fast-paced innovation, empowering staff, cutting overheads and bureaucracy, and inspirational leadership.

Competitive Strategy, Michael E Porter

Michael Porter's expertise is in *competitive strategy*, which means being clear about what you're going to do, for whom, and how you're going to do it. In *Competitive Strategy* (Free Press), Porter identifies the direct relationship between clarity of purpose and business success. Strategy must be founded in a core, foundation, or generic position – either cost leadership or advantage, brand leadership or advantage, or else a close focus on precisely defined niches. Your business strategy must be capable of being implemented effectively in response to the activities of competitors, and within the constraints of what Porter calls 'the five elemental forces of competition':

- Supplier power
- Buyer power
- The threat of substitution
- The threat of entry of new players
- The actions of close rivals

These forces are then set against the expertise and precision with which the competitive and operating environment is analysed, understood, and accommodated as a whole. If you get all of this right, you give yourself the best possible chance of success; if you don't, you simply create uncertainty in the minds of everyone involved – especially staff and customers.

In Search of European Excellence, Robert Heller

Robert Heller is the founding father of British management. He was the first editor of *Management Today* and since then he has written, consulted, and advised extensively on all aspects of management. *In Search of European Excellence* was written in 1998 (HarperCollins), and is a substantial and enduring evaluation of the strategic and operational management of UK and European organisations. The book concentrates on the key aspects of leadership, change, culture, control, organisation structure and design, renewal, motivation and teamwork, and quality. In particular, the book introduces *total quality of management* – the need for personal commitment as well as professional and occupational expertise.

Mastering Customer Relations, Roger Cartwright

Throughout this book we refer constantly to the critical importance of customers. Cartwright's book is the best guide to understanding fully the nature of customers and their behaviour. One of very few books to tackle this subject in full detail, *Mastering Customer Relations* (Macmillan) deals with customer types and managing them, offering value for money, handling complaints, and building profitable and lasting customer relations. Cartwright gives detailed illustrations of customer relations in action, and shows how to develop an effective customer relations strategy.

The Rise and Fall of Marks and Spencer, Judi Bevan

Marks and Spencer is a prime example of what happens to companies and organisations when they lose focus on what's important. Bevan's book (Profile Books) illustrates the rise of Marks and Spencer over a period of well over a hundred years, and explains the attention to every detail that was so critical to its initial growth and lasting success. The book then goes on to show just how quickly things can and do go wrong when managers begin to pursue their own agendas, start fighting amongst themselves, and concentrate on their own benefits at the expense of the business. The constant changes in leadership and direction of Marks and Spencer, and the ways in which these were implemented, have led to a downturn from which full recovery is demonstrably slow and incomplete to date.

Ryanair: How a Small Irish Airline Conquered Europe, Siobhan Creaton

Ryanair (Aurum Press Ltd) is the story of the effect that one person can have on an organisation if they have the right mix of expertise, energy, enthusiasm, commitment, and determination. Michael O'Leary, the CEO of budget airline Ryanair, delivers all of this, as a larger than life and controversial character. Creaton looks into how Ryanair confronts problems and issues, takes difficult decisions, and backs judgement with expertise rather than status.

The book is also a good illustration of the problems of succession. When Michael O'Leary leaves Ryanair, the next CEO needs to be chosen very carefully.

Made in Japan: The Sony Story, Akio Morita

Made in Japan (HarperCollins) illustrates the sheer hard work and commitment necessary to make businesses work. The book also shows the many barriers that you have to overcome if you want to build your dream into one of the world's most recognised and respected companies.

During the Second World War, Akio Morita served in the Japanese navy and it was here that he was first introduced to magnetic recording tape. Afterwards, rather than going into the family *saki* (rice whisky) business, he became convinced of the commercial potential and value of magnetic tape as a consumer product. For well over ten years, working out of the garage at his father's home, Morita and his partner Masaru Ibuka worked to perfect the tape to a commercial standard. After they perfected it, Morita took the then revolutionary step of concentrating on profit margins rather than high market share. The company expanded to include other electrical goods and subsequently into music, film, entertainment, games, and computers.

Maverick, Ricardo Semler

Maverick (Random House) is a revolutionary tale of organisation transformation, turning a dying and bureaucratic white goods manufacturing company into a fully responsive and dynamic entity – by placing the staff and customers at the heart of everything. Nothing too unusual in that, except that this took place in Brazil, against a *daily* inflation rate of ten per cent, and in a business environment riddled with patronage and corruption. On top of all that, the industry company failure rate was one in three.

To overcome these obstacles, Ricardo Semler engaged a fully open style of management and, in his own words, 'made the company thrive, by refusing to squander our most important resource – our people'. The results in any situation would be remarkable. The results achieved in this context are truly astounding – and yet all that Ricardo Semler has done is to concentrate on what's important, and to ignore or discontinue what's not.

Enron: Anatomy of Greed, Brian Cruver

Enron (Arrow) is an insider's story of the world's largest corporate failure and (alleged) fraud. Brian Cruver was an executive who worked for Enron both during its rapid growth and its spectacular fall. He tells of the collective corporate culture (the bad and the ugly as well as the good); the actions taken to try to ward off the crisis; and the actions taken by top executives who realised that the firm would collapse. *Enron* shows what happens when everything and everyone becomes corrupted, and of the processes leading to corruption – the assurances and the lies; the transition from strength to vanity, from vanity to arrogance, and from arrogance to greed and corruption. Cruver also details the more personal consequences of loss and bankruptcy, suicides, family breakdowns, alcoholism, and blame and counter-blame.

Index

• *H* •

• *I* •

• *S* •

• U •

• V •

• W •

FOR DUMMIES®

Do Anything. Just Add Dummies

UK editions

PROPERTY

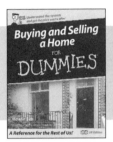

0-7645-7027-7

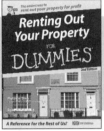

0-470-02921-8

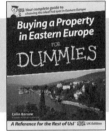

0-7645-7047-1

PERSONAL FINANCE

0-7645-7023-4

0-470-05815-3

0-7645-7039-0

BUSINESS

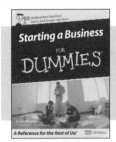

0-7645-7018-8

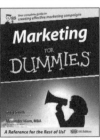

0-7645-7056-0

0-7645-7026-9

Answering Tough Interview
Questions For Dummies
(0-470-01903-4)

Arthritis For Dummies
(0-470-02582-4)

Being the Best Man
For Dummies
(0-470-02657-X)

British History
For Dummies
(0-470-03536-6)

Building Confidence
For Dummies
(0-470-01669-8)

Buying a Home on a Budget
For Dummies
(0-7645-7035-8)

Children's Health
For Dummies
(0-470-02735-5)

Cognitive Behavioural Therapy
For Dummies
(0-470-01838-0)

Cricket For Dummies
(0-470-03454-8)

CVs For Dummies
(0-7645-7017-X)

Detox For Dummies
(0-470-01908-5)

Diabetes For Dummies
(0-7645-7019-6)

Divorce For Dummies
(0-7645-7030-7)

DJing For Dummies
(0-470-03275-8)

eBay.co.uk For Dummies
(0-7645-7059-5)

European History
For Dummies
(0-7645-7060-9)

Gardening For Dummies
(0-470-01843-7)

Genealogy Online
For Dummies
(0-7645-7061-7)

Golf For Dummies
(0-470-01811-9)

Hypnotherapy For Dummies
(0-470-01930-1)

Irish History For Dummies
(0-7645-7040-4)

Neuro-linguistic Programming
For Dummies
(0-7645-7028-5)

Nutrition For Dummies
(0-7645-7058-7)

Parenting For Dummies
(0-470-02714-2)

Pregnancy For Dummies
(0-7645-7042-0)

Retiring Wealthy For Dummies
(0-470-02632-4)

Rugby Union For Dummies
(0-470-03537-4)

Small Business Employment
Law For Dummies
(0-7645-7052-8)

Starting a Business on
eBay.co.uk For Dummies
(0-470-02666-9)

Su Doku For Dummies
(0-470-01892-5)

The GL Diet For Dummies
(0-470-02753-3)

The Romans For Dummies
(0-470-03077-1)

Thyroid For Dummies
(0-470-03172-7)

UK Law and Your Rights
For Dummies
(0-470-02796-7)

Winning on Betfair
For Dummies
(0-470-02856-4)

FOR DUMMIES®

Do Anything. Just Add Dummies

HOBBIES

0-7645-5232-5

0-7645-6847-7

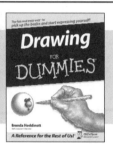

0-7645-5476-X

Also available:

Art For Dummies
(0-7645-5104-3)

Aromatherapy For Dummies
(0-7645-5171-X)

Bridge For Dummies
(0-471-92426-1)

Card Games For Dummies
(0-7645-9910-0)

Chess For Dummies
(0-7645-8404-9)

Improving Your Memory
For Dummies
(0-7645-5435-2)

Massage For Dummies
(0-7645-5172-8)

Meditation For Dummies
(0-471-77774-9)

Photography For Dummies
(0-7645-4116-1)

Quilting For Dummies
(0-7645-9799-X)

EDUCATION

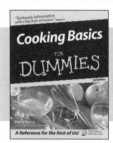

0-7645-7206-7

0-7645-5581-2

0-7645-5422-0

Also available:

Algebra For Dummies
(0-7645-5325-9)

Algebra II For Dummies
(0-471-77581-9)

Astronomy For Dummies
(0-7645-8465-0)

Buddhism For Dummies
(0-7645-5359-3)

Calculus For Dummies
(0-7645-2498-4)

Forensics For Dummies
(0-7645-5580-4)

Islam For Dummies
(0-7645-5503-0)

Philosophy For Dummies
(0-7645-5153-1)

Religion For Dummies
(0-7645-5264-3)

Trigonometry For Dummies
(0-7645-6903-1)

PETS

0-470-03717-2

0-7645-8418-9

0-7645-5275-9

Also available:

Labrador Retrievers
For Dummies
(0-7645-5281-3)

Aquariums For Dummies
(0-7645-5156-6)

Birds For Dummies
(0-7645-5139-6)

Dogs For Dummies
(0-7645-5274-0)

Ferrets For Dummies
(0-7645-5259-7)

Golden Retrievers
For Dummies
(0-7645-5267-8)

Horses For Dummies
(0-7645-9797-3)

Jack Russell Terriers
For Dummies
(0-7645-5268-6)

Puppies Raising & Training
Diary For Dummies
(0-7645-0876-8)

FOR DUMMIES®

The easy way to get more done and have more fun

LANGUAGES

0-7645-5194-9

0-7645-5193-0

0-7645-5196-5

Also available:

Chinese For Dummies
(0-471-78897-X)

Chinese Phrases
For Dummies
(0-7645-8477-4)

French Phrases For Dummies
(0-7645-7202-4)

German For Dummies
(0-7645-5195-7)

Italian Phrases For Dummies
(0-7645-7203-2)

Japanese For Dummies
(0-7645-5429-8)

Latin For Dummies
(0-7645-5431-X)

Spanish Phrases
For Dummies
(0-7645-7204-0)

Spanish Verbs For Dummies
(0-471-76872-3)

Hebrew For Dummies
(0-7645-5489-1)

MUSIC AND FILM

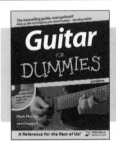

0-7645-9904-6

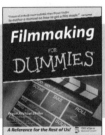

0-7645-2476-3

0-7645-5105-1

Also available:

Bass Guitar For Dummies
(0-7645-2487-9)

Blues For Dummies
(0-7645-5080-2)

Classical Music For Dummies
(0-7645-5009-8)

Drums For Dummies
(0-471-79411-2)

Jazz For Dummies
(0-471-76844-8)

Opera For Dummies
(0-7645-5010-1)

Rock Guitar For Dummies
(0-7645-5356-9)

Screenwriting For Dummies
(0-7645-5486-7)

Songwriting For Dummies
(0-7645-5404-2)

Singing For Dummies
(0-7645-2475-5)

HEALTH, SPORTS & FITNESS

0-7645-7851-0

0-7645-5623-1

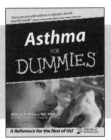

0-7645-4233-8

Also available:

Controlling Cholesterol
For Dummies
(0-7645-5440-9)

Dieting For Dummies
(0-7645-4149-8)

High Blood Pressure
For Dummies
(0-7645-5424-7)

Martial Arts For Dummies
(0-7645-5358-5)

Menopause For Dummies
(0-7645-5458-1)

Power Yoga For Dummies
(0-7645-5342-9)

Weight Training
For Dummies
(0-471-76845-6)

Yoga For Dummies
(0-7645-5117-5)

Available wherever books are sold. For more information or to order direct go to www.wiley.com or call 0800 243407 (Non UK call +44 1243 843296)

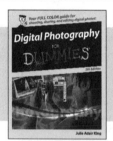

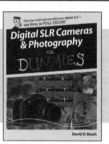